Design through Dialogue

A Guide for Clients and Architects

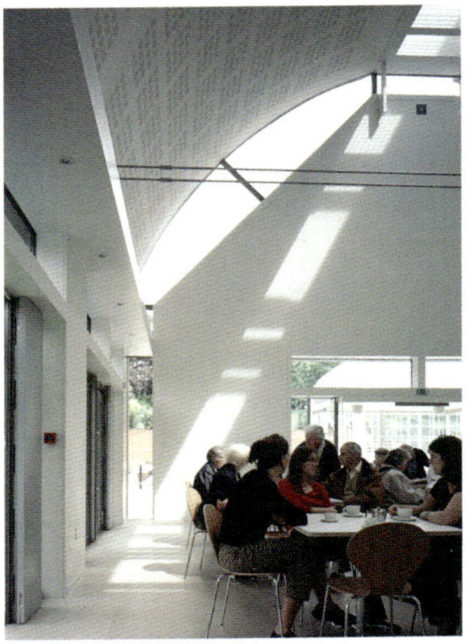
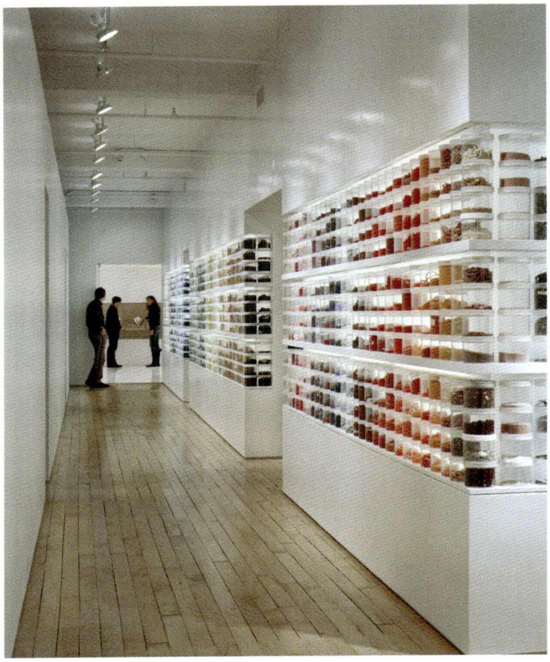
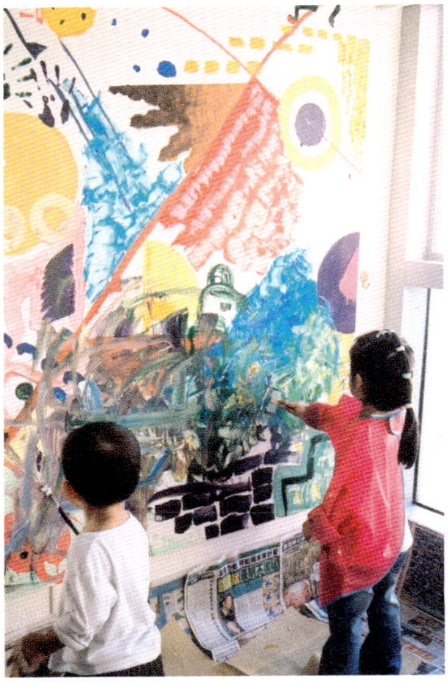
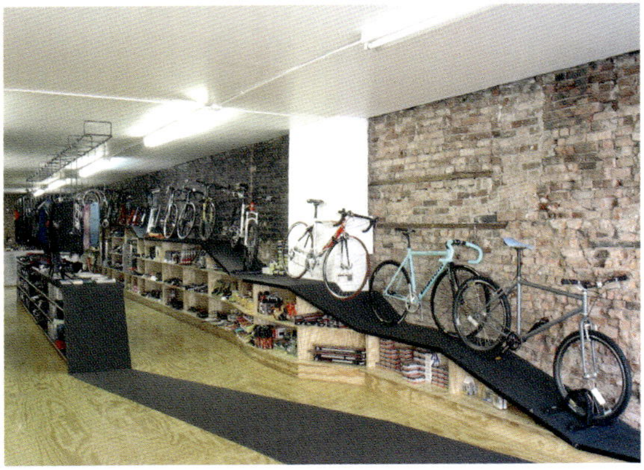

Design through Dialogue

A Guide for Clients and Architects

Karen A Franck
Teresa von Sommaruga Howard

WILEY
A John Wiley and Sons, Ltd, Publication

© 2010 John Wiley & Sons Ltd

Registered office
John Wiley & Sons Ltd, The Atrium, Southern Gate, Chichester, West Sussex, PO19 8SQ, United Kingdom

For details of our global editorial offices, for customer services and for information about how to apply for permission to reuse the copyright material in this book please see our website at www.wiley.com.

The right of the author to be identified as the author of this work has been asserted in accordance with the Copyright, Designs and Patents Act 1988.

All rights reserved. No part of this publication may be reproduced, stored in a retrieval system, or transmitted, in any form or by any means, electronic, mechanical, photocopying, recording or otherwise, except as permitted by the UK Copyright, Designs and Patents Act 1988, without the prior permission of the publisher.

Wiley also publishes its books in a variety of electronic formats. Some content that appears in print may not be available in electronic books.

Designations used by companies to distinguish their products are often claimed as trademarks. All brand names and product names used in this book are trade names, service marks, trademarks or registered trademarks of their respective owners. The publisher is not associated with any product or vendor mentioned in this book. This publication is designed to provide accurate and authoritative information in regard to the subject matter covered. It is sold on the understanding that the publisher is not engaged in rendering professional services. If professional advice or other expert assistance is required, the services of a competent professional should be sought.

Executive Commissioning Editor: Helen Castle
Project Editor: Miriam Swift
Publishing Assistant: Calver Lezama
Content Editor: Françoise Vaslin

ISBN 978-0-470-72190-2 HB
     978-0-470-87071-6 PB

Cover design, page design and layouts by Liz Sephton
Printed and bound by Printer Trento, Italy

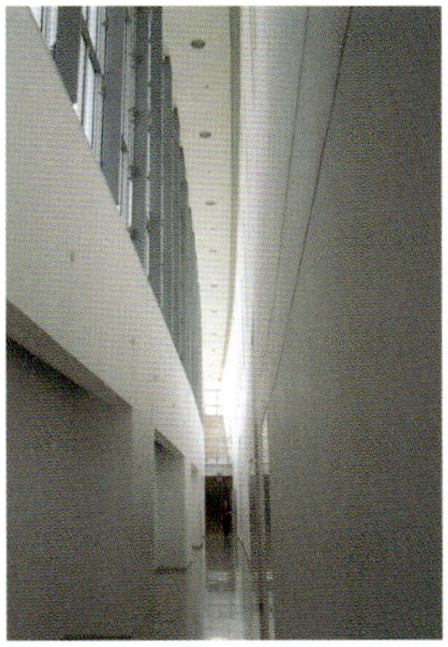

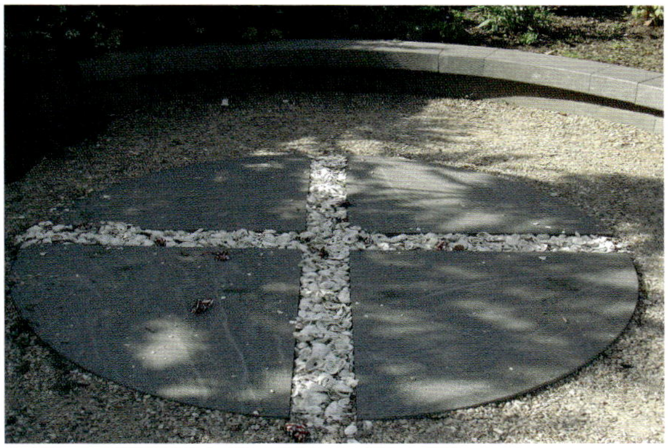

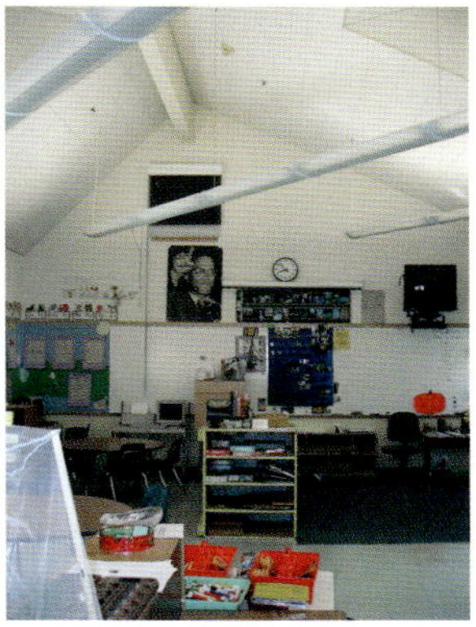

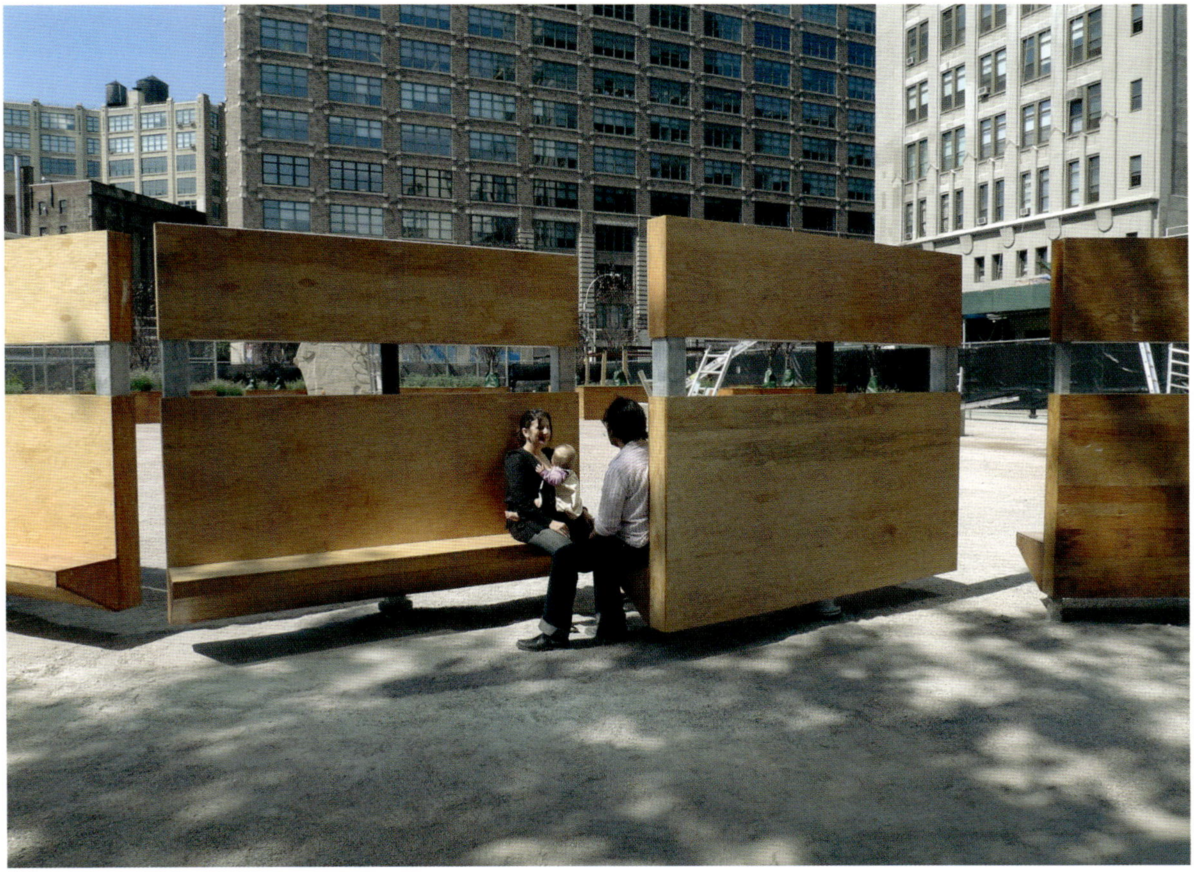

Contents

Chapter 1   Introduction   **9**
    A Dialogue between Client and Architect   10
    A Relational Approach   15
    Our Dialogue   18
    Thank You   20

Chapter 2   In Dialogue   **25**
    Client and Architect   25
    Briefing and Designing   36
    The Brief and the Design   41
    Use and Form   46
    Inner Worlds and Outer Worlds   51

Chapter 3   Relating   **61**
    Beginning the Relationship   62
    Creating a 'Good Enough' Relationship   70
    Maintaining a Facilitating Environment   81

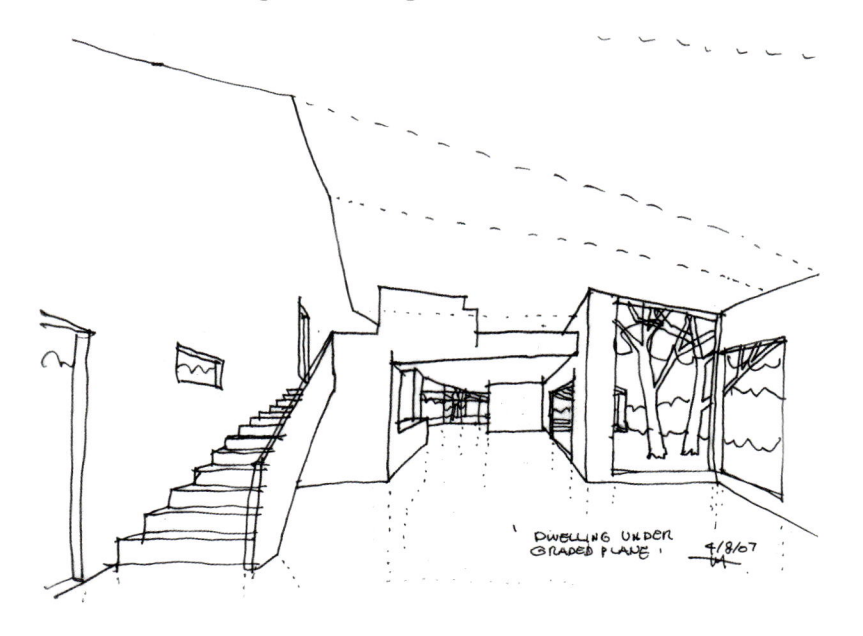

Chapter 4   Talking   **93**
      Creating Meaning Together   93
      Talking in Groups   102
      Attending to Silence   111
      The Words Matter   115

Chapter 5   Exploring   **129**
      Exploring as an Attitude   130
      Exploring as Actions   136
      Deciding What to Explore   146

Chapter 6   Transforming   **165**
      Transforming at the Human Scale   166
      Looking Beneath the Surface   169
      Treating Type as a Question   172
      Scrutinizing Form and Use   182
      Transforming through Dialogue   187

Architects and Clients   **196**
Bibliography   **198**
Index   **205**
Image credits   **208**

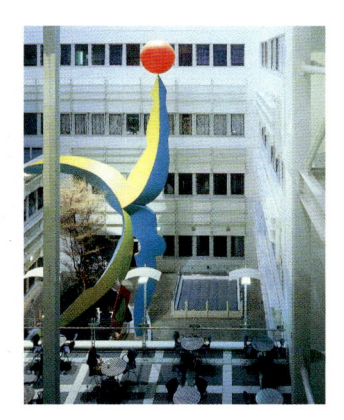

Chapter 1　Introduction

After years of anticipation the new museum opens. Architects and critics scrutinise all aspects of its design with great excitement. Visitors throng to the building to experience its innovative features first hand. Pictures and commentary appear in major magazines and newspapers and on the web. The architects are praised for their skill and the museum board is congratulated on its progressive choice of designers, but nowhere is the complicated and sometimes contentious process of the museum's creation described. As so often happens, the building's form receives all the attention; what happened behind the scenes, over a period of many years, remains invisible.

In this book we explore that largely hidden process, focusing on the exchanges between client and architect and how these help to shape design. Often, but perhaps not often enough, the exchanges between client and architect take the form of a *dialogue*: that is, they *think together*. From the contrasting contributions of client and architect something new emerges, from tensions generated by difference, possibly by conflict, a transformation occurs. How this happens, who is involved and how design results is the subject of *Design through Dialogue: A Guide for Clients and Architects*.

In recent years, as the size and complexity of architectural projects have grown and more building professionals participate, variation in who fulfils the roles of architect and client has increased, with contact between architect and client becoming more attenuated. Fortunately, there are still architects who are responsible for design and who meet face to face with clients. For us, 'architect' refers to this person or persons; 'client' includes

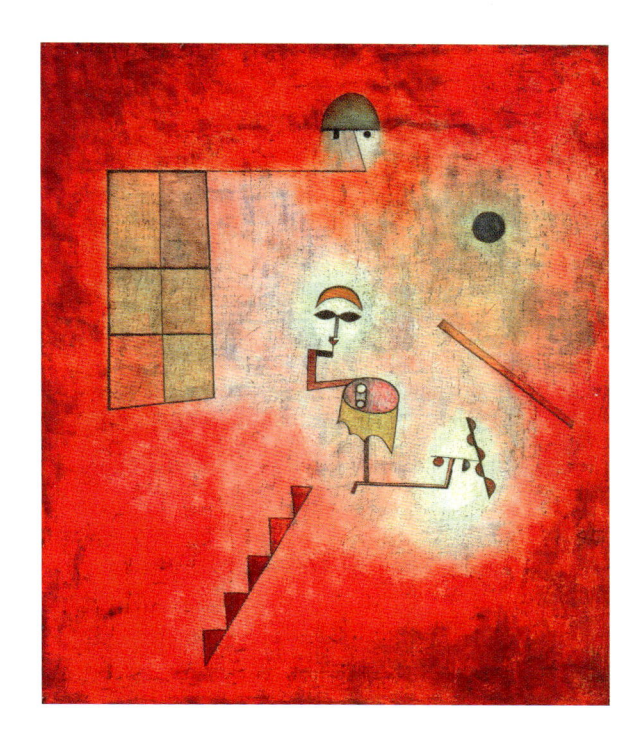

Paul Klee, *Conjuring Trick*, 1927. Two figures appear to float in dialogue. The whole is in a balance, supported by the frame of their relationship. Klee often explored relationships between opposites, which he portrayed in delicate, momentary balance as he tried to reconcile the frictions within an enveloping tension. (Philadelphia Museum of Art: The Louise and Walter Arensberg Collection).

those who commission a project as well as those who are consulted during design whose lives it will affect.

Our intention is to help clients and architects enter a dialogue with confidence and pursue it with success. Instead of presenting instructions, rules or specific techniques, as a manual might, we draw examples from actual architectural projects, both large and small, from different countries. We interpret, support and extend material from these cases with concepts drawn from various fields: group dynamics, psychoanalytic psychotherapy, communication theory, developmental psychology as well as architecture. Our book is a guide that suggests how clients and architects might find their way through what is always new territory: designing an architectural project together. While we focus on the relationship between client and architect and the activities they undertake, the book should be useful to all those who participate in the design and construction of environments.

Some, possibly many, architects pursue design primarily as the creation of form without giving sufficient attention to patterns of use and how the new environment can enhance the lives of occupants. This purely aesthetic orientation, which is also promoted in the education of many architecture students, leads to the mistaken view among potential clients, particularly for commercial projects, that architects are only image-makers, cannot be trusted to work within time and budget constraints and therefore must relinquish many of their traditional responsibilities to others, including project and construction managers. That view and the resulting decrease in the centrality of the architect to the design and construction process severely reduce opportunities for architects and clients to discover how design can enhance the quality of everyday life.

Fortunately, there are architects who still consider both form and use as well as the connections between them, exploring how design can meet people's needs and desires in innovative ways. These architects engage in dialogue with the client, pursuing design as both a social and an aesthetic process. By presenting the ways that such architects work and the projects that result, we hope to give architects, students of architecture and future clients a greater understanding of how design is achieved through dialogue and of the many benefits that ensue.

A Dialogue between Client and Architect

The term dialogue is often used as a synonym for conversation but dialogue is more than just conversation. Dialogue is a collaborative activity; participants talk with rather than to each other; certainly they may disagree but they do not aim to 'win' or persuade. Instead, through talking they explore and discover, staying with the tensions and conflicts that arise, to allow the unexpected to surface. Such a process depends on an attitude of not knowing and a tolerance for uncertainty. Just as importantly, dialogue relies on a relationship that Jewish philosopher and theologian Martin Buber called 'I-thou', in which each person fully acknowledges and respects the other's humanity including that person's knowledge and ideas.[1] Buber, who developed a philosophy of dialogue, recognised that instead of an 'I' that only knows objects and ends, dialogue requires an 'I of relation' that he later termed the 'I of love'.

Architect Louis Kahn found that he had many beliefs in common with his client Dr Jonas Salk, inventor of the polio vaccine, including a belief in the distinction between what Salk called the 'measurable and the 'unmeasurable'.[2] Architect and client came from very similar backgrounds and shared a vision of creating community and linking human intellect and spirit. The result of their collaboration, the Salk Institute for Biological Studies in La Jolla, California, is a remarkable building. Many of its outstanding features can be traced directly to the dialogue between client and architect which began when they first met in 1959.

Each respected and listened to the other. While Salk was sympathetic to Kahn's design approach, from the very beginning he was able to reject some of the architect's key ideas and present his own. Based on his understanding of the needs of research scientists, Salk rejected Kahn's first proposal for laboratories in towers similar to those at the Richards Building Kahn had designed for the University of Pennsylvania. Instead, Salk required open-plan laboratories.[3] For his part, Louis Kahn was sensitive to needs that the scientists had not recognised themselves: he proposed a small study for each principal scientist as a refuge from the noisy, spartan labs and persuaded the scientists of their value.

The construction contract had already been signed when Salk realised he could not accept Kahn's second scheme of four laboratories organised around two courtyards; he requested instead just two lab buildings facing each other across a single open space. The design that followed led to the creation of a dramatic space: between two three-storey laboratories a single, hard-surfaced plaza stretches without interruption to the Pacific Ocean. The fact that the central plaza is hard surfaced without any planting is the result of advice offered by Mexican architect Luis Barragan. The teak study cubicles

Louis Kahn, Salk Institute for Biological Studies, La Jolla, California, 1965.
Many of the outstanding features of the design emerged from the dialogue between Kahn and Dr Jonas Salk. LEFT The two laboratory buildings face an open plaza. ABOVE Each principal scientist has a study, a quiet retreat from the laboratory.

CHAPTER 1 INTRODUCTION • 11

> … dialogue is a conversation in which people think together in relationship. Thinking together implies that you no longer take your own position as final. You relax your grip on certainty and listen to the possibilities that result simply from being in a relationship with others – possibilities that might not otherwise have occurred.
>
> William Isaacs, *Dialogue and the Art of Thinking Together*, 1999, p 19

Moore Ruble Yudell, St. Matthew's Parish Church, Pacific Palisades, California, 1983, Third design workshop.
Using large-scale models, Charles Moore discusses alternative schemes with parishioners

are stacked in towers at each end of the laboratory buildings, Kahn recreated with them some aspects of 'the monastic setting that had interested Salk and him from the start'.[4] Since the lab buildings were sunk below ground, the lowest floor of laboratories is at basement level. To bring daylight to them, Kahn designed long, sunken courtyards on each side of the plaza.[5] Today architects of large projects rarely work exclusively with just one person as Kahn did with Salk. It is far more common for architects to work with a client group or several groups as Charles Moore of Moore Ruble Yudell (MRY) did while designing St. Matthew's Parish Church in Pacific Palisades, California. After the small A-frame chapel of St. Matthew's burned to the ground, the congregation decided to rebuild. Partly as a consequence of acrimony over the recent selection of a new pastor, the congregation decided that, in order to be built, any final design for the new church would require a two-thirds vote of approval from all 350 members. Charles Moore was one of the few architects willing to accept that requirement, writing in the proposal submitted to the selection committee in 1979 that ' … the most important act of the architect is listening, and the successful building grows out of an intimate and continued relation with the clients'.[6] In his proposal Moore outlined a series of workshops to give all parishioners an opportunity to participate directly in the design process.

After MRY was chosen, the architects held three design workshops on Sunday afternoons, a month apart. Structured with care and usually including a shared meal, each workshop set out specific tasks that required a combination of talking and showing by the architects and the participants. For instance, during the first workshop parishioners walked the 37-acre site, pausing at certain points to record their thoughts, impressions and desires for the new church. Later they developed briefing and design preferences, using materials for making models which the architects provided. During the second workshop participants proposed plans for the church, making their own drawings, sketches and rough models. Moore also showed them slides of many churches, modern and historic, asking them for their likes and dislikes. It was at the third workshop that MRY presented three alternative designs arising from the previous workshops. Six of the seven groups within the workshop agreed on the same alternative.[7]

The participatory process of designing St. Matthew's illustrates several characteristics of an effective dialogue between client and architect. The architects were observably open to the possibilities and desires expressed by parishioners, even when they were contradictory, enthusiastically drawing design implications from differences rather than proposing alternatives or trying to reach consensus between opposing views. Charles Moore recalls:

'An important discovery we made early on was that when we really pushed something we lost it. It worked best to let the parishioners generate the ideas and then to coax them into architectural expression.'[8] It is notable that Moore used the word 'let'. Letting allows something to happen; it does not impose or direct the action in a certain direction to achieve a predetermined outcome. Allowing things to emerge is a key feature of dialogue that requires time and patience as well as the stance of being open. This stance has been called 'suspending' one's opinion and, as importantly, 'the certainty that lies behind it'.[9]

Early in the participatory design process for St. Matthew's the architects discovered that the parishioners held very strong and conflicting preferences: some wanted a 'simple parish church' while 'other people wanted a noble, almost cathedral-like space'.[10] Another apparent contradiction was a shared desire for intimate seating in the half round but also for a traditional sanctuary. Many parishioners wished for connections to the outdoors through the plentiful use of glass but other participants, concerned about good acoustics for the new organ, argued for hard, heavy surfaces and not glass. And another group of older members, expressing nostalgia for the former wooden church, preferred a wood interior.[11]

The architects were able to hold these apparent opposites in mind, in balance, to generate design proposals that accommodated them all. In the

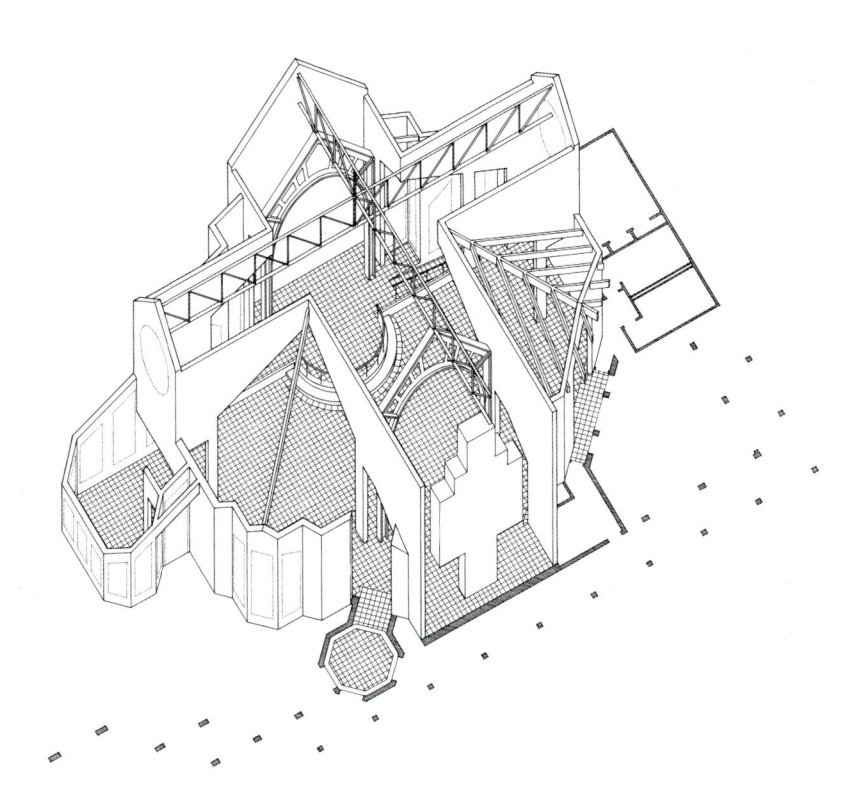

Moore Ruble Yudell, St. Matthew's Parish Church, Pacific Palisades, California, 1983.
To respond to contrasting requirements, the architects designed a modified Latin cross roof to create a lofty space inside with additional hipped roofs to allow the church to look modest from the outside.

> ... people creating something, working together to make something, have a much easier time working with each other, and find the experience far more exciting and positive than people on committees, who are cast automatically into a kind of critical role of wondering whether what's already in front of them is alright or not.
>
> Charles Moore, *Working together to make something*, 1988, p 103

St Matthew's Parish Church. The design addressed its location in a residential neighbourhood and the desires of the parishioners.
BELOW Entrance to the church is through a courtyard and along a covered walkway. BELOW RIGHT Windows give views to the garden. The pews and exposed timber roof give the impression of a wood interior.

final design seven rows of seating in a half ellipse create intimacy while a modified Latin cross roof provides a tall, even a grand space. Hipped roofs, starting low at the eaves rise to a cruciform in the centre: thus a lofty space is formed inside while the church looks modest from the outside. The church site was in a residential neighbourhood so an imposing, cathedral like structure would have been inappropriate. Two solid plaster walls, addressing the requirement for sufficient sound absorption, are faced with wood battens about two (61cm) feet apart. These, along with the internal timber roof and wooden furniture, give the overall impression of a wood interior. At the same time vertical windows next to the altar, a glass narthex and a bay window in the chapel create an impression of lots of glass.[12]

During the development of the schematic design for St. Matthew's the pastor of the church and the future occupants of the new church who participated in the workshops served as the client for the project. Subsequently, to develop and refine the design the architects worked with several committees of congregation members. Approval of the final design came from almost the entire congregation: a full 83 per cent approved, far higher than the requisite two-thirds.

At St. Matthew's architect and client were able to contribute in the best way they could from their respective areas of knowledge and experience. As in any successful dialogue each respected the knowledge and ideas of the other and the outcome grew from their joint efforts, a process that was immensely satisfying to all. Charles Moore has written, 'Being a part of making that church was an opportunity to work toward an architecture filled with the energies not only of architects but of inhabitants as well, and helping people to find something to which they can belong'.[13] As importantly, the architects were able to respect and contain the differences expressed by parishioners to find a new path to the unexpected and the remarkable.

Over the course of the entire design process, from initial conversations through design refinement, the clients for the Salk Institute and St. Matthew's worked directly with the architects who were designing the building. That is not always the case. Sometimes other staff members in the architecture firm complete the tasks of collecting information and determining client requirements before design proposals are made. Or these tasks may be completed by outside consultants hired by the client before the architect is commissioned. In these situations the design architect is at least one step removed from the client, reducing and sometimes removing the possibility for dialogue between client and designer to take place. In this book we are interested primarily in this direct dialogue, between those on the client side who are most knowledgeable about what is needed and desired and those an the architect side who are responsible for the design.

A Relational Approach

As Charles Moore observed in his written proposal to the selection committee at St. Matthew's, a successful building grows from the relationship between client and architect. In fact, it grows from an entire network of relationships among myriad participants. Just a short list could include: the architect (or more likely several architects and other design professionals), the client (often an entire client team), future occupants, members of the local community, engineers and consultants in specialised areas, contractors and subcontractors, city officials and other municipal authorities, representatives of financial institutions, fabricators and other producers of materials and products. Despite the significant impact that the quality of these relationships has on the ease of the entire design process and the quality of the final project, historically little guidance has been given to clients or architects on how best to engage in these relationships and how to manage different perspectives and inevitable disagreements. That is beginning to change.

The web sites for both the Royal Institute of British Architects (RIBA) in the UK and the American Institute of Architects (AIA) in the US use the word 'dialogue' in their general recommendations to clients who are choosing architects. The RIBA calls its recommendations 'Working with an architect on your home' and states, 'Good architecture needs collaboration and dialogue. You need to respect each other's views.'[14] The AIA also suggests cooperation in its title 'You and your architect: A guide for a successful partnership' and states, 'There is no substitute for the intensive dialogue and inquiry that characterize the design process'.[15]

Two recent publications in the UK give more comprehensive and detailed guidance to clients of both small and large projects. Each offers well-organised and well-illustrated recommendations to clients for finding an architect, creating a brief and participating in design decisions. *Creating Excellent Buildings: A Guide for Clients* by the CABE is very clear in its instruction to the client regarding responsibility: 'You should retain responsibility for seeing that the brief describes unambiguously and clearly what you want the project to accomplish. You should review it, be sure it says what you want it to …'[16] The *School Works Tool Kit* by Jane Seymour recognises the importance of the active role clients can take in working with architects on

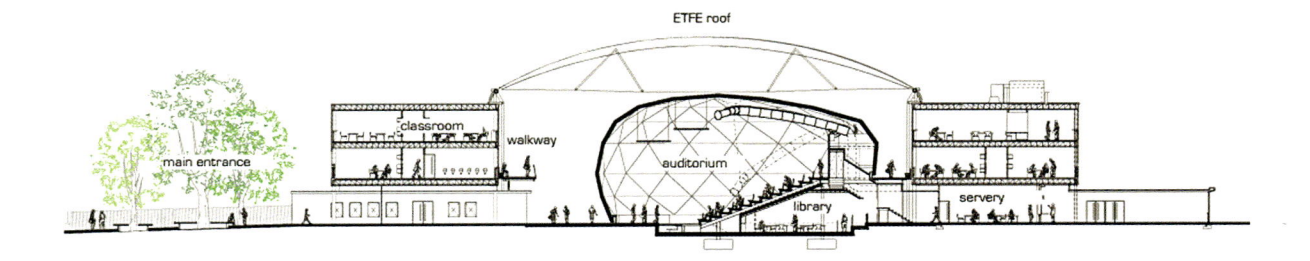

de Rijke Marsh Morgan Architects, Kingsdale School, Dulwich, London, 2004.

A large, mixed-use courtyard accommodates a geodesic auditorium, dining facilities and aerial walkways and bridges instead of corridors and stairs. This radical renovation of a 1960s building involved students, teachers and the larger community, a process that generated the *School Works Tools Kit*.

school design. It stresses the importance of building a 'thinking space' to help the community generate its own design ideas instead of 'being asked for their reactions to a preconceived design agenda'. The Kit suggests clients 'link design issues with questions of purpose', 'take account of management and organisational implications' and 'look below the surface'.[17]

Works published in the US present cases showing how architects, landscape architects and planners have worked relationally with clients. In *Architecture: The Story of Practice* Dana Cuff analyses how the design of three outstanding buildings grew from a collaborative design process rather than from the hand of a single genius. In *Placemaking: The Art and Practice of Building Communities* Lynda H Schneekloth and Robert G Shibley use case studies from their practice to present a theory and a method for professionals working cooperatively with client communities. In *Designing Public Consensus* Barbara Faga examines the public participatory process that occurred in a wide variety of projects, extracting 'tips' for planners and designers to make that process more manageable and more useful. In *Curing the Fountainheadache: How Architects & their Clients Communicate* architect Andrew Pressman and other contributors tell stories of architect-client interactions, both frustrating and exhilarating, with pointers for clients and architects.[18]

In the fields of construction and business management the question of how to build effective working relationships is receiving more attention. As the process of designing and constructing buildings becomes more complex and includes ever more participants and as new technologies enable people to communicate more rapidly, there is growing recognition that good business practice requires a high level of coordination between different parties. Such coordination could benefit from a collaborative relationship between architect and contractor, replacing the more traditional adversarial one.

In 1994 the UK government and the construction industry, recognising the positive impact collaborative relationships can have on both process and product, jointly commissioned Michael Latham's report, *Constructing the Team*, which led to the establishment of the Construction Industry Board to oversee reform. In 2001, in a follow-up report, Latham noted that partnering had made great strides, particularly in the housing association movement and other parts of the public sector but that many commercial clients still did not understand that fiercely competitive tenders and the practice of accepting the lowest bid do not produce value for money.[19]

Adversarial approaches produce high levels of litigation and conflict, low investment and negligible margins, well-documented drawbacks that have stimulated an increasing number of collaborative relationships in design and construction in Britain. Such relationships are reinforced by new forms of partnering contracts that engage everyone on the construction team in the joint discovery of solutions to problems. Responsibility for risk is shared between contractor and client, further reinforced when open book accounting clauses are incorporated. These forms of contract ensure a successful outcome through an ongoing cooperative relationship.[20]

In the US, guidance offered to architects from a business and management perspective stresses teamwork and engagement of the client. In their concise manual *The Next Architect: A New Twist on the Future of Design* James Cramer and Scott Simpson single out three recent changes that affect design practice: (1) recognition that design is team-based and not the work of a solitary genius; (2) increase in the speed of tasks; and (3) development of technologies that allow designers to show their thinking and proposals in three and four dimensions extremely quickly. This third change makes 'the design process far more transparent and accessible to clients and the public alike, further encouraging (and in fact requiring) broad participation'.[21] The authors point to the significant role the client now plays and the importance of the architect's 'clientship skills' and list simple rules to follow. They also recommend radical changes to the entire design and construction process, with contractors becoming partners early on by joining the design development phase and participating in the preparation of construction documents.

In his discussion of the need to redesign architectural practice, Thomas R Fisher in *In the Scheme of Things* notes the extremely adversarial character of the relationships between participants in the design and construction process and suggests that the jargon used by different professionals hinders understanding and cooperation. He suggests that building cooperative relationships could well begin with language, with 'the words we choose and the way we use them'.[22] Another path to cooperation and collaboration is offered in the emerging, computer-based techniques of building information modelling (BIM). With BIM all participants in the project, from early on, can contribute and share information with the use of a single virtual model.[23]

How best to improve the relationship between professional and client is receiving more attention in business and the professions. In *The Trusted Advisor*, David Maister, Charles Green and Robert Galford extend guidance to all professional consultants who work with clients in an advisory capacity. Many of their suggestions on how to build a client's trust and confidence apply to architects as well: how to focus on the client, how to be a good listener, the importance of acknowledging and responding to emotions.[24] In the field of psychotherapy, therapists have been rethinking their relationship with clients, giving special attention to the inherent power differential and taking it into account in their work with clients. Based on the writings of the Chilean biologist Humberto Maturana and intersubjective psychoanalysts

> ... in the most ancient meaning of the word, logos meant to 'gather together' and suggested an intimate awareness of the relationships among things in the natural world. In that sense logos may be best rendered in English as relationship.
>
> William Isaacs, *Dialogue and the Art of Thinking Together*, 1999, p 19

> When someone reflects-in-action, he becomes a researcher in the practice context. He is not dependent on the categories of established theory and technique, but constructs a new theory of the unique case.
>
> Donald Schön, *The Reflective Practitioner*, 1983, p 68

such as Daniel Stern, many schools of therapy now encourage everyone in the room, including the therapist, to work together within the context of their evolving relationships.[25]

Design through Dialogue joins these initiatives in the call for more cooperative relationships between professionals and their clients. Rather than listing a set of rules or itemised tips for good practice, we encourage architects to adopt an overall attitude and methods of working with clients that will generate truly collaborative relationships and that will enable them to maintain those relationships through all the exigencies of design and construction. This is part of what Donald Schön called 'reflection-in-action' in contrast to an earlier mode of professional practice – application of 'technical rationality'. As reflective practitioners realise, 'Complexity, instability and uncertainty are not removed or resolved by applying specialised knowledge to well defined tasks'.[26] Instead, they approach each project with an open, inquiring attitude, discovering what is new to that project and responding, by thinking and doing, to the specifics of that case.

Our Dialogue

To gain greater insight into the way dialogue shapes design and to present details of a variety of projects, we interviewed architects and clients in the UK, the US, Sweden, Israel, Hong Kong and New Zealand. Some of the projects are large and well known (museums, a supreme court building, a central library, a hospital). Others are smaller and not so well known (schools, houses, shops, a local library). Some buildings: the National Museum of the American Indian, the Central Library in Seattle, Te Papa Tongarewa Museum of New Zealand, the Supreme Court in Jerusalem we selected because we already knew that the process of designing them would be illuminating for this book. Other times, often through serendipity, we met or learned of architects who relish their relationships with clients and who view their conversations with them not as a necessary burden but as a springboard for design. Even with such an attitude the process is not easy. We sought to discover how these architects work with clients and what the consequences are for design.

As in the dialogue between client and architect, we have each contributed to this work from our respective areas of expertise, experience and concern. Karen Franck is an environmental psychologist who teaches architecture students in seminars, design studios and courses on the social aspects of architecture at the New Jersey Institute of Technology. Karen has previously written about architectural design, urban public space, alternative housing and types in architecture. Teresa von Sommaruga Howard, who lives in London, is an architect who consulted with tenants in public sector housing well before that became a common practice. Teresa is also an interim manager and organisational consultant and a group-analytic psychotherapist with a specialty in conducting large dialogue groups.

Very much like the evolving design for a building, the form and content of this book kept changing as we kept ourselves open to new possibilities, holding the tensions and conflicts that arose, allowing them to generate new ideas. One of the biggest challenges we faced was how to structure the book. We wanted to integrate different kinds of material from a variety of cases and sources to illuminate particular approaches and concepts. Consequently, separating the book into discrete and complete case studies was not an option. Since we do not see the design process as a linear sequence of tasks but as a reiterative process of overlapping activities, it made no sense to organise chapters around steps in a linear sequence of what happens first, second etc.

After a great many outlines, much discussion and revision that continued as we wrote, we settled on a plan. Chapter 2 'In Dialogue', describes five different 'dialogues' that contribute to design: between client and architect, between briefing and designing as activities, between the brief and the design as outcomes, between ideas of use and ideas of form and between the inner and outer worlds of clients and architects. Subsequent chapters focus on four kinds of overlapping, often simultaneous activities that occur during the dialogue between client and architect: relating, talking, exploring and transforming. Examining each of these four activities offers a different lens for looking at design and dialogue, revealing a different set of issues and concerns.

From the beginning to the end of a project, no matter how large or small, and possibly after its completion, client and architect are *relating* to each other. They do so largely through *talking* and through activities closely connected to talking – showing and writing. During periods of briefing and designing, both client and architect are continuously finding things out; together and apart they are *exploring*. Often the client begins this activity before commissioning an architect, to determine needs, to select a designer, to consider whether a new building or a renovation is even necessary. It is in the architect's hands to take what has been learned with the client, to hold possible differences and possibilities and the tensions they generate and propose a design or several designs. This involves *transforming*. As with exploring, instances of transforming may happen anywhere along the way; a transformation is not necessarily a final or singular climax. Here again the client plays an important role for the client may well have asked, quite explicitly, for a different kind of building, for a transformation of the ordinary.

Since the activities of relating, exploring, talking and transforming do not happen sequentially, the chapters can be read in whatever order the reader prefers. Readers who seek all information about a given project are encouraged to consult the index since different aspects of the same architectural project often serve as examples in several chapters.

… thinking itself is born out of interpersonal relations

Peter Hobson, *The Cradle of Thought*, 2004, p 5

Another challenge we faced was finding the right words for translating a body of knowledge from other disciplines that have their own languages and concepts. As in all translations the new language we developed does not quite match the original. The intention is to open a door to new ways of understanding and reflecting that we hope many architects and clients will find illuminating. Endnotes and the bibliography offer sources for readers who wish to learn more.

Thank You

To create this book we engaged in the same activities that frame its chapters: relating, talking, exploring and transforming. In pursuing these activities we relied on the gracious participation of architects and clients around the world. From our interviews with them we gathered invaluable material – the details of projects and processes and their insights into design and dialogue. To the architects and the clients who contributed to this work, whose names are listed at the close of the book: Thank you for your time, your attention and your stories.

Our work benefited significantly from the contributions of others as well. Tony Holmes unfailingly supplied his photography and Photoshop skills, research assistance and his good humour. Nesbitt Blaisdell posed for the cover photograph with patience and grace. Lynn Paxson extended enthusiastic support and guidance particularly regarding the National Museum of the American Indian. Galen Cranz recommended architects to interview and supported our grant application to the Graham Foundation, as did Pauline Nee and Stephan Klein.

We are grateful to Helen Castle at John Wiley & Sons for her continuous encouragement and belief in this work and to Mariangela Palazzi Williams, also at John Wiley & Sons, who contributed suggestions just when we needed them. Each of them continued their tradition of nearly always saying 'yes'. We appreciate the generous grant from the Graham Foundation for Advanced Studies in the Arts that supported research for the book.

NOTES

1. Nahum N Glatzer and Paul Mendes Flohr, eds, *Martin Buber: A Life of Dialogue*, Schocken (New York), 1991, p 53.
2. Thomas Leslie, *Louis I. Kahn: Building Art, Building Science*, George Braziller (New York), 2005.
3. David B Brownlee and David G De Long, *Louis I. Kahn: In the Realm of Architecture*, Universe (New York), 1997.

4   Ibid, p 139.
5   Ibid, passim.
6   Charles Moore quoted in Richard Song, 'Charles Moore and his clients: Designing St. Matthew's', Eugene J Johnson, ed, *Charles Moore: Buildings and Projects 1949–1986*, Rizzoli (New York), 1986, p 48.
7   Ibid, for information about the content of each workshop.
8   Charles Moore quoted in Andrew Pressman, *Curing the Fountainheadache: How Architects & their Clients Communicate*, Sterling (New York), 2006, p 66.
9   William Isaacs, *Dialogue and the Art of Thinking Together*, Currency (New York), 1999.
10 Charles Moore, 'Working together to make something', *Architectural Record*, (New York) February 1984, p 103.
11 Ibid.
12 Song, 'Charles Moore and his clients, in Johnson, ed, *Charles Moore*, p 2.
13 See Richard Garber, ed, *Closing the Gap: Information Models in Contemporary Design Practice*, *Architectural Designs* vol 79, 2008, p 2.
14 'Working with an architect for your home', www.architecture.com/Files/RIBAProfessionalservices/ClientsServices/2007/WorkingWithAnArchitectureForYourHome.pdf p 17.
15 'You and your architect' www.aia.org/value/index.htm
16 CABE (Commission for Architecture and the Built Environment), *Creating Excellent Buildings: A Guide for Clients*, CABE (London), 2003, p 2.
17 Jane Seymour, Hillary Cotton, Grace Comely, Barbara Annesley and Sanjiv Lingayak, *School Works Tool Kit*, School Works Ltd (London), 2001, p 2.
18 Dana Cuff, *Architecture: The Story of Practice*, MIT Press (Cambridge, MA), 1991; Lynda H Schneekloth and Robert G Shibley, *Placemaking: The Art and Practice of Building Communities*, John Wiley & Sons Inc, 1995; Barbara Faga, *Designing Public Consensus*, John Wiley & Sons Inc (Hoboken, NJ), 2006; Andrew Pressman, *Curing the Fountainheadache*, Sterling (New York), 2006.
19 Michael Latham, 'Constructing the Team: Final Report of the Government/Industry Review of Procurement and Contractual Arrangements in the UK Construction Industry', HMSO (London), 1994.
20 The New Engineering Contract (NEC) Suite is a family of contracts developed to stimulate good management of the relationship between the two parties and hence the work included in the contract. Written in clear and simple language so that it is easily understood, the suite can be used for a wide variety of situations and types of work in any location. There are five Options; Option C is specifically for open book accounting.
21 James P Cramer, Scott Simpson, *The Next Architect: A New Twist on the Future of Design*, Greenway Communications (Norcross, GA), 2007, p 23.
22 Thomas R Fisher, *In the Scheme of Things: Alternative Thinking on the Practice of Architecture*, University of Minnesota Press (Minneapolis), 2000, p 113.
23 See Garber, ed, *Closing the Gap*.

24 David H Maister, Charles H Green and Robert M Galford, *The Trusted Advisor*, Touchstone (New York), 2000.

25 Humberto R Maturana and Francisco J Varela, *The Tree of Knowledge: The Biological Roots of Human Understanding*, New Science Library, Shambala (Boston, MA), 1987. Daniel N Stern, *The Present Moment in Psychotherapy and Everyday Life*, Norton (New York), 2004.

26 Donald A Schön, *Educating the Reflective Practitioner: Toward a New Design for Teaching and Learning in the Professions*, Jossey-Bass (San Francisco), 1987, p 19.

Chapter 2

In Dialogue

Design begins with conversation. This conversation becomes a dialogue when all participants listen and learn in an active to and fro, giving value to what the others have to offer. Then, from their contrasting contributions and resulting tensions and possible conflicts, something new can emerge. Carl Jung called this kind of outcome from an active engagement with opposites the 'transcendent function'.[1] The transcendent function can also arise from tension between other pairs of contrasting forces that are characteristic of the design process. Just as the client and the architect may engage in dialogue, so too can the activities of briefing and designing, the brief and the design as outcomes and ideas of use and form work 'in dialogue' with each other. Rather than one determining the other, each contributes to the creation of a transcendent third.

Another very different kind of dialogue also affects design. That is the dialectical relationship between a person's inner world of memories and desires and the outer world of experiences of places and relationships. Connections between the inner and outer worlds, while always present, remain largely invisible and unrecognised. Recognising that these connections exist can generate insight into the choices architects and clients make and can provide material to inspire and inform design. A more reflective and enriching dialogue can then take place between them.

> The confrontation of the two positions generates a tension charged with energy and creates a living, third thing – not a logical still birth in accordance with the principle of *tertium non datur* (take or leave it) but a movement out of suspension between the opposites, a living birth that leads to a new level of being, a new situation.
>
> Carl G Jung quoted by Jeffery C Miller, *The Transcendent Function*, 2004, p 38

Client and Architect

For the conversation between client and architect to be a dialogue, each needs to be present and engaged, precisely the opposite of what happens when architects are asked to develop design proposals without any contact with the client, as in design competitions which lack what architect Cynthia Weese described as 'The synergy developed by an involved and dedicated client interacting with the architect …'[2]

A dialogue between client and architect is possible when both parties bring their respective bodies of knowledge to the venture and encourage and respect the contributions the other can make. For this to happen the architect needs to recognise that the client's role is to inform and that the client's knowledge and opinions will help shape the design in crucial ways. The client needs to recognise that the architect's task is the transformation of knowledge about client needs and desires into the design of a place. From their strikingly different kinds of contribution and through thinking together, something new and unexpected is produced.

The Client Informs

Along with funds and a site, clients bring a set of needs and desires and a substantial body of knowledge about their organisation, its goals, its structure and its aspirations. The architect depends on this knowledge, which the client has and the architect does not. In his book *Design in Mind* Bryan Lawson quotes the architect Eva Jiricna, who describes what is both the problem and the reality: 'The client is not capable of knowing what the options are and we are not capable of understanding what the end product is for.'[3] Architects also recognise that having an active, engaged client can lead to a better design. Israeli architect Ada Karmi-Melamede of Ada Karmi-Melamede Architects, Tel Aviv told Teresa, 'If you have an intelligent, participating client, in fact you'll get a better product and he will be happier and you will be happier and then also he will live in this building the way you kind of envisaged it for him.'

Clients figure out their needs, desires and aspirations through a process called 'briefing' in the UK and 'programming' in the US. Through briefing clients *discover* their visions and objectives for a project as well as more specific spatial, physical and organisational requirements and preferences. During briefing clients have opportunities to reach agreement and set priorities. Briefing is more a matter of discovering what was previously unknown or poorly understood than of collecting information and ideas previously formulated. Thus briefing 'is the most important contribution the client can make to the building project. It is as creative as anything the architect or other designers subsequently do.'[4]

Briefing may precede or overlap the development of design proposals; it may be conducted before the architect who will design the project has been hired, afterwards or a combination of both. All kinds of people may be consulted including future occupants, neighbours, local organisations and professionals knowledgeable about that type of project. Focus groups, surveys, personal interviews, observations and design workshops are all possible techniques for gathering information and ideas. Clients may thoroughly scrutinise the building and site they presently occupy to learn

Southwark Building Design Service, Friary Estate Options Appraisal, London, 2002. Residents noted their suggestions for improving the estate's external environment directly on display boards that showed plans and photographs of the estate as it was.

what works and what does not and why, finding ideas for what can be different in the new project. Clients may visit projects similar to their own and talk with users there as the client group. Valuable briefing information is also generated in community design workshops where participants suggest their own design ideas as parishioners did during design of St. Matthew's Parish Church in Pacific Palisades, California (see Chapter 1).

Briefing often culminates in a written and illustrated document or series of documents, called a brief or a program. Large scale, public projects are the most likely to have detailed briefs completed prior to the start of design or during early stages of design. In smaller projects, clients may not compile a written brief at all. They may just make a list of needs or a rough sketch with more briefing occurring as design proceeds.

The nature of information in a brief varies from the more philosophical and qualitative to the factual and quantitative. Detailed briefs often include the project's purpose; client objectives and aspirations; expected patterns of use with characteristics and activities of occupants; types, sizes and relationships between spaces; furniture, equipment and other physical requirements, sometimes for each individual space; analysis of the site; budget; and even design concepts.

A brief can serve as a vehicle for on-going conversations between client and architect, possibly evolving as new decisions are reached. It can be used to ensure that design proposals meet the stated requirements or to enable a focused discussion for revising those requirements. If the brief is developed in phases, the completion of each phase can be a time when all parties reach agreement. If, over time, members of the client (or the design) team change, a written document helps to assure continuity, becoming a reference for all to use. The brief may also be used in applying for or raising funds.

As buildings have become more complex involving a greater variety of building professionals, briefing has become a specialty with attendant textbooks, guides for clients, architecture courses, professional organisations and consulting firms emerging to offer expertise and guidance.[5] Many architecture firms provide briefing and design as distinct services, frequently with one group of staff preparing the brief and another the design. Large organisations may have the staff and expertise to develop their briefs in

Participants in a community design workshop study options for the site planning of Gateway Commons in San Francisco designed by Pyatok Architects.

Creating a brief is an iterative process that may go to and fro a number of times. A good architect will probe and question the brief to find the best answer to your needs.

CABE, *Creating Excellent Buildings*, 2003, p 26

house or they may hire outside consultants who specialise in preparing briefs. This brief is then given to the architect who is to design the building or to those architects who will make initial proposals in order to be considered for the commission.

Whoever takes the major responsibility for briefing, it is essential that clients are centrally involved in these activities. Their engagement in briefing helps them become active and informed participants in the dialogue with the architect and ensures that the brief accurately reflects their intentions and needs. When clients hand over all briefing responsibility to outside consultants, without requiring the participation of their own staff, they relinquish a key aspect of their role in the design process. This disengagement from a dialogue with the architect becomes more extreme when the completed brief is presented to the architect to make an initial design without ever having any contact with the client.

Client and Architect Think Together

Some clients place great importance on being able to work closely with the architect to develop a design. They deliberately select architects who show an interest in, and an aptitude for, engaging in dialogue. In choosing an architect for the Seattle Central Library, the library rejected a design competition because, as Alex Harris, Director of the Capital Fund for the library reported to Karen, 'we didn't want someone to come up with a design concept for our project without working with us as a client'. After the first stage of the design competition for the Supreme Court building in Jerusalem, architects chosen for the second stage were interviewed. 'For the first time in Israel, priority was given to choosing an architect not only on the merits of the plans submitted, but also in anticipation of an on-going dialogue to continue throughout the design process.'[6]

Like clients, architects vary in how much importance they place on working closely with the client. Some design architects prefer to have other members of the firm act as the liaison with the client or even hire another firm to take on that role. The architects whose work is presented in this book recognise the value of working closely with the client, particularly one who wants and is able to contribute. Christie Coffin, of The Design Partnership, San Francisco and one of the architects for the Berkeley's Rosa Parks Elementary School, commented:

> It is always really wonderful if there is some small cohort in the client group that really cares about the place and is interested in learning more about how the place could be a tool for what they do and is supportive of thinking through the design in more detail. The best job is the job where there are people on the client side who take this as an opportunity to think like a designer and understand the environment.

Berkeley-based architect Rosa Lane is always eager to involve the future occupants of a building and a wide range of people from the community in design workshops as a way of generating design. This is her preferred approach to designing, as she told Karen:

> I love that process. If I'm in a process, I can't even imagine sitting at my desk and trying to come up with an idea. I probably can do it but it would be a very mechanical exploration of my own interior ideas of form. It would not have life in it and that is the key. To have a building … is to have the life of the community in it beforehand.

There is great variation in how, when and with whom a dialogue between client and architect takes place. For ease of discussion we describe three basic kinds: with a single individual, with a committee and with members of an entire community. To select an architect for the Supreme Court building in Jerusalem a detailed brief was prepared and an international design competition was held. The Israeli architects Ada Karmi-Melamede and her brother Ram Karmi were selected following a review of their proposal and an interview with the selection committee. After receiving the commission, the architects met regularly with a client committee but they worked most closely with one member – the Supreme Court Justice Meir Shamgar. In her interview with Teresa, Ada Karmi-Melamede described the intense conversations she and her brother Ram Karmi had with him: 'He was so intelligent … that it [the design] became better and we weren't that tired … It was something to do with the dialogue. You should never expect it to be available at the outset and you are lucky if it happens without effort.' Over the course of their discussions the architects developed a total of 16 different alternatives.

The architects' dialogue with the Supreme Court Justice focused on different possible routes to the courtrooms and the symbolic meaning of those routes. In their original competition submission the architects had placed the six courtrooms on the lowest level because 'we thought the law courts should be carved into the rock so that nobody could move the rock'. In this proposal the public descended to the courtrooms and, symbolically, to the law. But the Supreme Court Justice believed strongly that one should never descend to the law; one should always ascend. However, as the architects explained, having everyone ascend to the courtrooms would create a very different building. Eventually they proposed that the public reach the courtrooms straight on, that the judges descend to them from their chambers and that the accused ascend. 'At that time, there was silence all of a sudden in the room. We knew that we had hit upon a point that he understood – that the form or the section of the building had something to do with the way it looks. Since then he started to think like an architect. It was an amazing process, absolutely amazing.'

Design Group Collaborative holds a design charette for Maranacock Performing Arts Center, in Readfield, Maine. Teachers, students and staff are developing ideas for the schematic design.

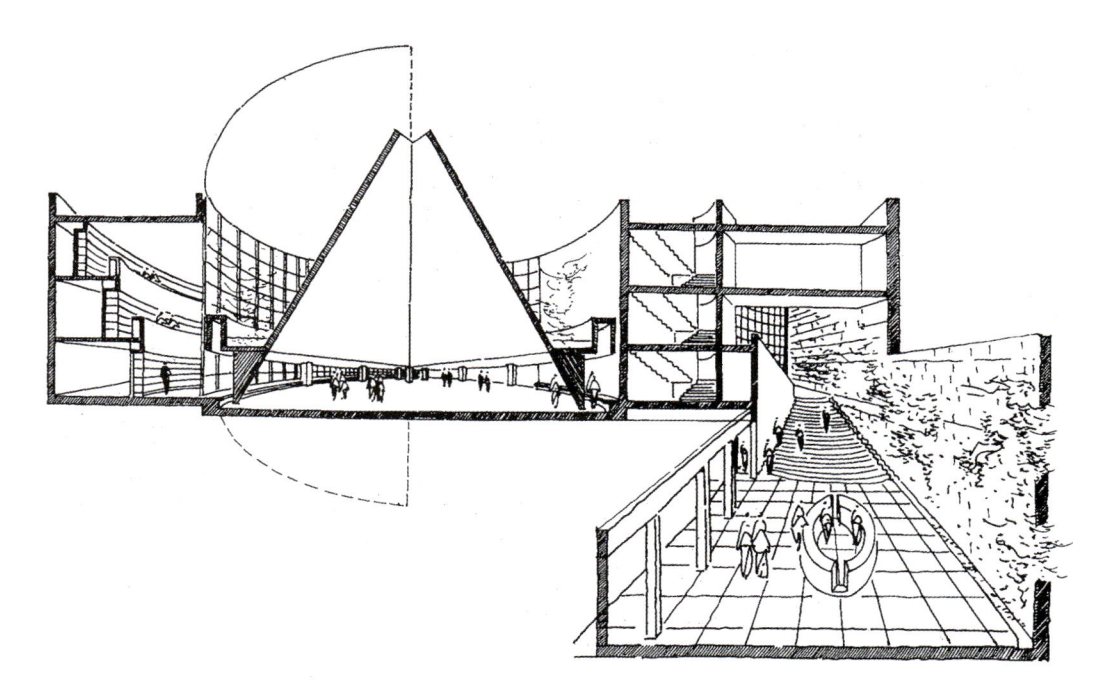

Ada Karmi-Melamede and Ram Karmi, Supreme Court, Jerusalem, 1992.
ABOVE The public passes through the foyer into the courtrooms on the same level while judges reach the courtrooms by descending from their chambers.
BELOW Entrance from the foyer to the courtrooms through a Jerusalem stone wall.

The Supreme Court Justice fulfilled the role of what CABE's *Creating Excellent Buildings* calls the 'design champion', that is someone who is willing to put in the time, energy and interest to learn about architecture and who can 'drive the design'.[7] The dialogue between client and architect works best when a design champion has enough authority and is willing to take risks or is a strong leader in the client group. In contrast, architects are often frustrated when they have to work with a project manager rather than with key people in the client organisation because they seek direct insights and responses, not mediated ones. Also, people in the client organisation with authority are likely to be better informed, more willing to take risks and have the power to make decisions.

Working with an entire committee or several committees can be more difficult than a dialogue with a single, empowered individual, particularly when meetings are attended by different members at different times or when the committee does not develop a clear position or opinions. Fortunately, client committees can be composed of hard-working, dedicated individuals who have strong opinions and are willing to devote time and energy and to learn about design so that a rich and fruitful dialogue can ensue.

From the very beginning the staff and the board of Seattle Central Library were determined to be a thoroughly engaged client, committed to clear communication and working closely with the architect. During the course of the project the City Librarian, Deborah Jacobs, the Director of the Central Library, Jill Jean and Alex Harris, Director of Capital Fund and representatives from the library board met with the architects frequently (even travelling to Rotterdam when necessary) and worked closely with Seneca Group, the project management firm they hired for the duration of the project. Throughout the process the client team and the architects engaged in a lively give and take, each side fully engaged with the project and attentive to the ideas and responses of the other.

The administrative client for the Rosa Parks Elementary School was the local school district but the district played a much less active role in the design process for the new school than a hard working and dedicated Site Committee composed of teachers from the old school and residents from the neighbourhood. The committee, led by community member Kristin Prentice, met weekly, starting from the period of interviewing potential architects and continuing right through to the end of construction.

During the community design workshops organised by the Site Committee key design concepts emerged and decisions regarding what facilities the school should include were reached. Just as for St. Matthew's Parish Church and other projects presented in this book, these sessions made it possible for members of an entire community to engage in dialogue with the architects and, as with St. Matthew's, the design emerged directly from those discussions.

Architect Kava Massih, who developed the design, participated in the community design workshops (see Chapter 4). He recalls how a key design concept, 'the classroom as a house', came from his participation and his commitment to the relationship with the client:

> Because of the process, the forms are very comfortable, everyday forms… I'm the one who came up with the form of each classroom because I kept hearing how the classroom is like a house; it's sort of a self-contained entity. I'm normally not so restrained, coming

Ratcliff Architects, Rosa Parks Elementary School, Berkeley, California, 1997.
Design of the school evolved from workshops with community members and input from students, teachers, librarians, social workers and local police.

up with forms that are a little more interesting. I thought I owed it to everyone not to do my own thing and impose it on them. I felt like it needed to be a little more familiar as if they had drawn it. It wouldn't be Rem Koolhaas drawing it. Again, it's this relationship that develops. You don't want to betray it.

Community design workshops are also held to elicit comments on design proposals that have already been generated by the architect. For the design of Bishops Square in Spitalfields, London, the developer of the site sought input to the initial landscape design from people who worked or lived in the surrounding neighbourhood. Participants in the community workshops expressed strong opinions: that the proposed plan was too corporate, with hard surfaces and sharp edges and it did not make connections to the rich history of the area. These comments led to significant changes in the project (see Chapter 3).

The Architect Transforms

The architect's major responsibility on any project is to transform a varied, often conflicting set of needs and constraints into the integrated design of a place. For the architect to accomplish this creative task, the client needs to trust the architect's abilities and not attempt to take over the designer's role. Dana Cuff, Professor of Urban Planning at the University of California, Los Angeles, found in her research that clients of outstanding architectural projects 'were actively engaged in the design process but when it came to expertise they did not command, they relied upon their consultants'.[8]

… clients do want designers to transcend the obvious and the mundane, and to produce proposals which are exciting and stimulating as well as merely practical. What this means is that design is not a search for the optimum solution to the given problem, that *design is exploratory*.

Nigel Cross, *Designerly Ways of Knowing*, 2007, p 52

The process of transforming is difficult, requiring patience, tolerance of uncertainty and an inner confidence that a design will emerge. Teresa describes her own experience of designing:

> I have the list of practical requirements and my impressions and feelings about what the client needs. I take them away with me; I start to let my mind wander to try to make some sense of it all. I draw or scribble on pieces of paper, draw the context to scale, take photos and gradually somewhere in my mind something begins to form. Often there are enormous tensions. It feels messy and uncomfortable, almost like being constipated or pregnant. It is often painful giving birth to the solution.

While design always transforms knowledge represented in written and spoken language into sketches and drawings, the best designs also transcend practical needs to achieve something more, something that both meets but also transcends programmatic requirements. Dana Cuff points out that this

Louise Braverman, Centro de Artes Nadir Afonso, Boticas, Portugal, 2010. The exhibition hall, to the left, carved out of a granite hillside, has a green roof serving as a park. The civic side of the building, on the right, includes a double height entry, auditorium, offices and gift shop. The cafe is both outside and inside.

creation of something beyond what the client could ever have imagined depends upon giving the architect 'some freedom to invent design solutions that the clients themselves could not conjure up'.[9]

New York architect Louise Braverman recognises the importance of meeting client needs and also achieving something more:

> … I bring other ways of extending their vision or amplifying their vision and they like it – the other larger ideas. Then I try to make it into an architectural whole that has architectural merit. I'm not here just to respond to needs. I'm here to take all this and make good architecture out of it.

Architects are deeply committed to this challenge of transforming an understanding of the client's needs and aspirations into an outstanding design. How exactly architects do, or should, accomplish this daunting task has long been the subject of theory, research and design directives. If one holds the view that designing is a sequential, linear process of distinct steps, one following the other, then one believes that the brief defines a problem that the proposed design solves. Observations of designers in action, however, suggest something quite different: that problem and solution emerge and evolve together, shaping each other, in an iterative process. Trying out solutions helps designers to understand stated problems or needs and to discover ones that have not yet been recognised. Nigel Cross, who has studied designers, calls this process a 'designerly' way of proceeding.[10] Kees Dorst, who has observed industrial designers tackling assigned problems, concludes that

> Creative design seems more to be a matter of developing and refining together both the formulation of a problem and ideas for a solution with constant iteration of analysis, synthesis and evaluation processes between the two notional design 'spaces' – problem space and solution space.[11]

Good design is transcendent. It moves beyond the practical, not as a direct solution to a problem stated in the brief but as an interpretation and exploration of the brief and, possibly, of domains beyond the brief. In this process of interpreting and exploring the many different facets of a project, architects often come upon particular aspects that serve to guide their design in significant ways. In observations of architecture students asked to design a children's nursery, given a written brief, one student commented immediately that 'the most important thing is that we are going to have children playing outside' and discussions proceeded from there to another student suggesting an L-shaped building to protect outdoor play areas. The first student's comment served to structure the project in a particular way.[12]

The creative designer interprets the design brief not as a specification for a solution, but as a kind of partial map of an unknown territory …

Nigel Cross, *Designerly Ways of Knowing*, 2007, p 52

Which aspects of a project come to the foreground to guide design depends upon the particular outlook, knowledge, concerns and values of the individual architect. It is this structuring of the project that explains how, given the exact same brief, architects develop quite different design proposals, often addressing quite different problems. In his published request for proposals from architects for the redesign of his Hong Kong apartment, Julien Grudzien did not mention his two young children. He received several proposed designs in response. In contrast, Denise Ho, the architect he eventually selected, did not simply send in a proposed design. Instead, she asked if she might visit him and his family before developing a proposal. During this visit she observed the lively activities of his two small children and their close relationship with both parents, circumstances that inspired her design.

Good architects frequently identify a need, a condition or a problem that the client had not voiced and that was not foreseen in the brief. The client's written program for a new Central Library in Seattle recommended a book collection on four levels, on the assumption that it is inevitable that books will be separated on different levels of the building. Architect Rem Koolhaas realised that such an arrangement on separate floors causes problems: the addition of new books often requires extensive rearrangement of the collection between different levels. Based on his identification of this problem, common to all libraries, which the clients had not presented, he proposed a continuous ramp with sufficient space for additional books to allow departments to expand without being relocated.

To guide design and to organise disparate and sometimes contradictory elements, designers often develop an organising spatial idea or design concept. A strong concept can sustain and focus energy and commitment through an arduous and frustrating design process. It also sustains the architect's interest and enthusiasm. Denise Ho describes the concept as

> the most magical part. For an architect, it is the most enjoyable, the most exciting. It's like meeting a boyfriend – thinking is he like this? Is he like that? Then suddenly one day you click. There he is – my partner. If it were not that magical, it would not drive architects to work so hard … After you have that concept, the rest is a matter of persistence to make sure the work can be done in accordance with the concept. The concept is what we look for.

The concept that emerged during Denise Ho's design of the Grudzien apartment in Hong Kong was a line that runs the length of apartment, on both floors. On the first floor this line divides circulation space (from the front door to the stairs and up the stairs) from the space of sitting, eating and working. When unforeseen problems emerged during the renovation, this concept served as a guide to choosing options: those options that followed the concept were chosen. Denise's explanation of the concept to her client enabled him to participate with her in the selection of options.

Denise Ho, bookcase/space divider, Grudzien apartment, Hong Kong, 2003. The organising concept is a line running the length of the apartment that divides circulation, on the left, from sitting, eating, working spaces on the right. Here the line takes the form of a bookcase/space divider.

During the early stages of design development for the National Museum of the American Indian Johnpaul Jones of Jones and Jones Architecture and Landscape Architecture, realised 'that we were going to have to use something to organise this whole thing around … If you organised all this complex layering and program around some wonderful space or spaces, it would come together in a way people could understand and move through.' The large central circular space, the Potomac, became that organising concept.

Established architects may draw from a family of related concepts to structure different projects, constituting what Bryan Lawson and others call 'guiding principles'. Lawson's interviews with well-known architects indicate that: Richard Burton is often centrally concerned with how people will move through the building while Richard MacCormac looks for geometric analogies such as a pinwheel, a courtyard, a grid or a circle.[13] Bringing natural light into interior spaces is a guiding principle in the work of Ada Karmi-Melamede as is the design of refined junctions between materials.

Even practices that specialise in small-scale projects pursue guiding principles. The New York architects Lewis Tsurumaki Lewis consistently seek to transform project and site limitations into design opportunities. The renovation of small, first-floor spaces in New York for restaurants offers few possibilities for innovative plans. Instead, the architects focus on surfaces, inserting new volumes into the existing spaces with an ingenious use of materials.[14] The architecture firm Freecell designs and builds interiors for exhibits, retail spaces, work spaces and apartments in New York. Much of this work reveals their guiding interest in integrating the display of items with efficient storage and easy access (see Chapter 5).

Freecell, Shortwave Bookstore, Brooklyn, New York 2002. A single, floor-to-ceiling structure, made of bent-steel conduit tubing, serves as book storage, book display and seating. The frame can be deconstructed and moved and is sturdy enough to climb on.

Briefing and Designing

The dialogue between architect and client consists largely of two primary and complex tasks: briefing and designing, with the client taking relatively more responsibility for briefing and the architect taking more responsibility for designing. The relationship between these tasks, which varies between projects, can be conceptualised in at least two ways: separate and distinct or overlapping and reciprocal.

A Linear Sequence of Separate Tasks?

One long-standing view, common in the US, holds that briefing should be separate and distinct from designing and, as importantly, should precede it in a linear sequence so that briefing is completed before designing begins. This view underlies the standard contracts between architect and owner recommended by the American Institute of Architects (AIA). In these contracts programming (along with feasibility studies, masterplans and prototypes) is listed as an 'additional service' distinct from the 'basic services' the architect provides and so must be contracted for separately. As part of basic services, the architect 'evaluates the program' while also reviewing other information in order to 'ascertain the requirements of the project' before proceeding to a discussion of 'alternative approaches to design and construction of the project'.

The model of briefing as preceding and guiding design in a linear sequence underlies the comprehensive and detailed programs, which are often presented to architects in the US after they receive a commission. For instance, architects selected to design courthouses must follow the *US Courts Design Guide*, produced by the General Services Administration of the federal government. Four hundred pages long, it presents all the spatial and other requirements and all the factors that need to be addressed in court design. Another document, *Facilities Standards for the Public Building Service*, specifies the information the architects are to submit in their preliminary concept designs (several are required). Information modelling techniques are now being devised to check that preliminary concept designs fulfil the requirements listed in the brief. [15]

The promotion of briefing and designing as distinct phases in a linear process derives from an underlying assumption that briefing *defines* a problem which subsequent design will *solve*. This assumption is the premise for many methods of architectural programming published in the US, including the method of 'problem seeking' that Caudill Rowlett Scott developed in the 1960s to use with their clients prior to beginning design.[16] Similarly, the purpose of the type of programming Robert Hershberger prefers is 'to completely define the architectural problem whether or not the designer is a participant in the programming process'.[17] Hershberger is critical of an overlap between briefing and designing for being time-consuming, expensive and too open-ended.

The assumption that briefing is the definition of a problem that design then solves is highly questionable since designing can involve not only the solving of problems but also the *discovering* of problems. Discovering often occurs during design, not only during a separate and distinct phase of briefing. In fact, some problems can only be discovered as design proposals are made. As design solutions emerge and architects present them to clients, the clients' responses reveal new information and new understandings are reached, a process that is not possible when the briefs are treated as completely fixed and unchangeable.

Interviews with architects demonstrate how much, in practice, briefing continues during design. Richard MacCormac says that there is 'the stuff of the thing which only comes out when you try … and produce a scheme and therefore the design process defines objectives in a way in which a brief could never do'. Because of this he says, 'In our office we design as a means of coming to terms with the brief and recognize a reciprocal relationship between the production of form and the definitions of the program'.[18] Architect John Outram reports that presenting several alternatives to a client has helped his firm identify more fully what the

> ... the programming process and the design process ought to be simultaneous and interactive ... the design process ought not to be a problem solution but a process of problem exploration, alternative generation and evaluation.
>
> Julia Williams Robinson and J Stephen Weeks, 'Programming as design' *Journal of Architectural Education*, vol 37, 1983, p 6

client was thinking about. Based on these and other interviews with leading architects, Bryan Lawson concludes that 'a conversation with the client mediated by the presence of proposed solutions can elicit more information than a purely abstract discussion about the problem ...'[19]

Briefing and designing seem to have a more reciprocal relationship in practice than the linear model allows. In recognising this reciprocity, Julia Robinson and Stephen Weeks at the University of Minnesota adopted an approach for undergraduate thesis projects called 'programming as design' that approximates more closely, through course assignments, what happens in professional practice.[20] Namely, their approach recognises that designing is a process of problem exploration, generation and evaluation of alternatives that often occurs simultaneously with briefing, each guiding and shaping the other, in a dialogue.

Reciprocity between Overlapping Activities?

In contrast to the AIA, the Royal Institute of British Architects (RIBA) recognises and supports a reciprocal relationship between briefing and designing by recommending the development of a brief over the course of a project, right up to the beginning of the design phase, after the development of a concept design. The RIBA's Plan of Work consists of five phases: preparation, design, preconstruction, construction and use. The preparation phase includes 'development of initial statement of requirements into the Design Brief by or on behalf of the client confirming key requirements and constraints'.[21] The design phase includes the implementation of the Design Brief and the preparation of additional data, preparation of a concept design, development of concept design and completion of the Project Brief (as part of design development). Thus, the design phase includes both development of concept design and completion of the brief.

In *Briefing Your Architect* Frank Salisbury presents the RIBA model: an outline brief that evolves into a detailed brief. He suggests that a brief needs to be developed over time and that it 'takes time before it becomes settled enough for a realistic design to be produced'. 'The building up of the brief should take place with the input of the architect' and, as importantly, the gradual development makes it easier for designers to absorb the client's needs and desires 'when they are revealed progressively'.[22]

> The detailed brief starts as a vision and outline brief and must be allowed to evolve during the early part of the project. In its final form, when detailed design is to be carried out, it evolves into a detailed brief.
>
> CABE, *Creating Excellent Buildings*, 2003, p 26

In its guide for clients CABE (Commission for Architecture and the Built Environment) also recommends a progressive, increasingly detailed development of the brief that extends in to the beginning of the design phase. In the first phase of the process is the preparation of a 'vision' statement of objectives developed to reach early consensus; this is followed by an 'outline brief' with more detailed requirements. Then, in the design phase, comes the development of a 'detailed brief'. 'At this stage the design team assumes a level of 'ownership of the brief'.[23]

These models that enable briefing and designing to be overlapping, reciprocal activities reflect more accurately what actually happens in practice than do linear models of discrete tasks. They build in opportunities for early design proposals to inform and shape the final brief; they give clients more time and possibly more information to determine detailed requirements; and they give architects, who may have been hired after preparation of early versions of the brief, an opportunity to learn more about client needs through submitting design ideas and a chance to shape the final version of the brief. Commissions and contracts that accommodate briefing and designing as overlapping and reciprocal activities allow design to include the discovery of problems and not just solutions to previously posed problems. The clarity of the RIBA and CABE models, with set stages and set outcomes for each stage, would address some of the concerns Robert Hershberger raises about an overlap between briefing and designing: that it is time-consuming and expensive and too open-ended.

Many architects prefer an overlap between briefing and designing so that they can work with their clients to discover more fully what is needed and desired. An overlap between briefing and designing is just what happens in community design workshops where future occupants and other project stakeholders suggest their own designs and the reasons behind them: they are both briefing and designing, at once.

In his conversation with Teresa, London-based architect Edward Cullinan of Edward Cullinan Associates suggested that the best briefs enable the architect to think through what is needed with the client. He believes that at the beginning there is only a broad outline idea of what is wanted. Briefing occurs throughout the project as more knowledge about what is required develops; briefing is fully complete only when all decisions have been made and the building is finished. Referring to the developers for whom he generated a masterplan for Canon's Marsh in Bristol, Cullinan exclaimed: 'Even with Cress Nicholson, the number of one, two and three bedroom flats was never decreed. It all just grew out of the conversations. It is the art of the possible!' (See Chapter 3)

During his meetings with clients, in response to their ideas, Cullinan makes quick sketches on the spot. He talks,

Edward Cullinan Architects, Lambeth Community Care Centre, London, 1985.
BELOW The client team accepted many aspects of the architect's original proposal: a two-storey building with a central conservatory and a causeway to a back garden.
BOTTOM View from the garden. The design evolved significantly in response to the client's critical comments regarding the symmetry and narrow internal corridors of an early proposal.

sketches and listens all at once, briefing and designing simultaneously. The client team for Lambeth Community Care Centre in London had developed in a written brief a very detailed vision for a new community hospital before they hired Cullinan. They accepted many aspects of his first proposal but they also made critical comments that shaped the final design in significant ways.

Often architects are presented with a completed brief, which they have not helped develop, and are required to make an initial design proposal without any contact with the client. This is true not just for most competitions but other selection processes as well where opportunities for a dialogue to occur, both between architect and client and between the activities of briefing and designing (at least for the initial proposal) are omitted. Sometimes after architects have received the completed brief and won the commission, they are able to extend briefing in to the period of developing design proposals, as Ram and Ada Karmi-Melamede did in their extended dialogue with the Supreme Court Justice in Jerusalem.

Other times architects are able to persuade clients to allocate extra time and funds for additional research and consultation, even though a detailed and comprehensive brief had already been written. An excellent example is the National Museum of the American Indian. The Smithsonian commissioned Venturi, Scott Brown and Associates to prepare a thorough, multi-volume brief for the museum. During the briefing process, they sought ideas and information in nine meetings with tribal groups and tribal leaders in different parts of the country and in six briefing meetings with a variety of others, including Native American artists, Indian educators, museum directors, librarians and archivists and experts in technology and communications. Yet, once the architects for the project were chosen, based in part on their initial design proposal, they persuaded the Smithsonian to provide time and funding to hold four design review sessions with Indian groups in different parts of the country and also to seek additional information in meetings with tribal elders with specific kinds of expertise. This took quite a bit of persuading. Johnpaul Jones, a member of the design team, reported that the Smithsonian felt 'they had put in enough information and they were ready to get going. "Now you guys are designers, start designing" … We felt we needed these "advisors" to keep us honest.' (See Chapter 6)

The evolution of Seattle's Central Library also reveals an overlap of briefing into what the client had presumed would be exclusively the design stage. The library had already spent eight years developing a detailed brief with input from a variety of groups. After the Office of Metropolitan Architecture (OMA) and their local partner LMN Architects received the commission to design the library, Rem Koolhaas persuaded the client team to join the architects in three months of additional research, including visits to recently completed public libraries with related discussions of what worked and what did not and seminars with a range of experts. Joshua Ramus, one of OMA's Partners in Charge, explained to Karen that this period of 'thinking together' allowed the architects and the client team to establish a series of problems and to agree on positions toward those problems. These positions then informed and shaped the architects' design. Joshua finds that when clients have developed a brief prior to commissioning an architect, they do not see the need at first for additional thinking and talking. 'They say "We've already done all that. Just go and make pretty pictures now." They don't understand that architecture can actually solve problems.'

The Brief and the Design

Just as briefing and designing may have different relationships with each other, so do their outcomes. Three possible relationships can be distinguished: the brief largely determines design; the brief is set aside and major design decisions are generated from other sources; or the brief informs and shapes design but does not determine it.

The view that a client's brief determines design falls within a functionalist tradition in architecture, which architect Sunand Prasad sees as influential in England after the Second World War.[24] In practice the functionalist approach often meant that design began only after the written brief was completed and fixed, making briefing and designing separate, distinct stages in a linear process. Working in an architecture firm specialising in the 1970s in hospitals, Prasad found that patterns of use received all the attention without consideration of the expressiveness of the design or occupant experience. This single-minded approach led to extremely utilitarian buildings.

At the other extreme architects propose designs that set aside key requirements in the brief concerning use (at least in the initial stages of design), concentrating instead on issues of form independent of use. The result can be a building with a very compelling appearance that also meets the requirements of use, such as the Guggenheim Museum in Bilbao designed by Frank Gehry or one that is visually compelling and also becomes an iconic building even though it poses problems for some of the intended uses, such as architect Jørn Utzon's design for the Sydney Opera House.

The third way is probably the most common: design proposals address client needs, expressed in a written brief or in conversations between client and architect, but also transcend them. Architect Louise Braverman described this relationship between needs and design in talking with Karen:

> At the end of the day, I want the architecture to be wonderful and fabulous and erudite and aesthetic and something that speaks to the architectural culture of the time ... But it's got to evolve out of and transform into one of those pieces of architecture from the source — from the needs of the people.

Louise's design for the Centro de Artes Nadir Afonso, in the small town of Boticas in northern Portugal, to house artwork of the well-known Portuguese artist Nadir Afonso, illustrates her design philosophy. In designing the museum, Louise responded to a variety of needs: those of the artist's family to create a legacy in his name in the area where he grew up and to exhibit his work to a larger audience; those of the mayor to create jobs and bring in visitors; and those of the town to have more of a civic and cultural centre. Her design does this and more. The exhibition hall, carved out of the

---

Design method was primarily focused on the literal and precise fulfillment of a well formulated and detailed brief which had to come first. All architectural moves had to be justified in functional terms. Any departure was derided as 'formalism' which became a pejorative term.

Sunand Prasad, *Transformations*, 2007, p 20

OMA with LMN Architects, Central Library, Seattle, 2004. RIGHT Program analysis. The architects gave each type of activity and media listed in the client's original program a colour (left). Then they re-organised the activities into a more inclusive set of categories (centre) and housed them in five platforms (right). BELOW Five platforms: derived from the architects' analysis and re-organisation of the library's activities, as presented in the program, and then shifted to create the building's form.

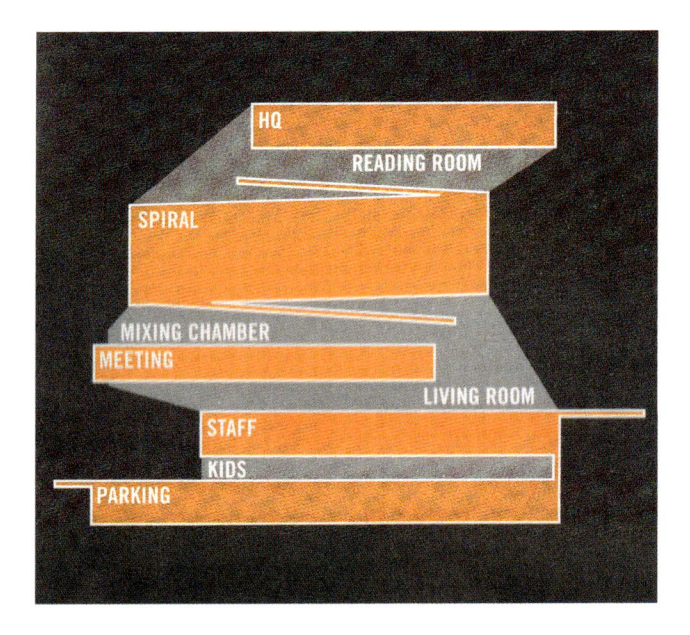

granite hillside, is below ground level covered by a sustainable green roof, which serves as a park. The civic side of the building includes a double height entry hall, an auditorium, offices and gift shop. The building appears to be emerging out of the ground, becoming what Louise calls a 'landscraper building'. Through this connection to the land, a relationship is created between the land and the paintings, giving visitors long views, through continuous space, to both landscape and art.

Design can evolve from a detailed, written brief and still transcend it. A dramatic example is the evolution of the design proposal for Seattle's Central Library (see Chapter 6). The Office of Metropolitan Architecture (OMA), through its lead designers Rem Koolhaas and Joshua Ramus and in partnership with LMN Architects, made full and careful use of the library's detailed program document and further discussions with the client team and other groups to develop a design that both used and transcended the program. The architects consolidated the many discrete activities and media listed in the library's program into a set of 11 categories, distinguishing

42 • IN DIALOGUE CHAPTER 2

them by colour in their graphic analysis. From additional analysis and by applying a new way of grouping activities, they derived five 'platforms' for the building, platforms of different sizes and conditions responding to the programmatic needs of the activities they housed and to the features of the site. They connected these platforms with in-between spaces or what they called 'trading floors'. These platforms are clearly apparent in the final form of the building, sheathed in diamond-shaped panels of glass.

Alex Harris, Director of Capital Fund for the Seattle Public Library, commented that this transformation of the brief into design struck one person in the client group as a 'parlour trick: where you had stripes of colour that were grouped together by function and out of that emerged this form'. One is reminded again of one of the English titles for Paul Klee's painting *Conjuring Trick*.

Architectural critic Herbert Muschamp applauded Rem Koolhaas's reliance on the architectural program for the design of the library and the organisation of space according to use. 'Because of the clarity of this example, the Central Library's impact on architecture could be profound. It makes art out of the relationship between architect and client.'[25]

Architects differ in the kinds of briefing information they find helpful and when. For the Seattle Central Library OMA made excellent use of a lengthy and detailed program from the client while for architect Michael Wilford the best brief is only one or two pages, even for large projects. 'We prefer the thinnest possible information so that we can get a grasp on the whole thing and then gradually embellish it with detail later.'[26] Some architects find briefs too specific, at least for gaining inspiration or developing an initial concept, and believe that it is most important that briefs present overall objectives and requirements.[27]

Architects are particularly disappointed when a brief contains only practical or technical requirements. Extensive lists of activities and spaces with size requirements and spatial relationships either require some kind of transformation into a concept, as OMA did, or are addressed further on in the design process. Ada Karmi-Melamede found that the competition brief for the Supreme Court building stipulated quantities for spaces and specific relationships between functions but said nothing about the dreams or beliefs of the client. She believes that 'what the building is about … has a lot to do with the aspirations of the client and the aspiration of the architect and none

OMA with LMN Architects, Central Library, Seattle, 2004. Early model of the project showing the five platforms and the connecting spaces, derived from the program analysis and re-organisation.

An early model shows the library's basic form, which did not change significantly as the project evolved past the research phase.

Ada Karmi-Melamede and Ram Karmi, public foyer outside the courtrooms, Supreme Court, Jerusalem, 1992. The brief listed a corridor to the courtroom. The architects fought for a more spacious and welcoming space with places to sit.

of these things are written in the program'. Regarding the program for the Supreme Court, she commented:

> You would think it was a kind of very pragmatic, mundane kind of institution because there wasn't one sentence that had anything to do with some kind of expectation on their part, neither was there symbolism nor the role of people, like visitors. In fact the foyer was something we fought for. It wasn't in the program. It was kind of a corridor to the courtroom …

The detailed program document for the National Museum of the American Indian prepared by Venturi, Scott Brown and Associates contained both pragmatic information and the dreams and beliefs of Indian groups from around the country, as expressed in their own words. The written language of the brief proved to have a significant impact upon design. Architect Johnpaul Jones found 'inspiration' in the title of the document (*The Way of the People*) and in the brief preamble written by Native American architect and author Rina Swentzell who presented four principles from tribal ways of being to guide the design and operations of the museum. What Rina Swetzell wrote 'is the inspiration for how this thing was put together'.

A section of the third principle in the Preamble reads: 'We embrace the cycles of our organic world, such as days, seasons – and our lives. Our life and death cycles connect us to the cycles of the sky, water and earth. We honor these cycles in our daily tasks, our subsistence patterns and ceremonial activities.'[28]

The organic world and its cycles are evident both outside and inside the museum. It is made of carved limestone, resembling rock formations worn away by wind and rain; the location of the main entrance faces east and the rising sun; water runs and cascades along the north side of the building in remembrance of Tiger Creek which still runs 20 feet below the site; inside, prisms of light catch the sun's rays; 40 rocks and boulders were placed on the site, called Grandfather Rocks.

The fourth principle in the Preamble in the program reads: 'We recognize our interconnectedness within this organic world and know that respect and sharing must pervade our thoughts and actions. Our reciprocal networks of hospitality connect our families, extended families, tribes and nations.'[29]

Visitors experience a sense of welcome and enjoy physical comforts from the moment they enter the site. The water on the north side gives a sense of coolness and the wall next to it, in the shade of the building, offers visitors a place to sit and touch the water. The generous overhang over the main entrance creates additional shade. Many places inside give visitors spaces to sit and rest while a cafeteria serves tasty meals based on regional Indian cooking. Perhaps the greatest sense of welcome is created by the four-storey atrium, the Potomac, which is the first space that visitors encounter. Johnpaul Jones commented that all these choices were intentional: 'We did all kinds of things to make you comfortable and that was different from any other place you went to on the mall.'

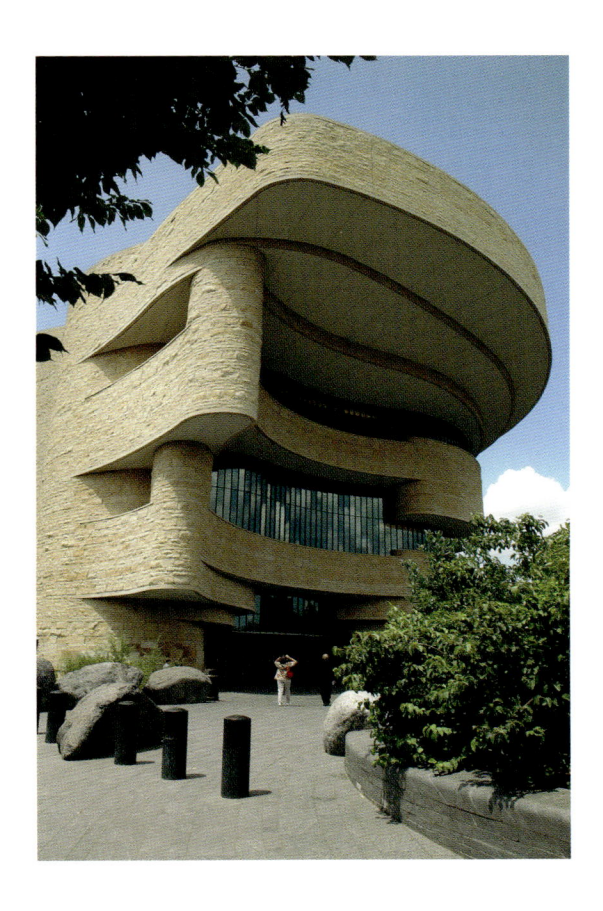

Douglas Cardinal and GBQC Architects, Johnpaul Jones, Ramona Sakiestewa, Donna House (project designers); Jones & Jones, Smith Group with Lou Weller and the Native American Design Collaborative, Polshek Partnership Architects and EDAW (project architects), National Museum of the American Indian, Washington DC, 2004. The main entrance has a generous overhang that shelters visitors. Made of limestone, the museum is intended to resemble a rock formation worn away by wind and rain.

Use and Form

Just as the relationship between briefing and designing, as activities, varies between projects and architects, so too does the relationship between considerations of use and determination of form. The brief records requirements of use and the design represents the suggested form, so the kinds of relationships that occur between use and form parallel those between brief and design.

The architect's major responsibility is the design of built form so it is not surprising that architects place great significance on the many physical design features of projects. Sometimes, however, their attention to form excludes the consideration of other important aspects of a building, including how it will be used. This tendency in architecture to privilege form over use is evident in two common practices. First, in the interest of designing arresting forms, architects may ignore or overlook particular programmatic requirements, making key and influential design choices independently of considerations related to use. Second, in evaluating a proposed design or a completed building attention to form may exclude any consideration of whether the design meets client needs.

When use is ignored during design, the completed building, while possessing striking formal characteristics, may actually impede tasks of daily life and work or make them more difficult. For instance, Mies van der Rohe successfully fulfilled his intention to create the most minimalist house possible but his design of a glass house did not support, and indeed frustrated, the fulfilment of the everyday practical tasks of living for his client and friend Edith Farnsworth.[30] And yet, since the degree to which a building meets occupants' needs is not considered in design evaluations, buildings may receive extensive praise and prestigious design awards, becoming canonical buildings in the culture of architecture and society at large.

Other well-known cases include Louis Kahn's Richards Building at the University of Pennsylvania, Jørn Utzon's Sydney Opera House, Peter Eisenman's Wexner Art Center in Columbus, Ohio and Zaha Hadid's Fire Station in Vitra, Switzerland. The clients for some of these buildings were, apparently, fully satisfied with the completed building despite the difficulties they generated for occupants. Other clients, however, found the problems so serious that they filed lawsuits against the architects or decided never to hire that architect again.

Even though it is widely accepted that these buildings caused problems for their occupants, their design is still held in high esteem in architecture. Such a stance seriously downplays the necessity of meeting client needs and, just as importantly, fails to recognise the complex and interesting relationships that do exist between features of design and features of use, relationships that many architects not only support but enhance through thoughtful design choices.

This for me is creativity, you know, finding solutions for all these things that are contradictory and the wrong type of creativity is that you just forget about the fact that sometimes it rains, you forget that sometimes there are many people and you just make beautiful stairs from the one idea you have in your head. That is not real creativity, it is fake creativity.

Herman Hertzberger in Bryan Lawson, *Design in Mind*, 1994, p 42

Disconnecting form from use, either in designing a building or in evaluating a completed one, gives design a poor reputation, generating suspicion that architects do not care about people and that 'design' is only a matter of aesthetics in a superficial sense. Such a belief casts doubt on the very talents that many architects bring to bear on understanding and addressing client needs, however pragmatic those needs may be. Joshua Ramus calls the separation of form from function one of the 'terrible schisms' that exist in architecture today.

Another orientation prizes not just form but, even more drastically, the visual image the form creates. In response to this emphasis some commentators have had to insist that architecture is *not* sculpture and that client needs (and budgetary requirements) should come first, not last. John Silber lays the blame on architects and architecture, not on clients who, he suggests, are bullied by architects.[31] While Silber places the responsibility on architects for excessive emphasis on image, the responsibility lies with clients as well – clients who want visually striking buildings and commission architects who are well known for designing them. This occurs more and more often in a global culture that gives so much significance to eye-catching images and expects the design of a single building to rejuvenate a city as the Guggenheim Museum did for Bilbao.[32]

That was precisely the client's objective in commissioning Frank Gehry, making the project an example of how client and architect can be well matched in the importance they place on form and outward appearance. Thomas Krens, Director of the Guggenheim Foundation, who served as the client for the project recalled:

> From the beginning, when we started talking about the program, I talked about the building in terms of Chartres Cathedral. I said that I wanted people, when they saw the building, to have the same reaction at the end of the 20th century and the beginning of the 21st century that somebody who approached Chartres Cathedral in the 15th century would have had.[33]

Fortunately, the design of the Guggenheim in Bilbao fulfilled that objective to a large extent but, in doing so, did not thwart the necessary activities and requirements of a museum.

Krens, like many clients of other large public projects, wanted a design that would make an impressive aesthetic statement for the institution and chose an architect for his strengths in that area. These clients look for architects with a strong record in form and image-making and often choose the one who arrives at the initial interview with a design proposal already in hand. Another client team may choose, instead, the architectural team that makes no design proposal so early in the process but suggests instead how it will explore needs and programmatic requirements with the client.

Clients may also look for a combination of both – a strong vision of form from the very beginning and a willingness to work with the client to develop and modify that initial proposal. This was true of the choice of architects for the Supreme Court in Jerusalem and the National Museum of the American Indian. Douglas Cardinal and his design team presented their concept model to the Smithsonian. Duane Blue Spruce, who served as design and construction liaison between the museum and the design team, commented about the selection process after the presentation: 'There was this strong sense that the building should have this awe-inspiring feeling to it. I think that came out very strongly in the initial architectural concepts

National Museum of the American Indian, Washington DC, 2004. The overall building concept remained largely the same throughout the design process and is apparent in the completed building.

In our office we design as a means of coming to terms with the brief and recognize a reciprocal relationship between the production of form and the definition of the programme.

Richard MacCormac in Bryan Lawson, *Design in Mind*, 1994, p 62

for the building … Everybody agreed that a bold gesture was the right thing, that we couldn't be tentative.' However, after they were selected the architects continued to gather input from tribal groups and experts in developing and modifying their initial proposal.

Aspects of use and features of form do not have to be treated as if they were unrelated to each other or, worse yet, as if they were in competition with each other (under the mistaken belief that arresting forms can only be created if use is ignored). Many architects do generate design from an understanding of possible or desired patterns of use so that form, in part, comes *from* an understanding of use. This kind of approach is apparent in the evolution of the design of the Seattle Central Library.

That form is often generated from an understanding of use is not to say that the relationship between use and form is one-directional or deterministic throughout the design process. What seems to happen is that form and use are addressed in connection to each other so that a kind of push and pull is generated between considerations of form and considerations of use. An ongoing dialogue takes place. As Sunand Prasad has written: '… rather than directly leading to form, function enters into a dialogue with form', into a dialectical relationship. By pushing against functional needs form is sharpened.'[34]

The evolution of the design of the interior for the National Museum of the American Indian illustrates this dialectical relationship. The overall form of the building with one large circular space was determined early on and is apparent in Douglas Cardinal's initial concept model presented in the first interview with the Smithsonian. With other members of the design team (Johnpaul Jones, Raomona Sakiestewa and Donna House), Cardinal created the shape of the building by carving away at a rectangular block made of layers of Styrofoam. This block corresponded to the three-dimensional space allowed by the height and setback limitations of the site. Johnpaul Jones recalls: 'If we took that three-dimensional space, imagined it as a chunk of rock, and carved into it, as wind and water would do, we could create a design that had a very natural quality to it.'[35]

In developing the design, however, it became clear that the large circular space the architects had envisioned for the centre of the building, called the Potomac, had to be moved to accommodate the program spaces on the different floors and for ease and clarity of circulation. Duane Blue Spruce described some of the concerns in Karen's interview with him:

> It was always seen as the central space but as the program started getting overlaid on it and seeing how oddly-shaped the galleries were,

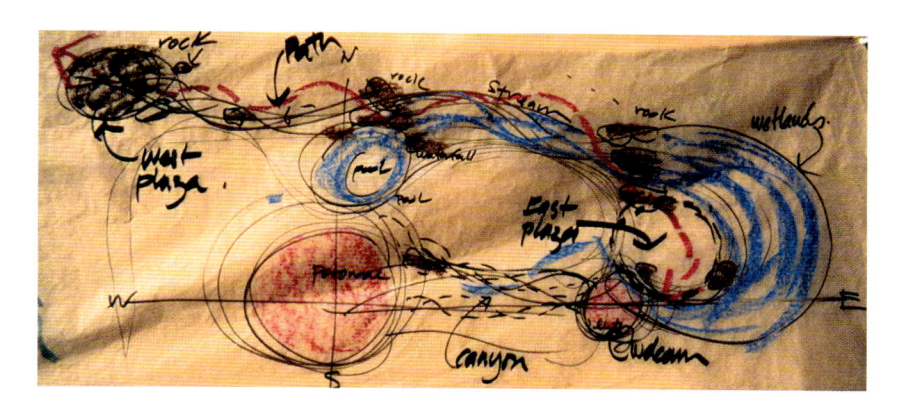

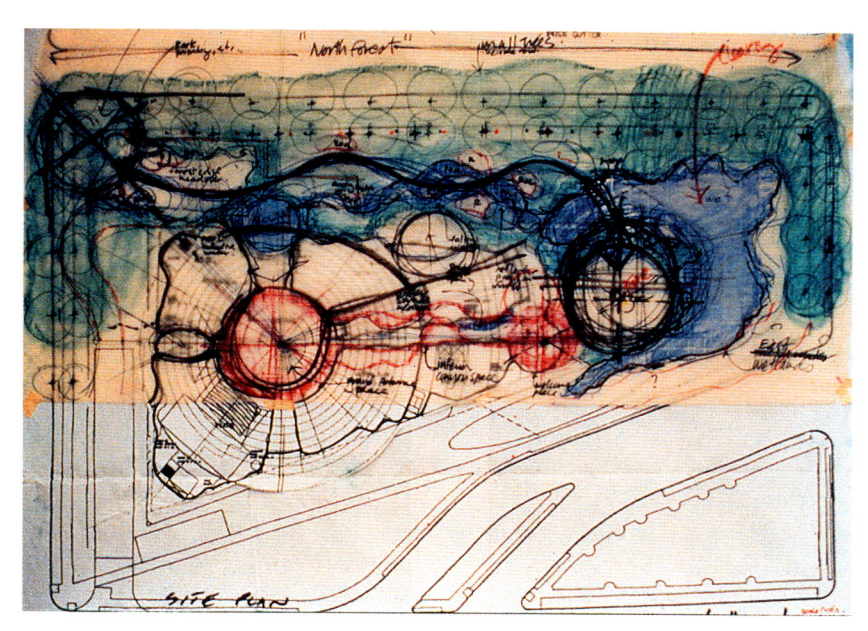

National Museum of the American Indian, Washington DC, 2004.
Early ideas show changes in the location and size of different circular spaces. LEFT The earliest sketch of the site and ground floor shows the Potomac space in the centre of the site and a circular space at the eastern end linked by an east/west passage called the Canyon. BELOW Once the area for the building had been determined, a smaller 'welcome place' was placed toward the east and a 'grand performance space' at the western side, again linked by the Canyon.

CHAPTER 2   IN DIALOGUE   •   49

National Museum of the American Indian, Washington DC, 2004.

The final plan shows the Potomac, a performance and welcoming space, at the eastern end of the building and a mid-sized theatre at the western end. The Canyon became a curving passageway, two-storeys high, from the south entrance around the theatre.

it was clear it needed to migrate more toward the east … These program spaces slid around. That's why you have a resource center and conference center on the north side. They used to be on the east side in a very forced kind of configuration. What we lost was that kind of understanding of the north edge of the Potomac being very transparent on the mall-facing side of the building, but it works.

In the final plan, the two-storey curving corridor on the ground floor, running from the south entrance around the theatre, is the remnant of what earlier had been a much taller space – the Canyon – running east to west and extending from the ground floor all the way up to the fourth that would be crossed with bridges. Duane Blue Spruce commented: 'It was unworkable mostly from a mechanical standpoint in terms of controlling the environments in the gallery spaces and so it eventually went away.'

As projects throughout this book illustrate, buildings that arise from a dialogue between form and use can be architecturally significant and visually arresting. The dialogue with use in no way diminishes the significance or strength of form. The Central Library in Seattle and the National Museum of the American Indian in Washington are just two examples. The overall form

OMA with LMN Architects, Central Library, Seattle, 2004. All external walls are angled surfaces composed of diamond-shaped panels of glass in a steel grid.

of the Rosa Parks Elementary School in Berkeley, although appropriately more modest, is still distinctive; it also emerged from dialogues between form and use, client and architect (see Chapter 4).

Inner Worlds and Outer Worlds

Walking into a beautiful building, hearing a stirring piece of music or smelling a strong scent can be powerful emotional experiences that arouse memories long forgotten. In those moments people may become aware of an inner reservoir of feeling that, at other times, recedes into the background. In such moments of heightened awareness a deeper level of the mind – the unconscious – makes its presence felt. Sensations, feelings, associations suddenly well up. This deep inner world, which begins when life begins, emerges from people's relationship with the external world – with people, places and experiences.

As life is lived, the inner world takes in and stores experiences and memories, which then exert a strong influence on attitudes, behaviours, choices and relationships. On a daily basis, people are primarily in touch with a conscious level of everyday practical thoughts, being largely out of touch with the inner world and the influence it exerts, all the time, on their responses and actions. These conscious thoughts are more accessible and can be imagined as being located closer to the surface of the mind.

> The idea of the unconscious is both difficult to grasp and commonplace … The idea that there is an influence operating in a person's life without them knowing about it is familiar, yet to get an idea of what that influence might be in a personal sense is difficult.
>
> Robert D Hinshelwood, *What Happens in Groups*, 1987, p 49

It is experiences in the outer world that form the inner world, that unconsciously influence how people make their way in the outer world and the kinds of spaces they seek or create. In *House as a Mirror of Self*, Clare Cooper Marcus shows the many different ways people express aspects of their unconscious and self-identity in their choice and decoration of home environments.[36] In *Some Place Like Home* Toby Israel explores how architects' important childhood experiences continue to shape their design choices in adulthood.[37] She also describes a series of exercises clients can use to uncover past experiences, preferences and needs that shape design choices. As clients and architects create outer spaces together, the inner space of each provides a wealth of material that can enrich and guide both briefing and designing.

The Client's Inner World

A client's desire and determination to create a new place, and even a new kind of place, often arises from past experiences stored in the inner world. Yvonne Westerberg grew up in a suburb that resembled a 'concrete jungle'. With no grandparents to visit or countryside within reach, she found respite in a nearby forest where, every spring, she would pick lilies of the valley for her parents. Years later, as a young occupational therapist, she helped an elderly man, Oskar, plant rhododendron seedlings. They only worked together for two hours and although he remained silent the whole time, she felt he was 'living life to the full'. To her surprise she discovered afterwards that he had been suffering from a brain tumour and died three months later.

Yvonne explained to Teresa that her experience with Oskar affected her deeply. It reminded her of the healing power of nature she had known as a child and with his sudden death she felt she had lost a new-found grandfather. She had always wanted to work with elderly people. Now she had discovered that gardens and gardening could give enjoyment of the present and hope for the future to people who had lost the will to live. It took her six years to raise sufficient funds and to ask the landscape architect Ulf Nordfjëll to work with her to realise her dream – the Garden of Senses in the existing garden of Sabbatsberg Hospital in Stockholm. (See Chapter 6)

When client and architect first meet, they may discover that their inner worlds fit, as in the case of the Sydney Opera House. When the competition

Ulf Nordfjëll, Garden of Senses, Sabbatsberg Hospital, Stockholm, 1998.
A chance encounter with an elderly man inspired the client, occupational therapist Yvonne Westerberg, to create this healing garden. While planting flowers with him, she sensed that he was 'living life to the full' even though, as she learned later, he had been dying of a brain tumour.

jurors selected Jørn Utzon, they intuitively picked up on his sensitivity to the sea. Utzon's father had been a naval architect and Utzon had always lived by the sea. It is likely that this aspect of his life provided him with an experience that enabled him so brilliantly to add expression to one of the world's most beautiful harbours with those glittering white sails. His proposed design matched the experience of Australians as people of an island nation but, sadly, the particular sensitivity that enabled his daring selection on behalf of the client, the New South Wales government, was unable to sustain a dialogue through all the exigencies of getting the building built.[38]

The inner worlds of architect and client can also be very different, sometimes diametrically opposed. Early in her architectural career Teresa was amazed to discover that not everybody enjoys the same environmental experiences that she does. For her, the sound of running water was a soothing reminder of the times she had spent as a child with her grandparents by the sea. The sounds of waves on the beach and the trickling river that passed through the garden had been a blessed respite from less happy times at home. She expected everyone to have this same reaction to the sea, to rivers and the sound of water until a client reacted very strongly to her suggestion for installing a small fountain in an entrance court. It took time to unravel that the sound and sight of water disturbed the client's emotional equilibrium since this family had lost a small child through drowning. The sound of water, then, had two very different meanings, soothing or distressingly re-traumatising.

Thus, exploring the clients' inner spaces can uncover past experiences, which, even if they remained hidden, would exert a strong influence on their responses to design possibilities and could also interfere with the design process. When Bob Mohr and Brodie Bain of Mithun Architects in Seattle began developing the masterplan for a campus for the Northwest Indian College on the Lummi Reservation in Washington state, they discovered something very important about the inner space of a whole community. The site chosen by the previous architecture firm for the first new building on the campus had been the location of several murders. The tribe felt that this site, associated as it was with such tragedy, was extremely ominous, a feeling the tribe had been unable to voice but that prevented the tribe from continuing the process with that firm (see Chapter 5).

Sometimes when painful memories emerge, they need to be worked through before design can proceed. This process becomes both a way of healing as well as a means of generating design possibilities. One example is the Donald W Reynolds Community Services Center in Pine Bluff, Arkansas. The building, sponsored by The United Way charity, was to house a variety of service organisations including The United Way, Girl Scouts and Boy Scouts, a counselling agency, a domestic violence support group and a local orchestra. Three hundred people participated in three days of workshops, including administrators and staff of the organisations that would occupy the building, their clients, local ministers and the mayor.

According to Rosa Lane, architectural consultant for the project, when the participants were asked to write down their visions for the building on the very first day, one of the ministers stood up and announced, 'I have to speak the unspeakable. This building can potentially heal wounds but I cannot sit here anymore and not bring up my concern about the racism in this community that's been going on for maybe 150 years.' So the group facilitators invited participants to write their own versions of 'the history they wanted and never had'. Rosa reports that this re-created history gave birth to the design; the building emerged from 'this re-visioning of their culture as a diverse community, as a healthy community that could recognize and respect each other in new ways'. The new building took the form of an old cotton factory that had once stood near the site, incorporating features of the former structure including a clerestory roof.

The Architect's Inner World

To generate design ideas architects depend upon a great variety of sources. One, often unrecognised source is their own inner world, a repository of experiences from childhood, from their architectural education and from their careers. Frances Downing's interviews with practising architects and architecture students demonstrate how these experiences are stored as mental images that carry emotional, experiential and objective information that can be drawn upon during design.[39]

An awareness of the connections between their own inner worlds and the outer spaces they design gives architects insight into their own motivations. Without such insight, they may be prone to imposing their own needs on clients who may have equally strong desires. In her design work, Teresa has always been fascinated by the possibility of creating a sparkling quality of light inside her buildings. From her early days at design school in New Zealand, she found herself incorporating windows at a high level, roof lights and clerestories in all her designs. Her clients, who often choose her because of this quality in her work, were the first to notice this signature move. Initially she shrugged it off. Much later she discovered that she had been born in an attic room with high-level dormer windows. Not surprisingly, Christopher Bollas, a British psychoanalyst, wonders 'whether there is an architectural unconscious'.[40]

While interviewing architect Michael Graves, Toby Israel noticed that the physical organisation of the warehouse Graves transformed into a home in Princeton was reminiscent of the Indiana stockyards where he spent time as a child and wondered if there could be a connection.[41] Graves noted that in the Midwest, there were no other real buildings apart from the library and church so these huge timber stockyard structures had made a big impression on him. He recalled the Stockyards Exchange Building in vivid sensory detail, especially the sound of footsteps on the

Teresa von Sommaruga Howard, house extension, Epsom, Surrey, 2004.
The client wanted a light-filled, family space that would bring the garden inside and would be more than a box stuck on the back of the house.

Michael Graves, San Capistrano Library, San Capistrano, California, 1983. The row of timber-trellised enclosures, for outdoor reading, is reminiscent of the pens in the Indiana stockyard where as a child Graves spent as much time as he could with his father and uncle.

wooden floors. It seems that both the warehouse that became his home, with its cellular structure and timber floors, and his San Capistrano Library in California, with its timber-trussed roof and steady rhythm of timber-trellised porticos, recreated aspects of the stockyards where he spent precious time with his father and uncle.

Michael Pyatok's childhood experiences, now carried internally, shape his design as well as his choice of clients and the kind of practice he pursues. In Karen's interview with him Michael suggested that the private outdoor spaces he always includes in his designs for affordable housing are most likely inspired by the fire escapes on apartment buildings in the Brooklyn neighbourhood where he grew up. He carries his experience of these spaces over to his design of low-income housing.

> We had landings on the fire escape outside the kitchen windows. It was a piece of outdoor turf in the sun away from the street where people could hang out. At these higher densities having a little outdoor space is very important. There are pressures now to do away with those things. There are long-term maintenance problems within tightening budgets. So we have to double our efforts to try to find money from the budget by doing something less expensively so we can release some of the budget to accommodate a very special need.

Pyatok Architects, Tower Apartments, Rohnert Park, California, 1993. Townhouse units above flats and parking provide housing for 50 low-income families. Each home has its own front and rear patio or porches.

CHAPTER 2 IN DIALOGUE • 55

While Michael was studying architecture at Pratt Institute, learning how to be a 'form maker and space shaper and the more exotic the better,' he was still living in the same apartment building where he had grown up. Each evening he returned to the same factory workers whom he had known all his life. For Pyatok, it only seemed natural to take his design talents back to those who had helped him along the way and whose factories were now closing down. Not surprisingly, he stresses the importance of thinking about clients who are not in the room – future residents and neighbours – not just the paying client and the developer (see Chapter 3).

Ram Karmi's youth also influenced his approach to architecture. He explained to Teresa that he grew up on a kibbutz and was horrified when he watched the Israeli housing ministry turn housing into a 'scientific process'. He saw that standard types were defined to match standard definitions of the client, resulting in a mass-produced urban landscape that focused more on cars than human beings. In contrast, his view is that 'you don't start with a *tabula rasa*. The inside is defined by the client and the outside, by the surroundings, topography and climate'.

Architect Rosa Lane learned a lot about space as a small child through sharing a bedroom with two sisters. As she told Karen, when she was 11, feeling the room was too crowded, she decided to build her own house. She carried out this construction project, in a grove of maple trees behind her family's house in Maine, without anyone knowing. Having found materials in the basement she took a few pieces at a time. Her father had already given her hammers and all the nails she wanted so she was able to build a 12 x 12 foot (3.6 x 3.6 metre) house with a living room and kitchen on the lower level and a sleeping loft on the upper level. She also put a window in the loft and another at the lower level. The structure stood from 1961 to 1988, when it finally collapsed.

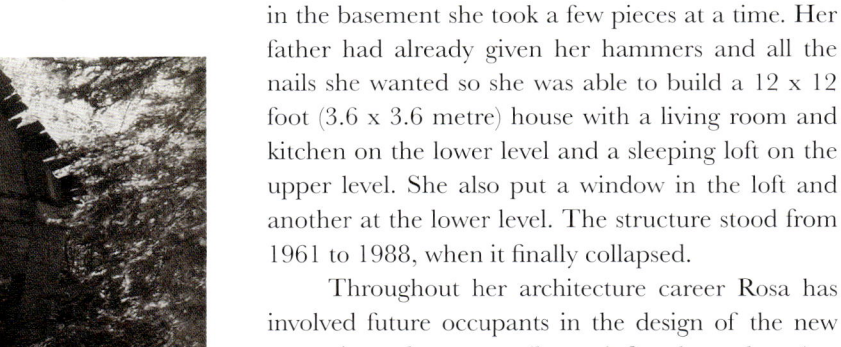

Throughout her architecture career Rosa has involved future occupants in the design of the new space in order create 'homes' for themselves (see Chapter 3). If the architects take full control, then they own the space rather than the people who are going to occupy it. Rosa seems to understand how important it is for people not to feel that constricting spaces are being imposed upon them. This innate knowledge comes from her own childhood experience that Rosa has internalised and now uses as a guiding truth.

The inner world of the architect shapes the way each architect practises architecture and the choices each makes during the design of a project, usually in unconscious ways. Becoming aware of the influence their inner world

Rosa Lane, House, Pemaquid Beach, Maine, 1961–1988. Using rocks for the foundation and timber frame construction, Rosa built this cabin when she was 11 years old, without her parents' knowledge.

can exert helps architects recognise some of the sources of their ideas. In a similar fashion clients can become aware of the influence of the inner world upon their stated requirements and desires. As a result, both will find that the reasons behind their preferences become more transparent and negotiable, enabling them to understand and work through difficulties that may arise between them.

NOTES

1. Carl G Jung, *The Transcendent Function*, trans AR Pope, Students Association, CG Jung Institute (Zurich), 1957, quoted in Jeffery C Miller, *The Transcendent Function*, State University of New York (Albany), 2004.
2. Cynthia Weese, 'Chicago Public Library', *Competitions 1*, Winter 1991, p 5, quoted in Shannon Mattern, *The New Downtown Library: Designing with Communities*, University of Minnesota Press (Minneapolis), 2007, p 16.
3. Quoted in Bryan Lawson, *Design in Mind*, Architectural Press (Oxford) 1994, p 50.
4. Frank Salisbury, *Briefing Your Architect*, second edition, Architectural Press (Oxford), 1990, p 46.
5. See the following books on briefing/programming: Theo JM Van der Voordt and Herman BR van Wegen, *Architecture in Use: An Introduction to the Programming, Design and Evaluation of Buildings*, Elsevier (Oxford), 2005; Alastair Blythe and John Worthington, *Managing the Brief for Better Design*, Spon Press (London), 2001; Edith Cherry, *Programming for Design: From Theory to Practice*, John Wiley & Sons Inc (New York), 1999; Robert G Hershberger, *Architectural Programming and Predesign Manager*, McGraw-Hill (New York), 1999; Salisbury, *Briefing Your Architect*; Robert R Kumlin, *Architectural Programming: Creative Techniques for Design Professionals*, McGraw-Hill (New York), 1995; Donna Duerk, *Architectural Programming: Creative Techniques for Design Professionals*, Van Nostrand Reinhold (New York), 1993; Wolfgang FE Preiser, *Programming the Built Environment*, Van Nostrand Reinhold (New York), 1985; Mickey Palmer, ed, *The Architects' Guide to Facility Programming*, Architectural Record Books (New York), 1981.
6. Yosef Sharon, *The Supreme Court Building, Jerusalem*, trans Alexandra Mahler, Yad Hanadiv (Israel), 1993, p 23.
7. CABE, *Creating Excellent Buildings: A Guide for Clients*, CABE (London), 2003.
8. Dana Cuff, 'The social production of built form', *Environment and Planning D: Society and Space* vol 7, 1989, p 441.
9. Ibid, p 445.
10. Nigel Cross, *Designerly Ways of Knowing*, Birkhäuser (Basel), 2007.
11. Kees Dorst and Nigel Cross, 'Creativity in the design process: co-evolution of problem-solution', *Design Studies*, vol 22, no 5, September 2001, p 434.
12. Fasal Agabani, *Cognitive Aspects in Architectural Design Problem Solving*, University of Sheffield, 1980 cited in Bryan Lawson, *What Designers Know*, Architectural Press (Oxford), 2004 pp 91, 92.

13 Lawson, *Design in Mind*.
14 Paul Lewis, Marc Tsurumaki and David Lewis, *Opportunistic Architecture*, Princeton Architectural Press (New York), 2007.
15 See Chuck Eastman 'Automated assessment of early concept designs', in Richard Garber, ed, *Closing the Gap: Information Models in Contemporary Design Practice*, *Architectural Design*, vol 79, 2009, pp 52–7.
16 William Pena, William Caudill and John Focke, *Problem Seeking: An Architectural Programming Primer*, Cahners Books International (Boston, MA), 1977.
17 Hershberger, *Architectural Programming*, p 34.
18 Quoted in Lawson, *Design in Mind*, p 62.
19 Ibid, p 72.
20 Julia Williams Robinson and J Stephen Weeks, 'Programming as design', *Journal of Architectural Education*, vol 37, 1983, pp 5–11.
21 RIBA Outline Plan of Work 2007.indd (pdf available through www.architecture.com).
22 Salisbury, *Briefing Your Architect*, p 50.
23 CABE (Commission for Architecture and the Built Environment), *Creating Excellent Buildings: A Guide for Clients*, CABE (London), 2003, p 55.
24 Sunand Prasad, *Transformations: The Architecture of Penoyre and Prasad*, Black Dog Publishing (London), 2007.
25 Herbert Muschamp, 'The library that puts on fishnets and hits the disco', *New York Times*, 16th May, 2004.
26 Quoted in Bryan Lawson, *How Designers Think*, Architectural Press (Oxford), third edition, 1997, p 8.
27 Lawson, *What Designers Know*.
28 Rita Swentzell, in Venturi, Scott Brown and Associates, *The Way of the People: National Museum of the American Indian (Master Facilities Programming, Phase 1)*, Office of Design and Construction, Smithsonian Institution (Washington, DC),1991 p vii.
29 Ibid.
30 See Alice Friedman, *Women and the Making of the Modern House: A Social and Architectural History*, Harry N Abrams (New York), 1998.
31 John Silber, *Architecture of the Absurd: How 'Genius' Disfigured a Practical Art*, Norton (New York), 2007.
32 Deyan Sudjic, *The Edifice Complex: How the Rich and Powerful Shape the World*, Penguin Press (New York), 2005.
33 Thomas Krens, 'Developing the museum for the 21st century: A vision becomes reality', in Peter Noever, ed, *Visionary Clients for a New Architecture*, Prestel (London), 2000, p 58.
34 Prasad, *Transformations*, p 15.
35 Johnpaul Jones, 'Carved by wind and water', in Duane Blue Spruce, ed, *Spirit of a Native Place: Building the National Museum of the American Indian*, Smithsonian Institution and National Geographic (Washington, DC), 2004, p 71.
36 Clare Cooper Marcus, *House as a Mirror of Self: Exploring the Deeper Meaning of Home*, Conari Books (Berkeley, CA), 1995.
37 Toby Israel, *Some Place Like Home: Using Design Psychology to Create Ideal Places*, Wiley-Academy (London), 2003.
38 Peter Murray, *The Saga of the Sydney Opera House*, Spon Press (London), 2004.

39 Frances Downing, *Remembrance and the Making of Places*, A & M University Press (College Station, TX), 2001.
40 Christopher Bollas, 'Architecture and the unconscious', *International Forum of Psychoanalysis*, vol 9, 2000, pp 28–42.
41 Israel, *Some Place Like Home*.

Chapter 3 — Relating

The relationship between client and architect forms the context for almost everything that happens. Consequently the quality of that relationship has a tremendous impact on the success of a project. Because this relationship is the medium through which design emerges and develops, it needs to be taken seriously and carefully nurtured, regardless of project size or available resources. Attending to the relationship is not a luxury but a necessity that requires continuing attentiveness, openness and a willingness to respond thoughtfully to whatever happens. A collaborative relationship requires special effort but generates a design and a set of experiences that bring rewards to both architect and client.

For many architects the relationship with a client is so important to their design process that they will invent one if necessary, as in design competitions that have detailed briefs but allow no contact with the actual client. This is what Israeli architect Ram Karmi did while developing a competition submission for the Supreme Court in Jerusalem with his sister Ada Karmi-Melamede. While Ram was sketching for this submission he had the television on. He already had the idea that the law should be accessible to everyone including children and he had already decided to design a bridge from the bus station to make an easy pedestrian link to the court. Then a news item came on the TV. An ice cream vendor's licence had been confiscated. In a single stroke he had lost his livelihood. A lawyer witnessing the event told the vendor, 'Don't worry, we'll go to the High Court!' and as a result he got his licence back. He became Ada and Ram's imagined client (see Chapter 2).

While architects are extremely adept at managing the relationships between design elements, they are not usually as adept at managing relationships with clients and the emotions that are involved. Their focus is more likely to be on the physical and spatial quality of connections between

Ram Karmi and Ada Karmi-Melamede, Supreme Court, Jerusalem, 1992. View from the bridge leading to the entrance area.

spaces, between the inside and outside of buildings, how the interior looks and feels and how the building sits in its surroundings. They enjoy inspiring an emotional response and a sense of exploration and delight in the physical world. Frank Lloyd Wright is famous for his ability to create reciprocal and engaging relationships between indoors and outdoors but often he seemed far less interested in reciprocity with his clients, even ignoring their stated requests. Luckily many of his clients were knowledgeable and demanding enough to ensure that he responded to their wishes.

Fortunately many architects do take the relationships with their clients seriously but, nonetheless, clients often feel they are not heard or respected. When clients feel unacknowledged, it is difficult to collaborate or to ensure the kind of outcome they want. In Britain the RIBA has demonstrated its concern over the failure of architect–client relationships by devoting several pages on its website to explaining what to do when things go wrong.[1] It is architects who develop the design and who most often set up and supervise the building contract. Consequently it is vital that they take responsibility for the health of the relationships involved.

Relationships are the fuel of life and creativity but they do not just happen. They need on-going attention, continuous self-reflection and courage to sustain them through inevitable ups and downs. Just as people who go into marriage with full hearts, are often told, 'You have to work at it!' And if they do, they reap the rewards. So, too, architect and client will discover that the more they put into their relationship, the more they will benefit.

Beginning the Relationship

Beginnings are crucial. If a relationship starts out on a good footing, the rest is likely to take care of itself. The opening phase of any professional relationship is fragile – from the client interviewing and choosing a professional through to preparing the way forward and then starting to work together. Like the beginning of a love affair, this period is full of possibility as well as hidden obstacles resulting from unrecognised intentions and perceptions. These can lead even the most relationally thoughtful architect and client into difficulties along the way. It helps to create a smooth ride for the rest of the project if architects and clients treat this period as though they were handling a crystal vase full of water and flowers. Time spent carefully arranging the flowers and settling the vase down on the table will be time well spent.

Choosing an Architect

Choosing an architect is a daunting decision to make. Clients have to make a leap of faith, entrusting their dreams to professionals whom they do not yet know and, in public projects, taking the risk of sharing with relative strangers decisions involving the expenditure of public funds that will eventually affect an entire community or city. Given these risks many clients realise how important it is to have a sympathetic and generative relationship with the architect. Consequently they deliberately seek out architects who, when they are interviewed for a project, show a strong interest in the client's needs. It is surprising how often architects do not pass that test.

Judy Green and her partner Carl Berg told Teresa that when they were looking for an architect to design their new house in Columbia County in New York, they interviewed several. Judy jokingly explained that they chose the one who was the least narcissistic. They are both psychologists and Carl said they soon discovered that some architects were more comfortable with the physical world than the relational world. It was as if these architects viewed the prospective house as theirs instead of the clients'. One architect had even refused to speak to them because she considered their budget at $400,000 too small. Carl and Judy eventually found Jeremiah Eck of Eck MacNeely Architects through a magazine article and were not disappointed. Eck was not concerned about the size of their budget. As Carl explained,

> He came over to walk the land with us and started a dialogue that was longer than the whole building process. He was interested in getting to know us and discovering why we wanted this house in this place. After two years, he came over with a model demonstrating his concept of a tent on a platform. So, we have big decks and it sure works.

Especially for large projects clients may seek to understand how particular architects work and how they would manage the kinds of situation that are likely to arise during the project. As part of the selection process for the Seattle Central Library the five firms being considered were invited to Seattle for a public presentation of their work, for an interview with the selection committee and the library board and for a design charette. For this, the architecture teams were asked, within a 24-hour-period, to develop ideas for a library on the assigned site and to make a brief presentation of those ideas to an audience of 1,500 members of the public. This process was appropriate for a project that, from the beginning, would involve a lot of public participation and scrutiny.

Eck MacNeely Architects, Berg Green House, Columbia County, New York, 1997. Jeremiah Eck's vision for this house, located on top of a hill in rolling farm country, was a 'tent on a deck' perched above the fields. The ample covered deck provides a sheltered space to sit outside.

Architect Joshua Ramus, then working at OMA, felt the charette was successful in revealing the approach the different architects would take. Steven Holl, for example, showed watercolours he had painted. OMA presented what Joshua called 'a kit of parts' to demonstrate different methods they would use depending upon what turned out to be important, since at that time the architects did not know 'anything about the client or anything that's important about the library system'.

An unplanned situation that occurred during these public presentations proved informative. Competitors had been told that the overhead projector would be oriented horizontally but, as it turned out, the images had to be oriented vertically. So pictures prepared for horizontal viewing would not fit. None of the architects knew this in advance nor did they attend any of the other presentations. Joshua only learned later that several of the competitors 'threw fits'. In contrast, OMA simply made do. Joshua remembers, 'We walked in and we looked at it and we turned, in front of the entire group, and said, "Do you have scissors?"' Then they simply cut their presentation so it would fit the vertical orientation of the projector. Although unintended, the situation turned out to be a revealing test. Subsequently the selection committee commented to Joshua that OMA's response of 'adapting to the situation and moving on' had 'an enormous impact on everyone'.

In order to reduce the uncertainty and the risks associated with the choice of an architect and the project overall, clients often pick architects whom they already know because they have worked with them before or because they have met them already in a different context. Maria Nordenberg in Stockholm explained that she felt she could trust architect Mats Fahlander because she had already met him at a dinner party and liked him. 'It was the way he talked because he listens very carefully and I could see that he, the things that came out of him were really according to my thoughts.'

In choosing an architecture firm for the Rosa Parks Elementary School in Berkeley the selection committee was keen to hire architects who would be able and willing to conduct a participatory design process with the community, as Christie Coffin and Kava Massih, then of Ratcliff Architects, were (see Chater 2). It was probably also important that Kava, who lived in the neighbourhood and had already been attending neighbourhood meetings about the new school, had come to know the key players just as they had come to know him. So members of the selection committee already knew him and were pleased that he lived in the neighbourhood. As Kristin Prentice, chair of the Site Committee, commented, 'it was his neighbourhood, it was his school'. A basis for trust was already in place.

A shared design sensibility often draws clients to particular architects. This common aesthetic becomes a significant element in the relationship and a shared basis for coming to decisions. Diana Gordon and Michael Keating were planning to buy, not build, a house in Greenport, New York when they saw a small, blurred black and white photograph in a local newspaper of a house designed by studio a/b architects. Diana remembers that the house looked 'very modern' and also like a 'lot of farm buildings thrown together'. From conversations with the author of the article, Diana and Michael discovered that the house, located nearby, was the home of the architects who had designed it, Glynis Berry and Hideaki Ariizumi of studio a/b. They drove by it several times and eventually visited. Diana recalls:

studio a/b architects, house on the North Fork, Orient, New York, 1995. After Diana Gordon and Michael Keating visited this house, they decided both to build a new house and to hire studio a/b to design it.

It was their house that generated the certainty that we should build, that we should build modern, that we should use architects, and that we should use these architects. We jumped over all these stages ... I think the two things that were important in the decision were the house and the fact that we liked them and had a very quick sense of what they would like ... We saw right away a kind of whimsy in their aesthetic and a warmth that would temper what is sometimes cold, modernistic architecture.

Preparing the Way

Giving thoughtful attention to a project's context and to arrangements for meetings with paying clients and others who are related to the project can encourage a participatory process and a more successful outcome. Often the context for a project frames people's perceptions of it and those perceptions, if not addressed, may significantly constrain possibilities and even prevent a project's completion.

Canon's Marsh had remained a derelict area of Bristol since the Second World War. Over the years the city's planning department rejected several masterplans, mainly because the homeowners who lived on the hill overlooking

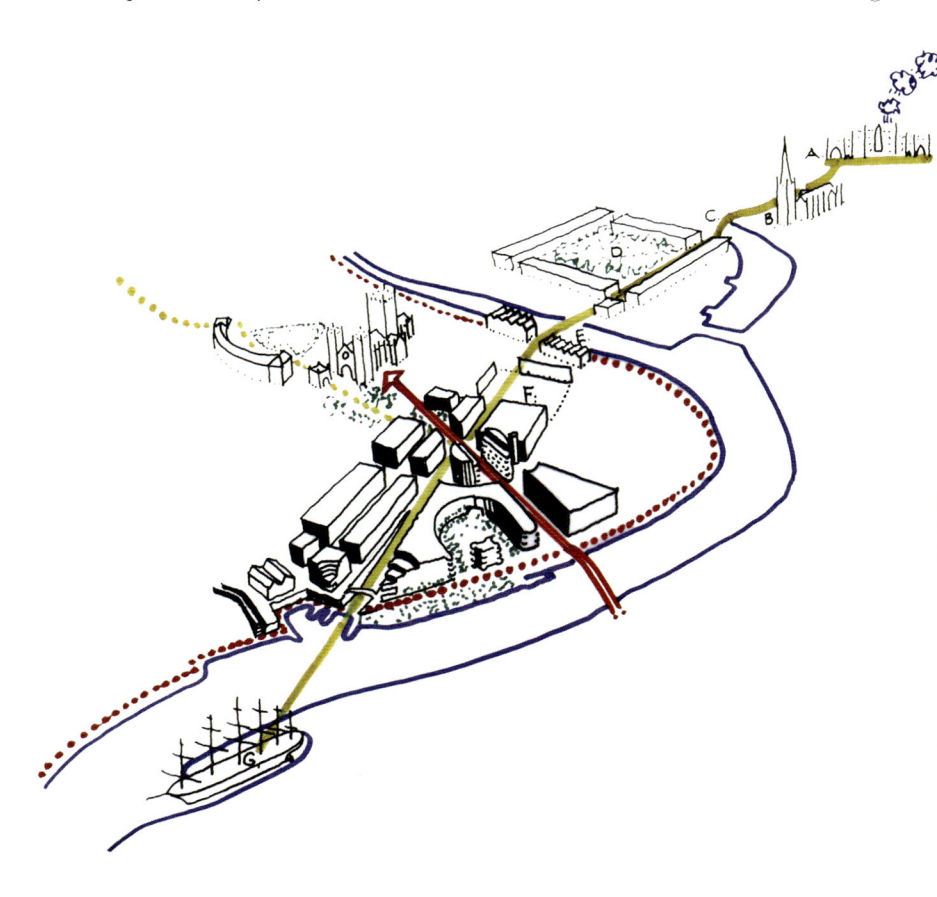

Edward Cullinan Architects, Canon's Marsh, Bristol, 2000. The masterplan shows the new cathedral walk and the completion of the Brunel Mile linking the new harbourside, where Brunel's SS *Great Britain* is moored (G), through the newly developed marsh area (F), Millennium Square (D), over the river (C) and past St Mary's Church (B) to Bristol Temple Meads, the first covered railway station (A).

CHAPTER 3 RELATING • 65

the site vetoed them. When the developers Cress Nicholson took on the redevelopment of the area, they hired an opinion research company to ensure that a large demographic cross section of the entire Bristol community could participate in determining what was needed. Edward Cullinan of Edward Cullinan Architects, hired to develop the masterplan, attended weekly meetings with different groups throughout the city. He told Teresa that it was the most intentionally democratic process he had ever experienced.

> The result that we got was extremely interesting. For once it did not rely on the opinions of those who are usually asked. The diverse groups all said they wanted public through routes, no closed enclaves, housing for everybody, cafés, play places and playgroups and a way down to the boat harbour. That was our brief. Beyond that it was to do a leisure building, some student housing, some offices and about 600 houses and to convert the old gas building in such a way that it worked for the developers, the planners and the general public.

When the West Berkeley District School Board officially agreed that the original school that preceded Rosa Parks Elementary School should either be rebuilt or substantially repaired, the community feared that if the school were to be demolished, it would never be rebuilt. This perception had a long history. Despite desegregation of US schools in the 1960s, the school had remained largely black because white families in nearby areas tended to send their children to private schools rather than to those that had been historically all black. This caused resentment. Then the District allowed the school to deteriorate physically even as the surrounding neighbourhood became one of the most integrated in the city of Berkeley. Kristin Prentice, chair of the Site Committee for the new school reported that, 'Years and years of abuse by the school district left many people in West Berkeley very jaded. They all pay the same taxes everybody else pays and don't see the benefit of it.'

Kristin also recalled that the community had every reason to remain distrustful even after public funds had been allocated for rebuilding specific schools. In a meeting with Kristin one school superintendent 'said flat out, the school shouldn't be rebuilt. "Who wants to go to a school down there?"' Even after the architects had received the commission for the new school, neighbourhood residents remained distrustful and deeply sceptical. Kristin remembers that in community meetings people still said '"Yeah, right. this is gonna happen". It did not matter if they had an architect and a plan, they still didn't really believe it was going to happen.' Persuading people who were understandably distrustful even to consider participating in community design workshops took a lot of work by the Site Committee and other volunteers. 'There was one guy in particular who lives half a block from the school. That was kind of his forté. He would go door to door and chat with old ladies and with young mothers and try to get them to come and let them know what was going on.' Then through the workshops the neighbourhood grew connected to the project, came to believe in it and reached agreement about what the new school should be like.

The community design workshops for the Rosa Parks Elementary School were carefully planned. Leaflets were distributed to a large area and anyone who was interested was invited to come. The meetings were always set for Saturday mornings, with continental breakfast and snacks. Translation into Spanish was provided as was childcare. This kind of preparation reduces anxiety and creates a more conducive working environment. SH Foulkes, the British

studio a/b architects, Gordon House, Greenport, New York, 2008. When the architects asked Diana what she loved about her former house, she described the way the light fell on the pine floors.

originator of group analysis, recommended providing a dependable and steady situation for meetings. He advised making sure that the size of the physical space, seating arrangement, light quality and warmth are all appropriate to the task and to ensure, if possible, that all meetings are held in the same space.[2] Times and duration of meetings should also be agreed upon in advance. Paying attention to what Foulkes called 'dynamic administration' provides a fixed and stable frame to help people feel safe enough to work together.

Starting Out

Client and architect start out on their journey together in many different ways. On some projects their first meeting is at the client's interview with the architect, during the selection process. In fact, it may be the quality of that first encounter that persuades the client to choose that architect. What can architects do, in that very first meeting with the client, to merit this leap of faith? One answer is for the architect to respond to the potential client in such a way that the client feels understood and senses that the architect will continue to respond in a sensitive and attentive manner over the course of the project. The architect can also alleviate normal client anxieties about issues such as costs, timeframes and the design process itself by acknowledging them and talking them through with the client.

This was Diana Gordon's experience of her first meeting with Glynis Berry and Hideaki Ariizumi, which took place before she had fully decided to build a new house rather than purchase an existing one. She and Michael Keating invited Glynis and Hideaki to visit them on nearby Shelter Island in Diana's summerhouse that she was planning to sell. Diana told the architects how much she loved that house and how difficult to was going to be to move. She remembers that the architects asked, 'What is it you love so much about this house?' which she felt 'was a wonderful question. It really started off the sense that they were really interested in the way we lived.' (See Chapter 4)

During that first conversation about the project Glynis and Hideaki also addressed Diana's concern about costs:

> I'm very nervous about money. So we started to talk about that right away and I think that was very good. They said you should assume $225 per square foot. I wouldn't even have known there was a standard that you apply. Knowing what the standard was reduced my anxiety level right away. And we did that early and I think that was important.

Indeed, the budget is nearly always a source of anxiety for both client and architect. The client worries whether there will be enough money to complete the project; the architect worries about realising the client's dreams while holding responsibility for managing the budget. It is always a sensitive process. Two clients of the Swedish architect Mats Fahlander told Teresa that they chose him because of his commitment to creating sophisticated and carefully designed spaces within their budgets. They knew he would do this because, unlike the other architects his clients approached, Mats was willing to work out prospective costs in detail before receiving the commission.

Michael Mostoller, Princeton architect, believes that, 'at the first meeting it's important to try to be interactive as well as to focus on the business side of it.' Clients may believe they know what they want but, actually, they may not. 'You have to work well with people in order to get this right.' At the first meeting Michael always 'walks through' what he is going to do with the client and tries to set up a relationship where they both understand exactly what they are going to get. He sees his role as one of educating the client 'about what is going to happen, what the project is going to be, what the issues are'.

Often clients and architects start working together only after the architect has been selected and has accepted the commission. Only then do they start their journey together. How architects start this journey varies. Some take the client's initially stated needs or written brief at face value. Others use that information just as a starting point for gathering more information and for gaining a deeper understanding of the client's needs and of possibilities the client may not have envisioned. This was true of the approach OMA took on the Seattle Central Library commission. After receiving the commission, the architects embarked, with the client group, on three months of what Joshua Ramus calls 'speaking and thinking'. Although the library had already developed a lengthy and detailed brief, the architects felt that they, with the clients, needed to develop a 'common language' and 'common positions' otherwise, as they explained to the clients, 'when we put architectural proposals before you it's not going to be clear if you are reacting to the architecture or to the idea'.

When a group comes together to work on a set task people are usually eager to get on with the task at hand and not to 'waste time'. But, as OMA realised, failing to give time to learning 'where everyone is coming from' is a false economy. When individuals have no chance to reach an understanding of what brings each of them to the current situation before they begin to 'work', any disagreements that subsequently arise will be much more difficult to resolve. Even when people already know each other, it is important that they discover each other in this new situation. Learning about each other first makes it possible for the group to think and work together. Forming a 'working alliance' based on real exchange at the start of a project will help lay a foundation for the rest of the commission.[3]

A working alliance can be formed in different ways. Denise Scott Brown of Venturi, Scott Brown and Associates told Karen that there will always be conflicts. She makes the first meeting with a client a party to establish lots of good feelings at the start to help them through the difficult times 'so we can hold hands and fight'. To begin the first of three workshops to solicit community input for the design of Bishops Square in Spitalfields, London, Teresa invited the group of residents and workers from the area to construct a shared history of the neighbourhood. She invited participants to find out from each other how long they had lived or worked there and to organise themselves in a line in ascending

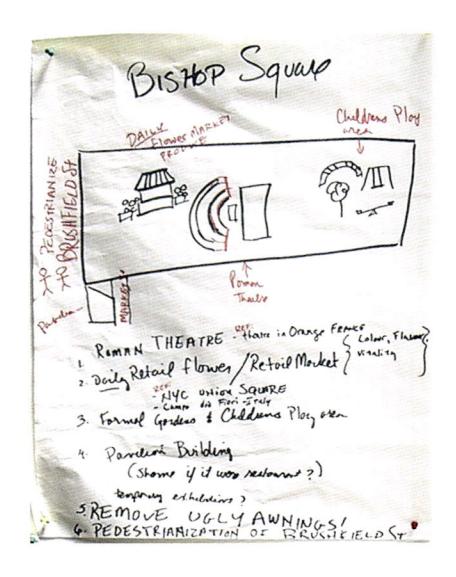

Townshend Landscape Architects, Bishops Square, Spitalfields, London, 2007.
LEFT In the second community design workshop in a series of three, participants developed ideas that influenced the landscape architects' final proposal. BELOW LEFT Every day people gather under the tent in the square to seek shelter from sun or rain, to eat a snack or to chat. BELOW Children enjoy playing on the green and around the water in the middle of the city.

CHAPTER 3 RELATING • 69

order: the earliest resident at one end and the latest at the other. Then they pooled and recorded their memories. This exercise revealed much that had been lost about the history of the area and so provided a new, shared basis for thinking about the future design. It also enabled individuals to get to know each other better and to build more confidence in the group so they could dare to share their different worldviews.

Creating a 'Good Enough' Relationship

As the British paediatrician and psychoanalyst Donald W Winnicott observed, there is never a baby alone but always a baby in a relationship with a consistent carer, usually the mother. When there is no mother and no adequate substitute available, the baby will not thrive and, in extreme situations, will not survive. Previously research and parenting guidance had focused exclusively on the baby, alone.[4] Winnicott recognised that it is the nature and quality of this first relationship that are key for child development.

Similarly, once an architecture project is underway, there is never an architecture client alone but always a client in relationship with an architect. And, given an actual project, there is rarely an architect without a client. The quality of the relationship between client and architect has a strong influence on the quality of the finished project. While both client and architect bear responsibility for ensuring their relationship is good enough, it is the architect who bears major responsibility both as the professional who knows how the design and construction process works and as the one who is legally responsible for the final design.

From his careful observations of mothers with their babies Winnicott developed a model of the 'good enough' mother who is 'ordinarily devoted' and able to provide what Winnicott called 'a continuity of being' for her baby.[5] She is not expected to be perfect, just ordinarily 'good enough'. Winnicott's model suggests a symbolic role for architects to adopt to help them develop the best possible working relationships with their clients.

Since designing and constructing buildings is an extremely complex process, gaps in understanding and outright disagreements between architects and clients are inevitable. For them to be able to talk through these unavoidable differences arising from their contrasting positions, the relationship needs to be 'good enough'. Architects will discover that their relationships become less problematic and more creative when they adopt an emotional attitude of being carefully attuned and responsive to their clients. Without the basic intention to commit emotionally, there will be insufficient stability for building a good enough working partnership to enable creative thinking to emerge.[6]

If the infant verbalizes, the mother vocalizes back. Similarly if the infant makes a face, the mother makes a face … the dialogue does not remain a … boring sequence of repeats, back and forth, because the mother is constantly introducing modifying imitations.

Daniel N Stern, *The Interpersonal World of the Infant*, 1985, p 139

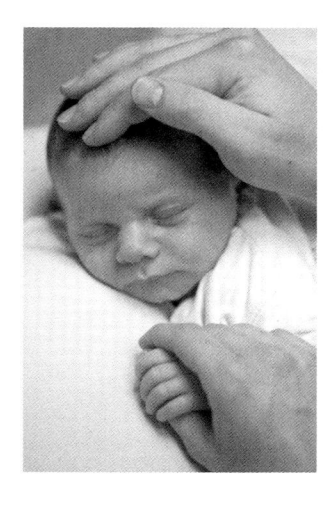

The ordinary devotion of a 'good enough' mother suggests a symbolic form for the architect–client relationship.

Being There for the Client

Winnicott noticed that when a mother's relationship with her baby settles down and is going well enough, she is in a 'state of reverie' or 'temporary preoccupation'.[7] It is now understood that fathers can be similarly preoccupied. If we take this as a model for what should happen in the relationship between architect and client, we can see that the client needs the reassurance and preoccupation of the architect. Architects are often preoccupied with the design and building of a project but they may not be similarly preoccupied with the client and the client's needs during the design and building process. Nurturing the relationship with the client in the service of the 'healthy project' requires a shift of emphasis for many architects – keeping the client as well as the project in mind.

As they focus on developing the design, the client's need for numerous explanations and reassurance may feel like an additional burden on the architect's time and energy. Without regular reassuring contact, clients often feel they are being ignored or forgotten, that their requests have gone into a deep hole. Without the experience of being held in mind, the client is likely to get more anxious than necessary and 'bug' the architect. By providing sufficient 'continuity of care' architects promote the creative development of both the relationship and the project. Yet the architect's ongoing concern for both the client and the project may go unrecognised by the client, as Mats Fahlander found. His sleepless nights are never paid for. His experience is not unlike that of a mother whose sleepless nights ensure the baby's physical and emotional survival.

Architect Rosa Lane understands how important it is for her to 'be there' as a reassuring presence for clients. In community design workshops she does not provide answers but gives gentle encouragement for people to respond with their own ideas. 'I will be there. I will just give them the space to explore.' She believes the most important thing in the relationship with clients is to make it safe enough for them to explore, 'to go as far as they can'. Rosa reports that workshop participants are often scared to jump in, unable to trust that they can work ideas out themselves. The community needs to know that she is 'there to give them confidence'. 'They need to know that I am hand holding and that I am with them as we go through this process.' When the architect is emotionally present for the client, creativity is facilitated.

Rosa remembers that when she was working with parents, teachers and community members to design a new elementary school in Maine, workshop participants would ask, 'I don't know Rosa if this space is large enough. Help me understand.' She would respond by suggesting that they could go to the gym in the old school with a tape to measure it off and then imagine the walls. She then asked them to stand in the 'as if' space and tell her how they felt.

Mother and father swing their child into sea giving confidence to try something new.

> How do you get 'inside of' other people's subjective experience and then let them know that you have arrived there, without using words?
>
> Daniel Stern, *The Interpersonal World of the Infant*, 1985, p 138

Often clients cannot find the words to express their distress and disappointment when their needs are not met. Careful, attuned attention is needed to help clients find appropriate words to express their hopes and their worries and to help architects explain what they intend. Without sufficient care huge misunderstandings can be generated. Sometimes not understanding the design or construction process leads clients to try to read the drawings, often difficult to understand, to make sense of what is happening. It can feel shameful not to understand, making it is impossible to ask for clarification. Architects need to notice small signs of confusion, uncertainty or doubt.

If architects are not fully attentive to their clients' responses, even those that are quite subtle, they may be misled. Architect Michael Mostoller described to Karen how clients can appear to have understood everything the architect has said all along and seem to accept the design even though it turns out later that they 'hate' it. To avoid this situation Michael keeps showing clients what the building is going to be like and how it will meet their needs and desires while constantly checking that they have understood. Although it is difficult to maintain such meticulous attention, the reward is a committed client.

As Michael recognises, clients may be unable to tell architects either that they do not understand a design or that they have doubts about it. This was Helen Hitman's experience when she reviewed the designs of the first two architects she worked with for her house in the Bay of Islands, New Zealand. She told Teresa that she was so impressed with their creativity and ability to draw that she was unable to tell them that their proposals were not what she wanted. In the end the only way she could solve the problem was to find a third architect.

Helen had ample reason to feel doubtful even though, at the time, she was uncertain how much she had contributed to the gap in their understanding. She told all three architects that she wanted something resonant with the traditional New Zealand 'bach' (a simple beach house) that was not an 'eyesore' and was appropriate to the site. When Teresa looked at the sketch plans of the first two architects, it was evident that these explicitly stated needs had not been heard. Both had suggested single box-like structures placed on a flat platform on piles to compensate for the steep slope. Neither resolved the issue of the steeply sloping site or the conflict between the direction of the best views to the bay, and the bay's location on the site's sunless south side.

The third architect, Nick Taylor of Francis Associates in Auckland, which is four hours drive away, started out by spending a weekend with Helen, getting to know her in her former house and studying the site. Nick told Teresa that when he first met Helen, he felt that they were on the same wavelength. During his visit Nick noted the steep slope and the conflict between sun and view. In response the house he designed ascends the site, piece by piece and is organised around a small, decked courtyard that opens the house both to views of the bay and to light coming from the north over the hill behind the house.

When the seeds of a cooperative relationship have not been planted, it may be impossible for clients to dissent or even express doubts. Unless architects allow ample space for reservations to be expressed, these may stay underground, establishing roots of dissatisfaction that grow into open dispute or prompt the search for another architect. At the same time being able to hear the client's reservations or outright criticism requires a high level of self-esteem on the architect's part.

Anyone who has spent any time in an architect's office knows of the intense planning that goes into preparing for client meetings, in an attempt to steer clients in a predetermined direction. The intention is to 'win' the client over. It is not part of this script to notice when the client, who is often mesmerised by the architect's skill demonstrated in drawings and models, shows signs of unhappiness. Architects toil long and hard on their designs and inevitably identify with these beloved productions. It takes a confident architect to put his or her own needs aside to be attentive to what will often be heard as criticism, to take a step back and to hear the client's concerns. Equally, it takes a confident client to say 'I don't like that'.

Nick Taylor, Francis Associates, Takapuna, Auckland. House for Helen Hitman, Long Beach, Russell, Bay of Islands, New Zealand, 2008. The house, settled into the site, always enables the bay to hold the eye. TOP LEFT View of the house from the beach. TOP RIGHT Full height glazing around the internal courtyard offers a view through the house to the bay.

Mother shows her baby a beautiful apple, which the baby then 'discovers' for herself. Architects often show their clients something new and not yet imagined that clients then have to discover for themselves to make their own.

Introducing Clients to the Unexpected

Infants engage in their first creative discovery when they endow an everyday object with special meaning and grow strongly attached to it. Although the parent has provided the discovered object, usually a toy or piece of blanket, the significant element in the discovery is that the child bestows this 'transitional object' with meaning. Like the carer for a small child, architects provide the best possible material for clients in the form of the design proposal. They need to allow clients to discover the significance it holds for them. If the clients are able to find meaning in the design, they will, like the architect, become strongly attached to it as if it were their first transitional object.

Through attentive explanation and demonstration architects can help clients understand something they have not experienced or considered before. To do this, architects need to be sensitive to whether the client has understood the design idea and to how to increase their understanding. To help his client

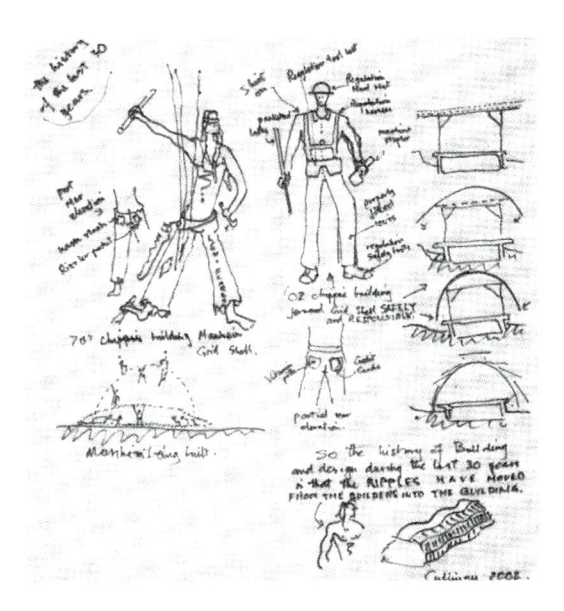

Edward Cullinan Architects, Weald and Downland Museum, West Sussex, UK, 2002. ABOVE Cullinan drew a cartoon sketch to explain to the client the change in gridshell design from the 1970s built by 'hippy' carpenters to the Downland Gridshell built responsibly to meet current health and safety standards. RIGHT The gently undulating shingle roof settles into its countryside context.

for the Weald and Downland Museum in Sussex, UK understand how the innovative gridshell lattice that he had developed with Buro Happold would stand up, Edward Cullinan drew a series of cartoon sketches to illustrate how gridshell construction had developed over the last 30 years from the 1970s' 'hippy' version to the Mannheim Gridshell and to the Downland Gridshell that meets modern safety requirements. As Cullinan jokingly describes in his drawing, 'So, the history of the last 30 years is that the ripples [in the builder's physique] have moved from the builders in to the building'.

During the design process for the B'nai Keshet Synagogue in New Jersey the architect, Michael Mostoller, sensed that the client did not fully understand his design proposal for windows in the sanctuary. Michael explained to Karen that the sacred text requires windows but every possible wall location for a window on the restricted site would have had a view of another building or a car park. One way he proposed to resolve that situation was to bring light in from overhead to 'bounce off the walls'.

> We drew that in all the customary ways – sections, elevations, prespective, little models and nobody understood it. You have to be aware when your client is not understanding. That's very important and we understood that nobody was getting this. So we made a model that was as big as this table. We put it up on a platform so people could put their heads up inside it and see how it worked. And they said 'Oh we love it!'

A parent's capacity to 'be there' in a 'devoted' way enables the infant to develop and 'come into existence'.[8] Gradually and inevitably over the course of their children's lives, parents become less attentive. However,

Michael Mostoller, B'nai Keshet Synagogue, Montclair, New Jersey, 2000. Small lights high in the sanctuary wall and etched glass windows bring in light without giving views of adjacent houses or the car park.

at periods of extreme difficulty, when nothing goes easily, mother or father needs to give special support to encourage the child to take the next developmental step. Eventually though they have to step back to allow their once tiny babies to move in to adulthood. Similarly the architect needs to support the client to 'come alive' in the relationship and, as a consequence, for the dreamed of building to come into existence. Just as infants grow up into adults, so clients mature and achieve greater understanding and insight into design as the project progresses. At the same time the architect needs to remain alert to what support and guidance the client requires at particular points in the process.

Joshua Ramus recounted to Karen that, 'A lot of people say "If we were so lucky to have your clients, we would do great stuff too."' And I say, 'What makes you think we got them great?' We have to make them great. We have to ask questions to expand their horizons and get them to think'. He spends several months at the start of a project talking and thinking with clients in order to identify key problems and develop collective positions regarding those problems.

Hong Kong architect Denise Ho understands the importance of timing in introducing clients to her design ideas. Early on, when she has started thinking about what she calls all the 'aesthetic things', she does not engage the clients in conversation about these concerns. Her experience is that early on clients are likely to be thinking about simple ideas such as 'I don't like red, I want purple!' So she waits until they are ready. Meanwhile, in order to gain their confidence, she restricts herself to talking about the practical issues that are uppermost in the client's mind, all the while thinking about what is important architecturally. As time goes by the conversations get deeper and she begins to explain her design ideas and the client will be able by then to add to her thinking. As Denise says, 'That is good timing!'

Give and Take, Push and Pull

Many architects appreciate clients who have the time, energy and capacity to engage in an ongoing give and take during the design process. New York architect Louise Braverman enjoys relationships with clients 'where we can have conversations all the time and bounce ideas off each other'. She appreciates a client 'who is an intelligent, forward thinking person who likes to communicate and has very strong opinions.' John Hartmann of Freecell wants 'to challenge clients and I want them to challenge me and I want that to shape design.'

Some clients recognise the value of trade-offs during the design process: if they agree to choices that are extremely important to the architect, they expect the architect to agree to choices that are extremely important to them. This occurred during the design of the Seattle Central Library. Alex Harris, Director of the Capital Fund, recalled, 'there were places where we put our foot down and places where we were willing to consider'. The transparent enclosure around the elevator core and the red corridors leading to meeting rooms were two cases where the library accepted the architect's wishes. Alex Harris commented, 'I think to some degree the board concluded that they had hired Rem to be Rem' and 'maybe they ought to just step back and let that happen'.

Clients need to be clear and determined in expressing and defending their needs and aspirations; they also need to take responsibility for ensuring that the proposed design is addressing their expectations. To guarantee such persistent clarity may take determined work but it is worth the effort. In her study comparing exceptional buildings with 'everyday practice' Dana Cuff found that clients of exceptional buildings not only showed 'respect for the architect's values' but also took a 'strong stand' to which the architect had to respond.[9]

Despite the stature of Frank Lloyd Wright, client Mary Palmer was able to express and fight for her wishes for a house for herself and her husband.[10] Contrary to their requests, Wright's first proposal included no dining room, only a tiny kitchen, and no study. Mary made an itemised list of all their reservations and changes and set off for Spring Green, armed with home-made jam to convince the 'great man' that she liked to cook and needed a proper kitchen and dining room. He seemed to listen carefully but it took several more meetings before they came to agreement about how the house should be planned. Thrilled to have Wright design the house, Mary Palmer was nonetheless determined that he pay attention to her wishes.

Without clients' active participation and willingness to make demands and, when necessary, to disagree with the architect, there can be no dialogue. Similarly, without architects' willingness to stand up for what they believe, rather than simply acquiescing, there can be no dialogue. This kind of push and pull occurred throughout the design of the Seattle Central Library and contributed significantly to the quality of the completed building. Sam Miller, one of the project directors at LMN, the joint venture firm that worked with OMA, places great importance on the 'creative tension' that existed between OMA and the client team. He commented that 'OMA was constantly pushing … which is what you want from them' but the library board and Seattle City Librarian Deborah Jacobs stood up to them.

> There was a long dialogue and creative tension and I think Deborah likes to say we won the right battles and they won the right battles.

OMA with LMN Architects, Central Library, Seattle 2004. The client required two full scale mock-ups of this book spiral, which resulted in an improved design.

CHAPTER 3 RELATING • 77

There was a tension and there was pushing and pulling and Deborah was strong and the board was strong enough to stand up to Rem and Rem was strong enough to stand up to them. It was a good balance of ideas and exchange of ideas … It was a dialogue all over.

One very clear outcome of the tension between client and architect at the Seattle library is the book spiral. Sam remembers that 'the library pushed back and said "We want to see it. We want to feel and test it."' The two full-scale mock ups then resulted in a 'better idea and everybody liked it more'.

Clients Take a Leap of Faith

Architects need the freedom to develop design solutions the client may not be able to imagine. In her study of the process that shapes the design of excellent buildings Dana Cuff found that 'clients avoided stepping into the designer's role'.[11] At some point in the design process clients need to take a leap of faith to allow architects to employ their expertise in the designing of form and space as fully as possible. The clients need to be able to trust that the architects they have hired will use their knowledge and skill to meet the clients' needs, possibly in ways they had not envisioned initially.

For Diana Gordon this leap of faith came fairly early on, before the design process began, when she was visiting possible sites with the architects. While visiting one dilapidated house she heard Hideaki Ariizumi say 'There's nothing here we could use.' Diana realised that he was not referring only to practical matters but that he wanted to 'start from scratch'. She grasped that 'In his head something was forming already and I felt great respect for that' and that this project she was undertaking would be an 'artistic endeavour'.

The building goes beyond their ability to imagine and perhaps to pay, which is a direct result of giving the professional some freedom to invent design solutions that the clients themselves could not conjure up.

Dana Cuff, 'The social production of built form', *Environment and Planning D: Society and Space*, 1989, p 445

studio a/b architects, Gordon Residence, Greenport, New York, 2008.
Diana Gordon 'let go' and let architect Hideaki Ariizumi's 'artistic conception flower'. He and his partner Glynis Berry also responded to their clients' needs and desires.
BELOW View from the street. RIGHT View from the back shows attached green house.

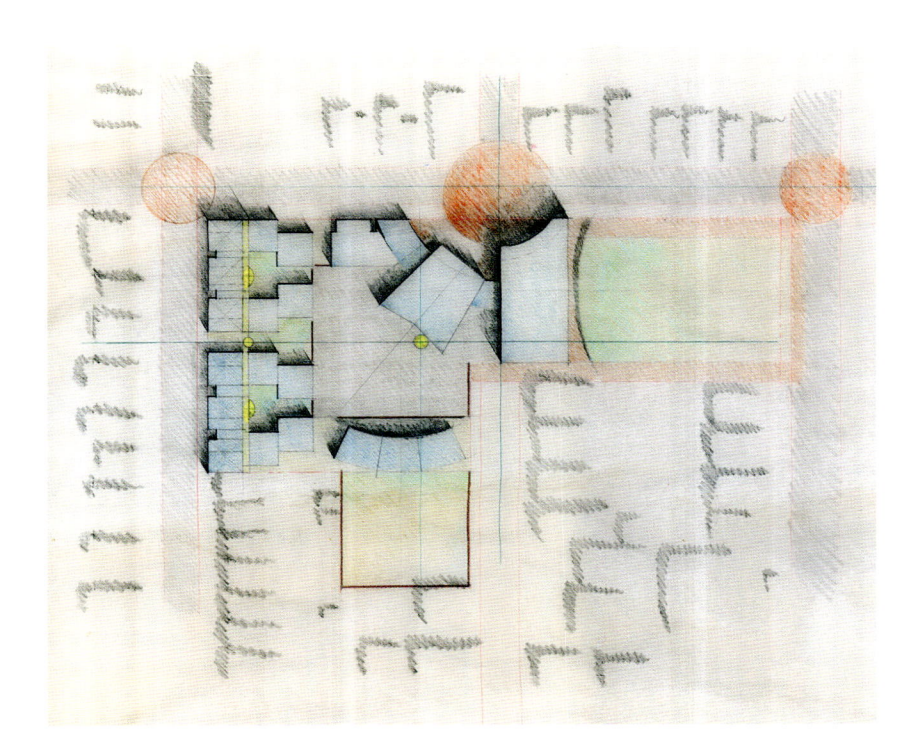

Ratcliff Architects, Rosa Parks Elementary School, Berkeley, California, 1997.
After participating in the community design workshops, architect Kava Massih drew this plan. As a consequence of the workshops, the classrooms are clustered around two small courtyards and then share a larger, enclosed open space. The gym, on the far right, can be opened to connect to the local park.

I believe in letting artists be artists and I thought well, I have to let go in ways other than not worrying about money. I have to let go and let his artistic conception flower.

For clients to take this leap of faith, they need to trust the architect and to have some insight into what architects do. In fact, it may be only after clients understand what architects face in designing that trust develops. That is one advantage of a participatory design process with workshops where people have direct experience of the design challenges architects face. When talking about his participation in the workshops held for the Rosa Parks Elementary School, architect Kava Massih commented that such a process 'demystifies' architecture and 'once they know what you have to do, they trust you more'.

There is a moment when they trust you and throw their hands up and say, 'You're the expert and you're the one who's getting paid to do this, you do it.' There's this level of trust … That is really, really important – that moment of trust then allows them to sort of sit back and let you do your thing.

In explaining how the process might work with other clients Kava commented, 'It's important to let them into the process and to use the space of it to get them to trust you to let you take the rest of it.' Throughout Karen's interview with him he used similar phrasing – 'I've always felt that the planning stage is where you let everybody in' and 'you let them in on your passes – that suggest a process that is primarily the architect's process which the client joins (or enters), the result being the client's greater understanding of design and a willingness to give the architect leeway to pursue it.

Joshua Ramus used the same phrase, with respect to both client and architect: '… both sides have to let the other in. It's not just the architect letting the client in, the client also has to let the architect in … You have to lift up your skirt. You have to say "This is what we do, this is how we work".' In Joshua's approach this involves an extended period of working intensely with the client to identify the outstanding problems and the positions they will take to address them. In describing that period working on the Seattle Central Library, Joshua said, 'We were actually collectively designing. We were fleshing out really, really important moves but we were not confusing anyone with "it looks like this" yet. And as long as everyone always knows that at the core it really works, they're willing to dream.'

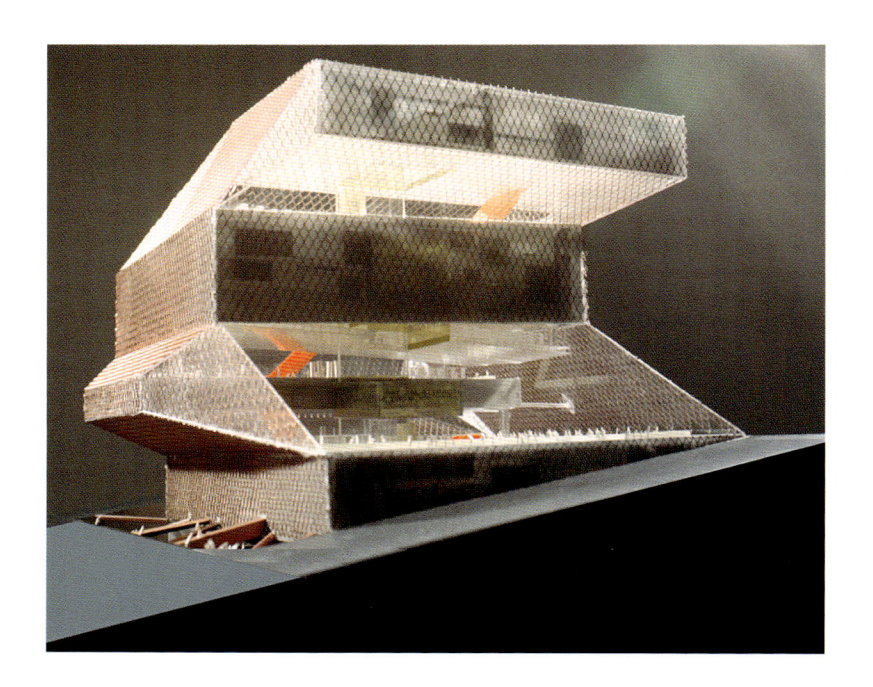

OMA with LMN Architects, Central Library, Seattle. 2004. The model the architects presented to the client team was a bit of a shock. But the clients realised that the design met all their needs and were willing to take the risk of accepting the unexpected.

Nonetheless, as Joshua tells the story, when the architects presented their design proposal in the form of a model 'the library board was deadly quiet'. The meeting was at the Lake Washington home of Gil Anderson, president of the library board. He asked the architects to give the board some time alone and suggested they wait on the dock by the lake. 'So it was like walking the plank. We didn't know if we were about to get fired from our first major American project. And they had us out there for an hour and a half.'

> Then Gil took an insane leap of faith. He said 'I don't know what that is. It doesn't look like a building to me. You guys may have a rarefied sense of aesthetics I don't have … That doesn't look like architecture to me. I don't even know where the entrance is.' (At that moment we thought we were done.) 'But we can see how it is everything we agreed so if you can promise me you can build that thing, what ever it is, for the budget we'll do it.'

Maintaining a Facilitating Environment

Because individuals think and work within the context of their relationships with each other, a supportive emotional atmosphere that ensures steady, responsive interactions encourages creativity. Such an environment is similar to what Donald W Winnicott called the 'facilitating environment' maintained by caregivers who are finely attuned to the needs of their infants, enabling them to grow to their full potential.[12]

Design and construction depend upon many different kinds of relationship; each of them needs to be carefully negotiated to ensure the project gets designed and built in the best possible way. To ensure the project's success it is important that one person in the team takes on the responsibility for providing emotional support. This might be the architect, the project manager or a member of the client team with authority who facilitates creativity. Within this facilitating relational environment the innovative design solutions are more likely to develop as the project grows almost organically.

Good gardeners know that once a seed is planted they can only wait for the plant to grow. Nothing appears to happen for what seems like ages even though the seed is germinating and sprouting out of sight, under ground. If they try to dig it up to have a look, the fragile sprout will probably die. To ensure its survival, it has to be left alone to allow it to grow at its own rhythm and in its own time. But gardeners do not remain passive: they create an environment that facilitates the plant's growth by keeping the temperature, light and moisture at just the right level and by placing the plant in a location safe from harm (by cats or children or other possible sources of disruption). Meanwhile, they watch and wait until suddenly the first shoots emerge.

It is just as important for architects and their clients to wait until ideas emerge from their relationship. It is the containing quality of the relationship that enables something new to be discovered or created. One architect who is able to allow the design to emerge from a creative relationship with her client is Denise Ho. She believes that it is vital to approach the client with her mind empty of any fixed images: 'Creativity is about starting from nothing and then generating with the client'. At the end of one project, her client took her in his arms and said, 'This is our baby. It's not just a product. It is the process of it. And that is unique.' As Denise then explained to Karen, 'It's not something he goes out to the shop, he likes and takes home. It is something of his own creation. So I think to be open-minded is the only way.'

People, like plants, need careful tending to grow strong and reach their full potential.

When the environment is experienced as facilitating, a 'place' becomes available for play and creativity. Donald W Winnicott called this play space between a good enough mother and child 'potential space' since it is here that the seeds of creativity are sown and grow.[13] It is in this 'area of experiencing' that the infant first makes the 'transition' from an 'inner emotional reality' to an 'actual or external reality' through the discovery of objects in creative play.[14] As long as the facilitating environment is maintained, creativity flourishes, but it is easily disturbed by overwhelming anxiety that is not addressed and by aggression or conflict that is not contained.

When Winnicott first introduced the concept of potential space, he quoted these lines from the poet Rabindranath Tagore to give a flavour of what he intended:

> On the seashore of endless worlds children meet. The infinite sky is motionless overhead and the restless water is boisterous. On the seashore of endless worlds the children meet with shouts and dances.
>
> They build their houses with sand and they play with empty shells. With withered leaves they weave their boats and smilingly float them on the vast deep. Children have their play on the seashore of the worlds.[15]

Containing Anxiety

Although some anxiety can provide a necessary spur for new ideas, too much anxiety is likely to overwhelm people and interfere with their relationships. Too much stress in turn poses a serious threat to establishing potential space and so inhibits creative thinking. Too much anxiety shuts down the limbic system in the brain triggering the centre of creative activity, the cerebral cortex, to also shut down so the capacity for innovation is lost.[16] One needs the support of a network of good enough relationships in order to be truly creative and to face the uncertainties of what one does not yet know.[17]

For every project to realise its potential, one person needs to protect the facilitating environment to ensure there is potential space for innovative thinking to occur. Often architects, as the professionals responsible for the outcome, perform this task, which Winnicott called 'holding'.[18] Whoever fulfils this role is responsible for maintaining a steady emotional

Jasmax Architects, Te Papa Tongarewa: Museum of New Zealand, Wellington, 1994. View of the museum from the harbour walk.

environment while ideas for the design are emerging and later while the new physical environment is being built. In large projects a leading member of the client team may assume this role, as was the case at Te Papa Tongarewa: Museum of New Zealand. Cheryl Sotheran, the Pākehā Joint Chief Executive of the museum, working closely with Cliff Whiting, her Māori counterpart, held much of the anxiety generated around the project.

Holding is a complex emotional task. Not only are the 'holding persons' responsible for managing their own natural concerns about meeting their own expectations, concerns endemic in all people engaged in a creative endeavour, but they also need to contain everyone else's hopes and natural anxieties. Perhaps more often than not on public sector projects, there is no one person who is naturally in a position to hold the systemic anxieties on behalf of the team. This is a role that project managers as well as architects could be trained to take on.

Early in the design process architects or clients or both together often develop concepts, positions or visions that guide the design of the building and serve as a basis for choosing between different options. These also serve to reduce uncertainty, confusion and anxiety.

Joshua Ramus, now of REX architects in New York, works intensely with the client at the outset of a project to establish what he calls 'positions', which will jointly take towards problems or issues they have already identified in the project and those that may emerge subsequently. These positions serve as a clearly understood and agreed upon basis for collectively making and explaining decisions to others. In talking with Karen, Joshua recalled one of the benefits of this approach during the design of Seattle's Central Library when he was working with Rem Koolhaas of OMA:

> ... in retrospect I think we took really good positions but that wasn't the most important thing. The most important thing is that we took decisions and we could justify why we took them. And we could stand before the public and say 'These are the decisions we took, this is why we took them and even if we're wrong, we can look you in the eye and say with confidence why we did it.'

At Te Papa the joint Chief Executives Cheryl Sotheran and Cliff Whiting held tight to the vision of biculturalism throughout the entire taxing process of designing and building the museum. Cheryl explained to Teresa that she took the government's expectations for a new type of museum very seriously. All her decision-making was framed by the intention to make the museum bicultural. In addition, she was determined that the museum would not be 'another over-spent and late public services project'.

Spotting Anxiety

Designing and constructing buildings is a process that inevitably provokes anxiety, so attention to its debilitating effects is essential. Anxiety is difficult to acknowledge since both its presence and its source are often hard to identify. Most people have been socialised to ignore anxiety and have learnt to ascribe such feelings to stress, being unwell or overworked. Learning to spot anxiety as it arises in the here and now means unlearning a lifetime of ignoring these feelings. All behaviour is a form of communication but the reason for a particular behaviour may not be immediately evident. Anxiety often underlies what seems to be inexplicable behaviour.

Clients and architects may become uncommunicative. Angry or antagonistic responses or an inability to meet deadlines may be expressions of fear.

Anxiety gives relationships a sticky quality. One feels constrained and unable to think. Architects and clients can make sense of this situation by paying attention to their own responses. Energy draining away, feeling stressed, angry or upset in the presence of particular clients is a strong clue about what is being felt but not expressed directly. Stepping back, not reacting overtly and monitoring their own inner reactions will enable architects to spot their clients' hidden anxious responses. It helps to acknowledge the other's feelings in a non-threatening way by asking questions about people's wellbeing. Often just listening and understanding is enough.

When Helen Hitman's house in New Zealand was nearing completion, the builder discovered that the fireplace selected for the house would not fit into the space designed for it. He proposed a solution but Helen was not at all sure it would work and was worried that it would cause a collapse. She could not understand what the builder was telling her and she was greatly concerned that costs would increase. She was reluctant to bother her architect Nick Taylor whose office was four hours away. Her anxiety became almost unbearable. Teresa, who was visiting at the time, helped Helen talk through what was worrying her. Subsequently when Teresa met with the builder and Helen, she was able to translate what he was saying so that Helen understood the solution. Like a good enough parent, Teresa was able to understand what it was Helen needed to know, how to meet that need and to contain her fears.

One frequent source of anxiety is continuous contradictory requirements, which often occur on large projects. A mismatch in expectations, as was set for Te Papa from the beginning, can induce an especially debilitating form of anxiety. The first expectation was that Te Papa should be a new type of museum. The second was an equal imperative: the building should not draw on the public purse more than necessary and must be built on time and within budget. Gregory Bateson called this kind of situation of contradictory expectations a 'double bind'.[19] Double binds create a pattern of communication so complex that it is extremely difficult to decide which message should be given priority. Thinking is constrained. Creativity is also limited and few reactions are actually possible as an enormous amount of energy is wasted trying to make sense of how to respond appropriately.

The contradiction in a double bind may be entirely invisible in the immediate context. The central symptom is intense tension, with no obvious origins. The resulting highly charged atmosphere makes it almost impossible to reflect on what might be driving the incessant tension and what might relieve it. People redirect their energy to ensuring that targets are met, no matter what they are, to the detriment of creating imaginative outcomes. In the case of Te Papa, it was extremely difficult to recognise the bind the team was in and to make space to think through what biculturalism meant for the design while simultaneously generating creative responses to the government's injunction to complete on time and within budget.

What makes a binding situation so difficult to unravel is the injunction against the expression of vulnerability in our society. Most people make sure they hide their stress and show their strength, particularly in working life. But as Bateson emphasised, the double bind is not only a matter of individual psychology but 'part of the ecology of ideas in systems or "minds" whose boundaries no longer coincide with the skin of the participant individuals'.[20] The bind becomes part of the fabric of the project, almost unnoticed in its ubiquity. It takes the skill of an experienced facilitator to untangle what is happening by asking all those involved what they are feeling and thinking. The facilitator listens to these powerful and uncomfortable feelings, makes sense of them and re-presents them to the group in an understandable form. Then the group develops a strategy for dealing with the contradictory messages.

Staying with It

To hold potential space open for new possibilities it is vital that architects or others in the holding position develop a capacity to withstand the effects of anxiety, possible aggression and resistance from other parties. If this person can manage to stay in this receptive place, creativity will flow and new solutions will emerge. Taking this stance needs almost infinite calm and determined patience, the capacity to tolerate one's own discomfort and the ability to know when it will be useful to take action and when it is better to wait, listen and attend.

Even though it was extremely difficult to meet the two contradictory expectations at Te Papa, and to withstand the double bind they were in, the team – architect and client – stayed with the frustration and tension and created a building that Cheryl Sotheran suggests is unique in New Zealand and possibly the world. The team worked together under Sotheran and Whiting to manage, through a shared determination, what at times must have seemed impossible. As Ken Gorbey, exhibition designer for Te Papa, explained to Teresa, 'Te Papa succeeded because it built a unique staff culture that was totally committed and created something extraordinary. They all just decided that they were going to do it. They were unsung heroes.'

When Edward Cullinan was commissioned to rebuild the parish church of St Mary's in Barnes, West London after it had burnt down, the parish had already divided themselves into two 'camps'. One camp wanted to

> It may be proposed that the true change in the organization ... took place not when we started the new program but when the language and the experience of those processes became part of the participants' assumptions about themselves and about the goals and practices of the organization.
>
> Carlos E Sluzki, 'A reflective consultation and some changes that resulted from it', *Human Systems*, vol 7, 1996, p 103

Edward Cullinan Architects, St Mary's Church, Barnes, London, 1984. BELOW After all the tumult in the community, the new building now relates gently to the old. BELOW RIGHT The old and the new sit comfortably together under one new roof.

rebuild the new church within the remaining walls left after the fire while the other wanted to take the opportunity to pull down the 19th-century walls to preserve the original medieval church and integrate it into the new building. The dispute caused a huge amount of confusion in the community and many sleepless nights for the architects. Edward remembers parishioners shouting at him. Once, after all the adults had finished screaming, one little girl stood up and said, 'What are you all so afraid of?' He told Teresa, 'You could have heard a pin drop. It was incredible.' (See Chapter 6)

Cullinan and his colleagues were able to be there to hear what everyone had to say. The essential component of the project's success was the architect's capacity to be involved enough with the community's concerns to stay with them through thick and thin. As he says, 'It didn't matter whether they opposed it or were for it. What mattered terrifically was whether they had a hand in it. People care about that and the reason they love it so much is that they were involved.'

In order to translate the client's dream into a building architects must put their own needs aside. This is not an easy step for anyone to take, especially architects who, like mothers, strongly identify with and gain personal satisfaction from the success of their endeavours. So architects, like mothers, need to be able to cope with a possible threat to their identity resulting from a challenge to their ideas. They also need infinite patience and an ability to tolerate aggression without retaliating.

When clients are upset and reactive, many professionals, to protect themselves, immediately make themselves unavailable, which is likely to exacerbate the situation and push the client to near panic. If, instead, architects gently seek to acknowledge what might be going on for the client and respond to their concerns without being defensive, reason will prevail. Mats Fahlander was able to maintain a good relationship with one of his more anxious clients because he was able to meet his mistrust and aggression with quiet acceptance. On this small project architect and client exchanged hundreds of e-mails. The client would often phone him and the conversation would always start with, 'I am very disappointed.' Mats said, 'It was very tough to hear that if you have the idea that you are going to solve things together!' Despite feeling a very strong need to justify his position, he refrained from doing so and protected his commission. After the project was completed the client admitted to Teresa that he has a deeply questioning nature and recognised the care that Mats put into creating a beautiful and exquisitely detailed new extension at a reasonable cost.

Architects need to be able to devote themselves to the project and to the people involved, to listen patiently and to contain what may be feelings of discomfort and frustration. By putting their own needs aside to be there

Mats Fahlander, extension to house, Täby, Stockholm, 2007.

for clients and for the project, architects can be 'good enough'. This approach is not easy but it facilitates a smoother ride through the long process and will create a better building and an appreciative client.

Edward Cullinan was commissioned to design the new £60 million building for the Faculty of Mathematics at Cambridge University on an open field site surrounded by houses. His initial design – a single, university-style building placed in the centre of the site – received ferocious 'not-in-my-backyard' opposition mainly from the university dons living around the site. They did not want a building on their open land. Rather than reacting in a defensive way, Cullinan turned his intense frustration towards the design. With the 300 mathematicians who would be occupying the building he developed a dramatically different design resembling houses set in a park, which was accepted by the surrounding community. A grass-topped hill was built over a very large underground room that is linked to an encircling series of separate pavilions (see Chapter 4).

Listening carefully and accepting clients' angry frustration requires a high level of emotional strength and self-awareness, yet such capacities are not easy to acquire. Even seasoned professionals can come unstuck. It is not easy to present a design and have it angrily rejected. Architects, unlike those who train in psychotherapy, are not usually required to develop knowledge about themselves in the service of their clients.

Some clients may be so doubtful about some decisions the architect makes that they decide to get additional advice. Louise Braverman simply accepts this approach and the differences of opinion that may arise. 'I just

Edward Cullinan Architects, Faculty of Mathematics at Cambridge University, Masterplan, Cambridge, 2003. The individual pavilions are set around the site like houses in a park. Pavilion A is partially underground.

CHAPTER 3 RELATING • 87

listen to them. Sometimes the other consultants have good ideas or not … Sometimes I feel that in some circumstances they've made a poor choice. It's their choice. They're the client.'

Supporting Each Other in the Office

When Winnicott was developing his idea of the 'good enough' mother, he recognised that she needed the father to support her. In one of his 1940s' radio talks he asked, 'What about Father?' and spoke about the importance of the father being there not only for the child but also for the mother who, particularly because of extreme fatigue and the difficult emotions that accompany early motherhood, needs support to sustain the necessary continuity of care of her baby.[21] Professionals also need someone to be there for them when weathering the difficult exigencies of practice.

In the caring professions this need is taken seriously enough to offer 'supervision'. Talking with someone, on a regular basis, in a professional capacity to make sense of difficult encounters is a good antidote to stress and burnout. It is also a form of personal development in the context of practice. As doctors have increasingly recognised, their relationship with the patient counts. They have learned that maintaining a 'good bedside manner' is not easy. In the early 1950s under the auspices of the Tavistock Clinic in London Michael Balint developed seminars for doctors to give them the opportunity to notice the 'emotional turmoil' they were drawn into and to explore the kinds of personal and professional resources available for dealing with this turmoil.[22] These groups have continued in various forms ever since.

Those professionals engaged in design and construction also experience great emotional strain. Managing relationships, responding appropriately to anxiety, conflict and aggression and, at the same time, getting the project completed demand a great deal of emotional resilience, as Cheryl Sotheran found at Te Papa. Having to reconcile available finance and time with design possibilities and weather continuous controversy was enormously stressful for her. Individuals who take leadership positions are often expected to shoulder enormous responsibility, often with a heavy personal cost. Without ongoing support and encouragement it is almost impossible to be strong, thoughtful, appropriate and responsive all the time. What helps is to have various forms of reflective support built into everyday practice.

A facilitating environment in the office requires not only support and encouragement from colleagues but also for every individual the provision of a stable and good enough emotional space to think and be creative. Ignoring feelings of frustration or discouragement and just getting on with the practical work was the common response to difficult situations in the architect's department of the London housing authority when Teresa was a team leader there. Under her guidance, design staff met with residents to seek their ideas for the major rehabilitation of Old Loughborough housing estate

---

Mothers who have it in them to provide good-enough care can do better by being cared for themselves in a way that acknowledges the essential nature of their task.

Donald W Winnicott, 'The Theory of the Parent-Infant Relationship' in his *The Maturational Processes and the Facilitating Environment*, 1960, p 49

Just as the mother needs ongoing, consistent support to enable her to care for her baby, so too do those people who 'hold' the complex process of design and construction.

in south London. Teresa noticed that after visiting the estate and talking to residents, staff would often return to the office drained and angry. Absence levels also increased. Teresa recognised that there was a connection between the personal encounters on the estate and the stress levels in her staff. These professionals needed time and support to find some perspective on their experiences so she suggested they describe their experiences with residents to each other at the regular staff meetings. Slowly they were able to share their experiences in a way that gave them the inner strength to carry out this difficult work and, for the first time, discovered appreciative tenants.

NOTES

1. Royal Institute of British Architects website: http://www.architecture.com/UseAnArchitect/Home.aspx
2. Morris Nitsun, 'Technical considerations in dealing with the anti-group', in *The Anti-Group: Destructive Forces in the Group and their Creative Potential*, Routledge (London), 1996, pp 155–60 for a more detailed description.
3. Working Alliance is a term derived from psychotherapy that can be applied to professional relationships generally. It is the product of the patient's and the therapist's conscious determination and ability to work together on the troublesome aspects of the patient's internal world, his or her relationships with others and/or other aspects of his or her life. No successful therapy can take place without a good working alliance, which, outside the therapeutic setting, is equivalent to a good working relationship in any team effort. Angela Molnos, 'A psychotherapist's harvest', 1998, http://www.net.klte.hu/~keresofi/psyth/psyhthr.html
4. Donald W Winnicott, 'The theory of the parent-infant relationship', in his *The Maturational Processes and the Facilitating Environment: Studies in the Theory of Emotional Development*, Hogarth Press (London), 1960, p 39.
5. Madeleine Davis and David Wallbridge, *Boundary and Space: An Introduction to the Work of D. W. Winnicott*, Karnac Books (London), 1981, p 125.
6. Peter Hobson, *The Cradle of Thought: Exploring the Origins of Thinking*, Macmillan (London), 2002, p 3.
7. Donald W Winnicott, 'Primary maternal preoccupation', in his *Through Paediatrics to Psychoanalysis: Collected Papers*, Hogarth Press (London), 1956.
8. Winnicott, 'The theory of the parent-infant relationship, p 54.
9. Dana Cuff, 'The social production of built form', *Environment and Planning D: Society and Space*, 1989, vol 7, p 442.
10. Grant Hildebrand with Ann and Leonard K Eaton, *Frank Lloyd Wright's Palmer House*, University of Washington Press (Seattle), 2007.
11. Cuff, 'The social production of built form', p 441.
12. Donald W Winnicott, 'Morals and education', in his *The Maturational Processes and the Facilitating Environment*, p 97.
13. Thomas Ogden, 'On potential space', in Dodi Goldman, ed, *In One's Bones: The Clinical Genius of Winnicott*, Jason Aaronson (Northvale NJ), 1993, p107.

14 Donald W Winnicott, 'The location of cultural experience', in his *Playing and Reality* (London), 1971, p 112.
15 Rabindranath Tagore, *Gitanjali: Song Offerings*, Full Circle (New Dehli), 2002, p 80.
16 Pierce J Howard, *The Owner's Manual: Everyday Applications from Mind-Brain Research*, Bard Press (Austin, Tx), 2000, p 616.
17 Nassim Nicholas Taleb, *The Black Swan: The Impact of the Highly Improbable*, Allen Lane (Camberwell, Australia), 2007, p xix.
18 Davis and Wallbridge, *Boundary and Space*, p 99.
19 Gregory Bateson, *Steps to an Ecology of Mind: Collected Essays in Anthropology, Psychiatry, Evolution, and Epistemology*, University of Chicago Press (Chicago), 1972, p 206.
20 Ibid, p 339.
21 Donald W Winnicott, 'What about Father?' in his *The Child, the Family and the Outside World*, Penguin (London), 1964, p 113.
22 Michael Balint, Enid Balint, Robert Gosling and Peter Hildebrand, *A Study of Doctors: Mutual Selection and the Evaluation of Results in a Training Programme for Family Doctors*, Mind and Medicine Monographs, Tavistock Publications (London), 1966, p 5.

Chapter 4 — Talking

From their very first meeting onward architects and clients talk. When clients interview architects during the selection process, when they figure out together what is needed and when they discuss possible alternatives, they talk, both in person and on the phone. As they visit sites or projects together, as architects make proposals and respond to client comments and as they reach eventual agreement on design, they talk some more. Very likely they exchange e-mail messages and text messages as well. The conversations often involve a number of people talking together in groups large and small.

Language, written and spoken, is the medium clients and architects use to get to know each other, to learn from each other and, along with sketches, drawings and models, to realise the clients' hopes and dreams. Consequently, the words used, the manner in which they are exchanged and the way visual material illustrates and supplements those words, all play a significant role in shaping both the dialogue between client and architect and the design that emerges.

> The crucial role of language to human evolution was not the ability to exchange ideas, but the increased ability to cooperate.
>
> Fritjof Capra, *The Web of Life*, 1997, p. 282

Creating Meaning Together

Different ways of talking are appropriate for different occasions. Some are highly formalised with specific protocols, as in courtroom trials, expert panels, lectures or press conferences. In these forms of social communication certain people speak as experts, giving out information, while others listen and absorb that information. A hierarchy of relationships operates with those who speak having more power than those who listen. Generally, only those listening ask questions and only the experts give answers.

Conversation is a dramatically different kind of communication: there is give and take between participants, an exchange. Everybody has the opportunity to both give and receive information. One of the reasons Jeremy Till gives for viewing participatory design as a conversation is precisely because in a conversation the architect 'moves … from being a detached observer into an engaged participant'.[1] Just as importantly, the

> The most important parts of any conversation are those that neither party could have imagined before starting.
>
> William Isaacs, *Dialogue and the Art of Thinking Together*, 1999 p 9

client is an active participant, not a passive recipient. Together they create the conversation as the project proceeds, not knowing in advance what the possible outcomes will be. A conversation allows for the possibility of new knowledge being generated.

When disagreements arise in conversations, individuals may attempt to persuade the others to agree with them and, if an argument develops, they may try to 'win' the argument or they may take offence and stop talking altogether. Taking another approach, participants may vote or work to reach consensus or compromise. When people engage in *dialogue*, however, participants aim to continue talking in an open manner and to stay with the disagreement long enough to allow new ideas to emerge. Talking together in this way eventually precipitates a shift from disagreement to the discovery of possibilities beyond anything anyone could have imagined. It is like the gathering of a critical mass of cosmic dust that suddenly generates a new star.

Dialogue is a form of 'shared inquiry, a way of thinking and reflecting together'.[2] In a dialogue, participants not only discover meaning, they also create it. This is an essential aspect of the dialogue between architect and client: it is a generative process. In contrasting a model of design as a search for solution with a model of design as conversation or dialogue, John Forester recognises the benefit of approaching design as 'making sense together in practical conversations'.[3]

To create meaning together and to work out differences as they arise, client and architect need to talk with each other. When they choose written modes of communication – emails, text messages or letters – in preference to conversation, the message is removed from its context, making the meaning more difficult to grasp. Anthropologist and linguist Gregory Bateson distinguished between two modes of communication: 'report', which conveys information, and 'command', which indicates the sort of message it is.[4] In written communication the report is more difficult to disentangle from the command. Hearing the other's voice, observing expressions and gestures and noticing silences all provide additional clues to what is being expressed. People often resort to writing to deliver difficult messages; this exacerbates a situation that may already be tense and full of possibilities for misunderstanding. Written communication can be effective for conveying very simple messages, for clarifying previous conversations or for supplementing them with additional information, but it should not replace talking.

'We're All in this Together'

People conversing with each other are *within* the conversation, in a reciprocal relationship with each other without the sense of 'us' and 'them' that other forms of communication may involve. As the conversation proceeds, a kind

Dialogue takes time to gather momentum like the gathering of a critical mass of cosmic dust that generates a new star.

… the models of conversation, dialogue and question-response interactions allow for the native, historically rooted competences of participants to create new meanings together, regarding both means and ends.

John Forester, 'Designing', *Journal of Architecture Education*, vol 38, 1985, p 17 of unity is created. It is very telling that earlier and now obsolete meanings of the word conversation emphasised inclusiveness: the action of living or having one's being *in* or *among* and the action of consorting with others, living together, commerce, society, intimacy. New York architect Louise Braverman recognises this quality of conversation and how important it is for the relationship between architect and client. She told Karen:

> We're all in this together. We're all people. That's why I hate that word 'user' – the architect over here and the user over there. That's ridiculous. If you're empathetic and you love people, you have a conversation. That's what your book is about!

This sense of being *with* others in a conversation, and even more so in a dialogue where there is a centre rather than sides, generates a sense of responsibility as well as a sense of togetherness. Family therapist Harlene Anderson cites this characteristic of collaborative therapy. From the give and take of people talking with and to each other, 'all members develop a sense of belonging. And, in my experience, a sense of belonging invites participation, which in turn invites ownership. Ownership, in turn, invites shared responsibility.'[5] Similarly, as architects and clients engage in extended conversations, a sense of shared ownership of the project and shared responsibility for its success develops. Architect Kava Massih describes such feelings arising from the participatory design process for the Rosa Parks Elementary School in Berkeley, California:

> That's the beauty of the whole process, that I feel ownership of it even though I wasn't the author of it. It allows a lot of people to feel ownership and that ownership is the thing that makes it all worthwhile. I used to say about this project that I could walk out of any public hearing about the project and there would be 50 people defending it as strongly as I would.

For clients to feel comfortable enough to participate in a free exchange with the architect, architects need to present themselves in ways that invite that exchange, to pay attention not only to *what* they say but also to *how* they say it. The 'how' ranges from dress to tone of voice to facial expression and gestures to the words and phrases they use. Either intentionally or unintentionally architects may be suggesting that, in fact, they are not 'in here together'. The

Louise Braverman, Chelsea Court, New York, 2003.
Studio apartments for previously homeless individuals provide full size kitchen appliances, dining tables and convertible bed/couches so residents may lead lives typical of many New Yorkers.

> An architect's presentation of self can also cause barriers and divisions and again begin to present the architect as the expert, the authority who is going to perhaps listen a little bit but mostly go off and do his or her own thing.
>
> Rosa Lane, Berkeley, October 2005

architect's way of talking, dressing and interacting can significantly shape the clients' perceptions and how much they feel that the architect prefers to remain remote or is inviting their participation.

Architect Louise Braverman recognises the importance of her manner of talking with clients, especially when she introduces an initial design proposal. 'I think the best way is talking one human to another. I tell them how I thought about it as a person – why if I were living in one room, I would want a kitchen or why it makes sense if it were my daughter.' Architect Rosa Lane is aware of how she may be seen by the community. In working with design workshop participants for a new elementary school in Maine she was careful about the attitude she took and the clothes she wore. She told Karen that she was there 'in a sweat shirt and rolling up sleeves and being part of it although still an outsider'.

Architects may tailor their approach to the kind of clients with whom they are working. Brodie Bain from Mithun Architects in Seattle learned how important it was to Native American clients that the architects approach them on an equal level, with very specific physical gestures. 'Normally we stand up to give a formal presentation. In this case it was important not to stand up, to be at their same level, at the table with them.' About meeting with the elders of the Lummi Reservation in Washington state, Bob Mohr, a colleague of Brodie's, commented on the importance of sharing a meal and being informal: 'We sat with them and we ate with them … . I tried to be kind of casual and conversational.' Brodie acknowledges that, to some extent, architects are always outsiders, adding "But also some architects act like outsiders. You know the arbiters of taste – "I'm not like you, I'm coming in here to tell you how to have good taste".' These architects, she believes, are more interested in expressing themselves through design than in collaborating with clients.

Architects need to consider how their clothing and manner are consistent with the approach they wish to take. Wearing nothing but black or glasses similar to those of Le Corbusier and Philip Johnson sends a message to clients that the architect wants to remain aloof, like a judge wearing a wig and a gown. If architects do wish to appear as 'arbiters of taste', then dressing in such a manner, to distinguish themselves from the general public, is appropriate and accurate. However, if architects wish to work collaboratively with clients, it is wise to choose an appearance that is less distinctive.

Even when they are required to make formal presentations to an audience, possibly a very large audience, architects can convey sufficient insight into the clients' needs that clients feel understood and that the architect is, or will be, on their side. Language can figure importantly in this situation. This was true of Rem Koolhaas's presentation to an audience of 1,500 in Seattle during the selection process for the Central Library. Sam Miller of LMN, the local firm that worked with OMA on the project, recalls that 'Rem is an amazing speaker and has an amazing command of the language. And for the library of course words were very important. I think that in large part that had a lot to do with how they clicked early on.' Alex Harris, Director of Capital Fund for Seattle's public libraries, believes that it was the intellectual rigour of the architects' thinking about libraries in general and this one in particular, displayed in their first presentation, that helped persuade the library board to select OMA. The architects were successful in receiving the commission not by 'snowing' the audience with beautiful images and impassioned talk but by already beginning a relationship with the client through demonstrating an understanding of the client's needs (see Chapter 3).

Listening and Hearing

Architecture firms commonly advertise on their websites that they 'listen'. Similarly, the American Institute of Architects recommends that after clients have interviewed potential architects and have chosen a leading candidate that, among other items, they consider whether 'the architect really listened to what you were saying'. The Royal Institute of British Architects states that at the initial meeting, after an architect has been chosen, 'your architect will listen carefully to your intentions …'. The word listen is used frequently enough to suggest its importance but it is also used loosely. Listening involves more than being silent and looking attentive. In conversations between architect and client, both need to listen in an active and interactive way, not only taking in information but also working hard to understand and to check that they have understood the intended meaning. Even the simplest requests and what seem to be clearly stated requirements often need clarification and confirmation.

A colleague of Teresa's recently commissioned an architect to add an extension to her house. She thought she had been very clear about the ceiling height she wanted. When the extension was finished, she discovered the architect had misunderstood, thinking that she meant the height and had applied her request to the exterior height. A friend of Karen's made it very clear to her architect that in the house he was designing for her the bathroom had to be big enough to accommodate a large-sized bathtub. After the plans were completed, she discovered that he had not followed her request, instead he used the space to create a larger dining area. His answer in response to her surprise was 'I didn't think it was that important to you.'

The ability both to listen and to hear prevented a premature end to one of the first projects Allies and Morrison ever undertook. The commission was a new building for a private school for girls in Belsize Park, London. The school had started life in a big Edwardian house and was planning to move to a new site. The designers started enthusiastically, producing different plan configurations to show the headmistress what they imagined. One proposal

Do not understand too quickly. Keep in mind that understanding is never-ending. Be tentative with what you think you might know. Knowing interferes with dialogue; it can preclude learning about the other, being inspired by them, and the spontaneity intrinsic to genuine dialogue.

Harlene Anderson, 'Dialogue', in Anderson and Gerhart, *Collaborative Therapy*, 2007, p 40

was for classrooms around courtyards and another placed a hall and dining hall together by an entrance with classrooms in a long line, all facing south and over looking the playground.

When the architects made their presentation to the headmistress, they could see her thinking, 'This is going nowhere. This is not my school!' What Allies and Morrison realised was that their proposals did not reflect her school. She was used to being right in the centre of things, in a big house where all the rooms, including her office, were located off a central staircase. In the new school they had proposed, her office was disconnected from the rest of the school. Allies and Morrison did not try to convince the headmistress to accept their proposals. Instead, they paid attention to her reaction and found an alternative that would draw everything more closely together. As Bob Allies said, 'We all had in our heads what a school should be like but what this head wanted wasn't one that we had thought about at all. In the end it worked out rather nicely.'

People tend to assume that everyday words have the same meaning for everyone. Differences in the meanings of a word, however, can be quite subtle and architects need to attend carefully to understand whether what they are hearing is what the client intended and to keep checking that they have understood. Also, interpreting statements literally is risky. Looking behind the words, seeing them in context and working to discover what they may stand for will help architects form a more complete picture. Hearing is as important as listening.

Fortunately, Swedish architect Mats Fahlander did not take Maria Nordenberg's desire for a 'traditional house' literally. He 'understood that it should be built with wood with nothing plastic or fancy like marble'. As Maria explained, 'Of course, it is not a traditional house but it has the values of a traditional house and Mats understood that.' He understood what she meant because he spent a lot of time talking with her about how she lives, how she uses her house and what is important for her. The point is that architects need to give themselves the opportunity to take in what is important to the client in terms of spatial experience and unspoken needs.

Mats Fahlander, house for Maria Nordenberg, Stockholm, 2007. A very modern house built in traditional timber.

Talking and Showing

During the design process visual, spatial and experiential qualities of the environment are essential sources of understanding and creativity for both the client and the architect. Words alone, while very important, are not sufficient either for exploring or presenting those qualities. Consequently, architects employ various means of showing themselves and their clients both what exists and what is possible. 'Showing' becomes an essential basis for talking, so much so that the two activities become intertwined.

Visits to buildings similar to the one being designed gives architects and clients a chance to discover particular features and aspects of use that may or may not work. Architects may also show images of other buildings and discuss what the clients like or dislike about them. If the client presently occupies a building that is to be renovated or replaced, walking around and discussing the existing building and its surroundings is another valuable source of information and insight. Diana Gordon found the architects' visit to her old house extremely important, she was able to tell Hideaki Ariizumi and Glynis Berry of studio a/b what she loved about that house, in particular the porches and the way the light fell on the pine flooring.

Architects choose different times in the design process to show clients their first ideas. Some architects prefer to rely on words alone at the beginning. As Bryan Lawson recounts, Eva Jiricna takes care to express in words what she understands her clients have said they want and only then draws it.[6] In this way she can make use of the ambiguity that verbal descriptions provide and drawings do not. Architects may also feel that an idea needs further development before it is drawn. Drawing may 'force us to clarify it too quickly. It sometimes seems better to let an idea mature a little before testing it too hard with the drawing.'[7]

Architects use drawings to serve different purposes. Those who wish only to persuade the client of the merits of their proposal and do not wish to engage the client in further exploration of possibilities are likely to present compelling, if not seductive, drawings and renderings, using the skill of presentation as a form of persuasion. A very different use of drawings is to discover more information and to stimulate the client's active participation in design decisions. Drawings can be exceedingly helpful for that purpose. Edward Cullinan, for instance, in his meetings with clients and sketches possible schemes, usually in three dimensions, on the spot in response to their input and revises those sketches as the conversation continues. He talks and draws simultaneously, showing clients how his mind is working.

Borough Development Department, London Borough of Lambeth, Ethelred Estate, London, 1997. Christine Flack, project architect, shows residents the proposed new layout and design for lift, landing and entrance area.

It's a question of dialogue. You need to build up a dialogue. If you only show a reduced solution as if built and finished, you lose an opportunity for communicating with the client. It is about participation.

Renzo Piano in Edward Robbins, *Why Architects Draw*, 1994, p 133

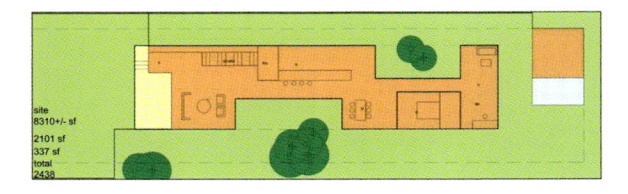

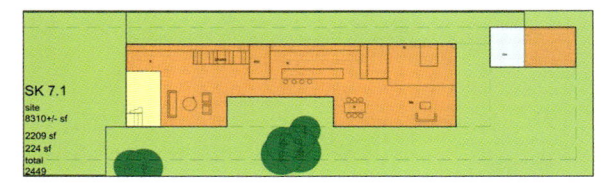

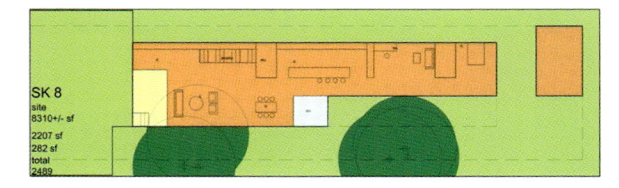

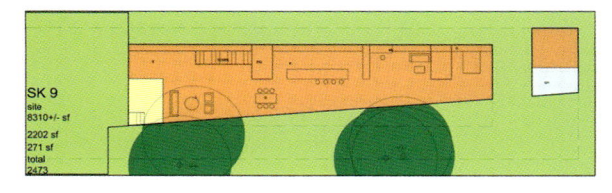

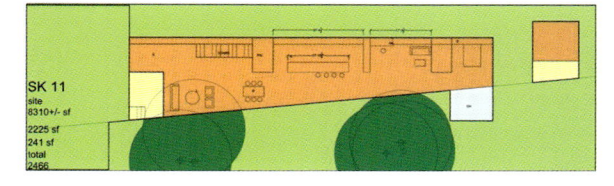

studio a/b architects, Gordon Residence, Greenport, New York, 2008. Hideaki Ariizumi developed a series of schematic designs to explain alternatives to the client. Early schemes retained more trees; later schemes simplified the footprint area of the house and explored different locations for the greenhouse, which was finally attached it to the house.

The precision and clarity of drawings or models can elicit valuable information that words alone may not. Architect Brodie Bain of Mithun in Seattle found that any drawings of campus plans for the Northwest Indian College that showed buildings in a straight line (arranged for passive solar orientation) stimulated immediate, negative responses, since to the client they looked too much like army barracks. 'There was a definite aversion to anything that looked like it was too organised, or, possibly too regimented.' Similarly, workshop participants immediately criticised the landscape architect's plan for Bishops Square in Spitalfields, London drawn in response to their initial suggestions. The proposed scheme had too many sharp corners. They wanted something softer with organic shapes that would be more accommodating to the human form.

As Donald Schön observed, architects also engage in a 'conversation' directly with their drawings independently of the client.[8] Santiago Calatrava describes this process as a 'dialogue': 'To start with you see the thing in your mind and it doesn't exist on paper and then you start making simple sketches and organising things and then you start doing layer after layer … it is very much a dialogue.'[9] All kinds of visual representations can serve as a partner in this conversation.

For Hideaki Ariizumi, drawing a series of alternative proposals allows him to explore different possibilities based on client needs and site requirements. As his partner Glynis Berry describes it, the drawings demonstrate to the client how 'we've looked at their concerns and how we have gone on to something else. Then they can look at the different weightings, because the options are not black and white, and see if they agree with the degree of importance. The drawings show how we got to a decision and become a way for them to participate.' (See Chapter 5)

Community design workshops draw upon many of these ways of showing and talking, along with additional approaches that engage participants directly in design. During the first workshop for the Rosa Parks Elementary School in Berkeley, which focused on the site, participants walked around the existing school and adjacent parts of the neighbourhood talking about what they liked and did not like. In teams of seven or eight, with a base

Ratcliff Architects, Rosa Parks Elementary School, Berkeley, California, 1997. Workshop participants recommended a better location for the entrance which helped maintain privacy from the entrance to a shared open space and smaller courtyards.

map of the site and blocks of foam core representing the different parts of the school (classrooms, library, cafeteria, etc) people indicated how they wanted to use the site, locating the best place for the front door, the playground and the classrooms.

Previously the school entrance had been facing houses and apartment buildings. Christie Coffin, one of the architects on the project, remembers, 'Everybody moved the door from where it had been at the old school to a new location, which turned out to be a terrific location in terms of making the school work – having very private parts and increasingly private parts.' There was a lot of discussion about what to do with the neighbouring park, which was managed by the school district and whether to move it or redevelop it. The group decided to preserve it.

The second workshop focused on the classrooms and the third on the school overall. In all of the workshops teams worked independently to develop their ideas and then showed them to the entire group, explaining their reasoning. During the fourth workshop, architects Christie Coffin and Kava Massih presented big coloured drawings of the options chosen. The group critiqued each option and agreed on what to preserve from each one and what to discard. One option became the focus for the final proposal, which was then developed and built.

Once ideas have been developed through dialogue between client and architect, drawings are an exceedingly informative and powerful way of communicating the key ideas. During the design of the Faculty for Mathematics

Edward Cullinan Architects, Faculty of Mathematics at Cambridge University, 2003. First the 'nest' for private study, then the 'perch' with a colleague then sitting on the 'branch' of a shared sitting room before launching into full 'flight'. A. Nest, B. Perch, C. Branch, D. Flight.

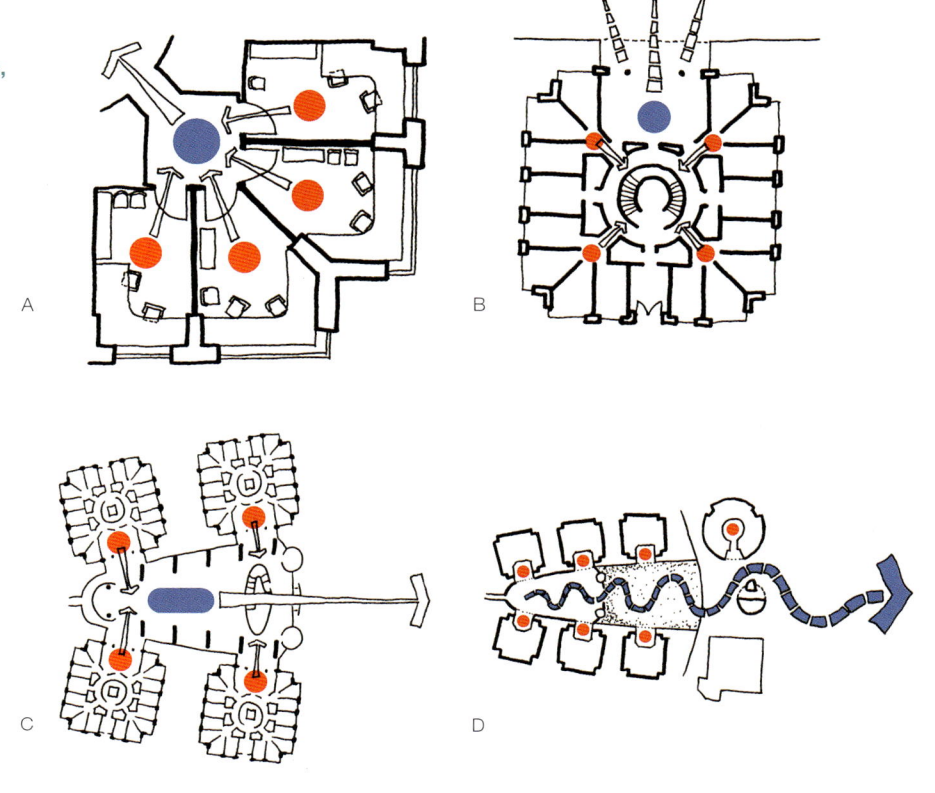

at Cambridge University, Edward Cullinan drew upon his emotional sensitivity to student needs. His drawings illustrate his thinking. Each pavilion is arranged for private study, for sharing ideas with a colleague next door and then with more colleagues in a shared sitting room, analogous perhaps to young birds graduating in stages from the safety of the nest to full flight (see Chapter 3).

Talking in Groups

These days, clients usually arrive in the form of a family, a committee, several committees or an entire community. The constructing team is rarely just two individuals. Often additional groups have to be consulted as well, including planning, zoning and historic preservation commissions and neighbourhood organisations. So architects spend a lot of time talking with groups of people, sometimes very large groups. Frequently in these meetings architects make formal presentations to an audience that may then raise questions and concerns, which can lead to heated arguments. In such meetings architects may become frustrated by what they perceive as opposition, grow defensive and try to persuade, reducing opportunities for open conversation or shared enquiry. To prevent angry exchanges, open discussion may be limited altogether, reducing even further the opportunity for significant contributions to be made.

Working with an entire group of people in a collaborative manner is more of a challenge than working with just a few. The shift from presentation/discussion to dialogue is difficult since there are more voices to encourage and to hear. For the architect, the client or whoever is managing the process, the shift in approach requires time, patience and a capacity to sustain connection despite conflicting needs and dreams. By helping the group to stay with and work through conflict, a shared basis for jointly conceiving the new or rehabilitated built environment can be established.

Lynda H Schneekloth and Robert G Shibley suggest that the first and most important task of collaborative planning and design is to structure a 'dialogic space' in which sustained conversation between all parties can take place.[10] They also recognise that in this space of sharing, which is open to many points of view, disagreement and conflict are very likely to emerge. In other settings this could be destructive but within a space of dialogue conflict can lead to new discoveries as long as there is continuing commitment to the process. As William Isaacs has pointed out, in Greek '*Dia* means "through", *logos* translates to "word" or "meaning". In essence, a dialogue is a flow of meaning.'[11] By adopting dialogue as a way of working, free-floating thinking is encouraged so that both process and content inform understanding in a constantly shifting figure and ground.

An Ancient Way of Working

In modern Western societies, for individuals to sit together in a circle to talk about problems in an open and inclusive manner is unusual. People are more accustomed to meetings that are hierarchically structured with a fixed agenda, where those who speak take 'positions', often in opposition to other positions, and where formal presentations, argument and attempts at persuasion, rather than shared thinking, are the norm. One barrier to shared thinking is the Western tendency to imagine that thinking is bounded by the limits of each person's mind. David Bohm points to a different form of thinking, which he calls 'participatory thought', that has been around much longer and is still evident in many tribal cultures.[12]

Indeed, gathering together in a circle to talk about problems affecting the community, to share thoughts and to make joint decisions is as old as humanity itself. Some American Indian tribes still use the Medicine Wheel or the Talking Stick to enable just and impartial hearing. The Māori in New Zealand invite everybody remotely involved with a problem affecting the community to a *hui* (a large gathering) held on the *marae* (a tribal gathering

A commitment to a relationship among all participants and to the space for dialogue creates a continuing story in which conflict can be accommodated … It is only when someone withdraws from the circle and refuses dialogue that the relationship and the potential power of placemaking fails.

Lynda H Schneekloth and Robert G Shibley, *Placemaking*, 1995, p 8

Dialogue begins when thoughts flow like a stream

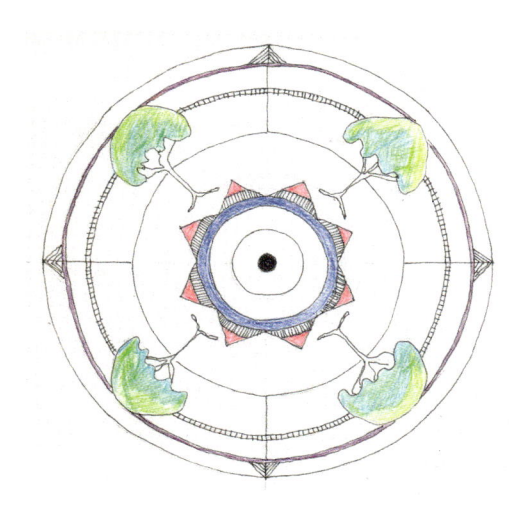

The Medicine Wheel provides a symbolic way to understand what happens in groups depending on where people sit in relation to the cardinal directions. East, west, north and south also symbolise the four elements, four aspects of human nature and four stages of human development.

[The marae] is the standing place of the present generation and will be the standing place for the generations to come. This spiritual aspect of the area is its most important facet … It is the place where I have the right to stand before others and speak as I feel. While I am on my feet, I know that others will give me their respect and allow me to speak without interruption. In return, I shall extend to them the same courtesy when they speak, whether I agree or not.

Hiwi and Pat Turoa, *Te Marae: A Guide to Customs and Protocol*, Reed (Auckland, NZ) 1998, p 19

place that serves social and spiritual purposes), where they meet together and come to agreed conclusions. The *hui* is conducted following long-standing protocols that determine the sequence of speakers and where they stand while speaking. They meet for as long as needed, extending through the day and night if necessary.

The *hui* is a well-established way of meeting and reaching decisions in Māori communities. When important decisions need to be made with another group or *iwi* (tribes), or tribe, they are invited on to the *marae* as *manuhiri* (visitors) to actively take part in the traditional ritual. If the *manuhiri* are architects or other interested officials this approach gives the people of the tribe some control over the consultation process and gives architects an opportunity to learn about the tribe's perspective experientially. When *iwi* (tribes) were consulted in preparation for Te Papa Tongarewa, the Museum of New Zealand, this process was followed. Other client groups, particularly those with indigenous origins, but not necessarily, may also have collaborative and inclusive approaches for making important decisions that can be used as a way of working with architects in those communities (see Chapter 6).

During briefing for the National Museum of the American Indian, 12 consultation workshops were held with tribal groups across the US. The architects joined in the preparation of these meetings, suggesting issues to be raised and questions to be asked but native facilitators led all the workshops while the architects listened and took notes. Justin Estoque, who served as the liaison between the Smithsonian (the client for the museum) and the architects, commented to Karen that with natives talking to natives, it was easy to follow protocols common to native culture. He reported that after the purpose of the project and the workshop had been explained, all participants introduced themselves, giving their names, their tribes and their reasons for coming to the workshop. People's spoken contributions were sometimes 'lengthy and rambling' but, following the native way, great respect was always shown when others were talking (see Chapter 2).

Carefully designed protocols that encourage participation enable creative work in all kinds of groups. To begin the design process for a primary school playground, Tony Ward led his students from the Auckland University School of Architecture through a guided meditation. As they lay in a circle on the ground of the site, they dreamed of possibilities for the playground. Afterwards they shared their dreams with each other and with the school children who participated in the playground's design. With funds the architecture students, parents and staff raised, the architecture students constructed a multi-use adventure playground environment by imaginatively incorporating second-hand and recycled materials and moving over 2,118 cubic feet (600 cubic metres) of earth shaped into landscaped mounds and planting 200 native trees.

For the community design workshops his firm conducts during the design of multi-family housing Michael Pyatok singles out two important factors: an explanation at the beginning the workshop of the entire process and then direct, active involvement of residents in design decisions. He invites the developer to explain who will be living in the new housing, how it will be managed and that people from the neighbourhood will be part of the design process and will be asked to join the governing board of the complex after it is built.

It is very important to Pyatok that participants in a community design workshop take an active role: 'They aren't passively sitting there and looking at a lot of drawings and saying, "I like that" or "I don't like that".' To enable participants to 'shape' the site plan and the units, each team in the group sits around a table and works with a kit of parts to represent the different elements the developer believes have to be there including the units, childcare centre and open space. After an orientation session and an introduction of the issues to be addressed, each team takes an hour and half to develop a scheme; the teams then present their schemes to the whole group and the merits and weaknesses of each scheme are discussed.

Auckland University School of Architecture Community Design Studio, Birkdale Primary School playground, Auckland, 1990. Tony Ward leads students through a guided meditation, dreaming of the possibilities, before they start work on their joint design.

Pyatok Architects, community design workshop for Paradise Creek Community, National City, California. The outcome was a masterplan for 300 units of housing with family counselling, youth and childcare centres and restoration of a tidal creek for recreation and education.

CHAPTER 4 TALKING • 105

There is often one person from the firm sitting in on each team to answer questions, but he or she remains largely passive. Pyatok reports that the residents are often more knowledgeable about housing than these young architects.

> It's very important that people take their housing histories to the table and talk about why the road should come in this way and not that way or that the open space looks too small for what the kids are really going to need. Before you know it, they're really into it and everybody's hands are on the table and they are pushing stuff around and they're arguing and talking and discussing things out.

Architects often gain essential information, insights and inspiration for their projects from participatory design workshops. At the same time, through their involvement in the workshops, participants learn about design and those who initially may have been opposed, sceptical or distrustful become committed to the project. This commitment can be extremely important when the actual building of the project comes under threat or when other parties attempt to change the design. Kristin Prentice, chair of the Site Committee for the Rosa Parks Elementary School, believes the community design workshops that were held helped the neighbourhood 'feel connected' so 'there weren't any little chinks for the school district to say "Oh well, we can't do this because you guys can't even agree".'

Many Inner Groups, One Outer Group

SH Foulkes, the originator of group analysis, noticed that when a group of people meet for the first time, they unconsciously bring with them expectations and beliefs based on their own life experiences, history and culture.[13] It is as though each individual brings along an inner group composed of assumptions and relationships through which that person views the outer group, the other people in it and the task. These individual inner groups combine to form the ground, which Foulkes called the 'foundation matrix', from which the group slowly evolves.

> … a more general application of the matrix idea can be linked to the heart of all creative activity
>
> Jeff P Roberts, 'Foulkes' concept of the matrix', *Group Analysis* vol 2, no15, 1982, p 114

As group participants interact with each other, they actively and consciously develop a new system of relationships based on how they actually experience each other in the group. The limiting assumptions they brought with them begin to lose their power. A 'dynamic matrix' that supports the work of the group gradually evolves. It can be thought of as an 'interconnecting web of relationships' that holds together the interactions of the whole group 'and gives meaning to material as it emerges'.[14] Like a womb, this dynamic matrix needs to be carefully nurtured in order for it to fulfil its function of bringing conception to fruition.

The dynamic matrix is like a delicate web that holds the interactions of the group together. As individuals talk to each other, they discover that the expectations they brought with them do not necessarily reflect the expectations

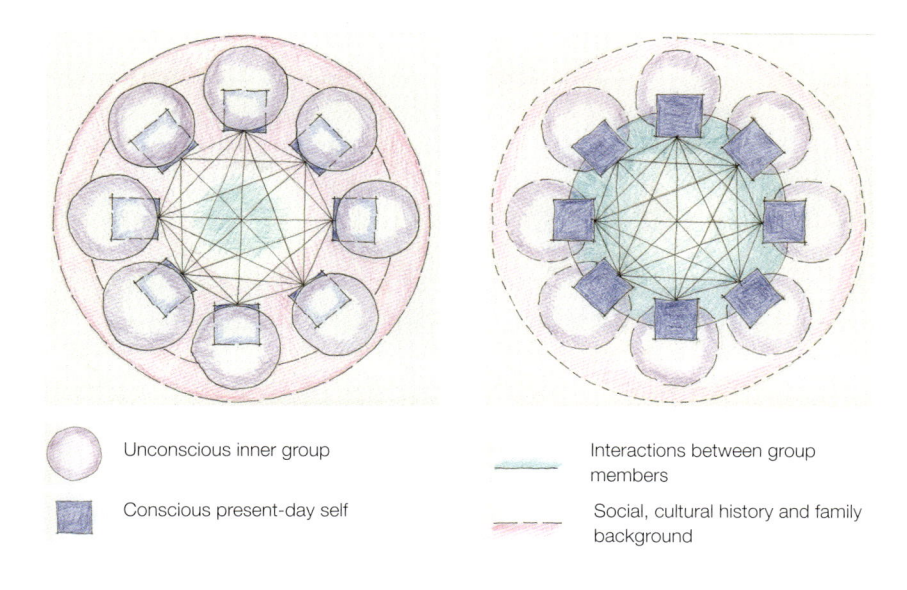

Foundation matrix. LEFT It contains everything that group members bring with them: history, culture, family background and life experience. Initially these often unconscious personal histories dominate the interaction among group members.

Dynamic matrix. RIGHT As participants work together and get to know each other, the foundation matrix recedes into the background and the dynamic matrix emerges to become increasingly influential.

○ Unconscious inner group

■ Conscious present-day self

— Interactions between group members

--- Social, cultural history and family background

and assumptions of other individuals in the group. As they weave the web of the dynamic matrix through their relationships within the group, they become conscious of the original foundation matrix they came with.

The foundation matrix, which is there from the beginning, provides a reference point for the dynamic matrix. Over time, as individuals understand their differences, the group's shared view of reality changes to provide a good enough basis for working together constructively. The dynamic matrix that emerges supports the work of the group. This process is rather like reading and updating a map of a constantly changing landscape.[15] As group members engage in sustained dialogue they notice that the atmosphere is changing. Slowly they realise that by speaking what is on their minds they are altering the climate of the group and, in turn, collective understanding alters. Noticing these changes is crucial. Individuals then realise that they have the power to change their situation.

At one time Teresa, who is a white and middle class, was in the position of managing three young black women from the Caribbean. For nearly a year Teresa noticed they were unwilling to follow her advice and were treating her offers of guidance as insulting. She finally plucked up the courage to ask the women whether they thought the fact that she was a white woman and they were black women was replicating the mistress/slave relationship from their ancestral past. Slow smiles crossed their faces and something profound shifted. They felt their experience had been acknowledged and were then able to seek out Teresa's guidance, follow her suggestions for getting additional training and come to work more regularly. From being unwilling to engage in any kind of conversation, one woman even began to call Teresa her 'white mother'. This small group had been stuck in a foundation matrix

The core dynamic of change in dialogue processes involves people getting some perspective on their own thoughts and thought processes, and on the way, those thought processes shape their perceptions of reality.

David Bohm, Donald Factor and Peter Garrett, 'Dialogue – A Proposal 1991', http://www.infed.org/archives/e-texts/bohm_dialogue.htm 2009, p 2

of interracial distrust. Noticing and talking about what was hidden and unconscious enabled a more supportive dynamic matrix to be generated that allowed the team to make use of the possibilities available to them.

Distrust is often a component of the foundation matrix, as Teresa has learnt in her work with residents on social housing estates. After watching from the sidelines for years while physical changes are made about which they are rarely if ever consulted, it is not surprising that residents have little trust. When finally invited to participate, residents often react with either lifeless apathy or barely disguised rage that often erupts with daunting ferocity. For designers such reactions may seem incomprehensible and give rise to the question, 'Why aren't these people glad that we are finally doing something?' The anger can be understood in terms of a foundation matrix engendered by past experiences of being consistently ignored or dismissed. When working with such groups, it is possible to change this foundation matrix, in which distrust is a given, by making time for all group members to talk about their experiences so that a dynamic matrix is generated and the possibility of trust becomes a given.

When Teresa started working with tenants on the Old Loughborough Estate in Lambeth, London, she encountered enormous anger and mistrust. Like many housing estates in the 1980s, this one suffered problems of leaking roofs, deteriorated brick facing, windows falling out and poor refuse collection facilities. The housing authority ignored these large-scale structural problems and, noting that the flats had become 'hard to let', designated the estate for interior refurbishment with new kitchens, bathrooms and central heating. To introduce this programme of 'package improvements', the Director of Housing invited everyone concerned to a public meeting, including the tenants, local councillors, the police, community workers and council officers. At this meeting, the tenants responded with outrage to the council's 'generous offer' to 'package improve' their flats, shouting that their intelligence was being insulted. (See Chapter 3)

As Teresa later discovered, many of these tenants had given up any hope of being listened to and taken seriously. They brought with them a foundation matrix full of mistrust that made if very difficult for them to trust anyone in authority. By not asking residents what they thought first, the housing department had further reinforced their expectation that nobody would listen to them. Teresa started by letting it be known that she would be in a particular flat on the estate at a regular time each week. Anybody could come and talk with her. Tenants came slowly at first, one at a time, drank tea and told her about their lives. This process continued over several months.

A group developed that continued to take an active role in working with her. Through talking and more talking the fragile foundation matrix full of mistrust became a dynamic matrix that enabled participants to believe that things could change for the better. These informal meetings reinforced Teresa's belief that the tenants knew exactly what the priorities were. They could make responsible decisions. As they desperately wanted to get the fabric of their homes dry, they decided to have the roofs repaired, the windows fixed and the brick facades re-pointed first and to defer the new kitchens, bathrooms and heating. Although with hindsight this seems a logical decision to take, at the time it risked losing funding for the more exciting improvements to the interiors of their homes. For that they had to wait patiently for another two or three years. Given life as many of them had lived it, this waiting was an exercise in trust but the dynamic matrix that had evolved allowed them to believe that the changes would happen. And they did.

Have a Group, Have Anxiety!

Wilfred R Bion, a pioneering British psychoanalyst, who was a tank commander during the Second World War, drew attention to the innate anxiety that accompanies any group endeavour.[16] Most people are immediately anxious when they enter a group and find it difficult to think and speak freely. It is not uncommon for individuals to discover that the only way they can screw up the courage to speak is to get angry first. But expressing raw anger may generate a persecutory atmosphere and so is likely to be counterproductive not only for the individual but for the group as a whole. Remnants of hierarchical groups experienced earlier in life may persist in the form of excessive obedience or rebellion. Either way it takes time to feel free enough from crippling anxiety to speak without having the vague feeling afterwards that one did not represent oneself well enough. Unless anxious feelings are acknowledged as being a natural reaction to the group setting, open dialogue leading to multifaceted creativity is seriously at risk.[17]

Whenever people are faced with change, as they inevitably are when an architect is involved, anxiety is raised and memories of previous upheavals return. Participating in workshops and meetings tends to exacerbate these anxieties yet they are rarely acknowledged. Instead, design proposals are 'talked up' so that fears about what the implications of the new plans might be tend to be buried, only to reappear later as extreme and rigid positions that are difficult to abandon because of possible loss of face. For those who have experienced many difficult moves in their lives, these anxieties are likely to be much greater and the ability to communicate about them directly and coherently is also likely to be more circumscribed. The result is likely to be a foundation matrix full of instability. Careful work needs to be put into creating a safe and stable environment in which a supportive dynamic matrix can evolve, as Teresa experienced first hand in working with tenants at the Old Loughborough housing estate.

Just being in a group fuels three universal 'basic assumptions' that Bion defines as 'fight/flight', 'pairing' and 'dependency'. These assumptions usually operate out of awareness and arise from the group's unconscious expectation that the leader will solve every problem. When the group is operating under the influence of these assumptions, it is unable to work on its assigned task. In this situation, the group feels tense, stiff, lacks a lively buzz and is unlikely to be able to complete its work. Bion referred to this state as a 'basic assumption group'. To free the group from the restrictions imposed by their anxiety, these basic assumptions need to be noticed, described and discussed in the group. It will then be freed up to work on its assigned task.

Most people recognise fight/flight. This nexus of instinctive reactions comes to the fore when there is fierce disagreement and shows itself in 'If you won't agree with me, I am leaving!' scenarios. Having the capacity to stay and

Man is a group animal at war with his groupishness.

Wilfred R Bion, *Experiences in Groups and Other Papers*, 1961, p 141

> Bion proposed that any group is really two groups – a work group and a basic assumption group. That is at any given moment, a group is either working on its task or acting as if it cannot work on the task due to the emotional tone of the group.
>
> Susan A Wheelan, *Group Processes*, 2005, p 10

'fight' through disagreement takes courage and the ability to think clearly in situations that feel threatening. Cheryl Southeran, Joint Chief Executive of Te Papa, found that capacity when she was negotiating the contract for operating the museum. In a meeting with the ministerial representative of the New Zealand government, she interrupted the representative's refusal to negotiate and an obfuscatory argument about how much notice had been given for meetings. She said, 'Can I just cut through this? You have *not* been waiting for months. This is a matter of *days* that we are talking about.' And then helpfully Cheryl charted a way forward. 'There are two ways this discussion can go. We can either negotiate this and get a steer from you now … or we can proceed to negotiate this directly with the minister.' She got her meeting with the minister and a successful agreement.[18]

The second basic assumption, pairing, is easily recognisable as are its energy-sapping consequences. Pairing occurs when people arrive in couples or form couples in the group by getting engrossed in deep discussion with each other. When others watch with interest or when a pair is encouraged to find a solution on behalf of the group, it is clear that the group is avoiding its assigned task. Some pairing is inevitable but if it becomes a default way of working, it is probably evidence that the group task is too challenging and the group is unable to say so directly. Time needs to be taken to talk about how the whole group can be engaged.

Although not as easily recognised, dependency usually shows itself early in the life of a group or at times of intolerable uncertainty. When community groups are asked to sketch or model their ideas, they often respond by saying 'You are the architect, you tell us what to do'. When the task feels onerous, anxiety will be high and will interfere with the group's ability to be creative. Participants seek to reduce anxiety by trying to find someone to complete the task for them. Teresa has noticed this dynamic many times. At the beginning of the second workshop she facilitated with a group of people who live and work around the old Spitalfields Market in London participants worked resourcefully, showing photographs and other images of what they wanted for the new Bishops Square. But then, when it was time to set priorities and develop these ideas, the group was unable to begin. Participants were anxious about how to proceed. The atmosphere became chaotic. It was a critical moment where the group seemed stuck and unable to think together about what they wanted. When she asked participants to put their dreams on paper, they balked.

Teresa recognised a kind of stage fright in the room. It was one thing for the group to come up with ideas, as they had in the first workshop, but it was quite another for them to put the ideas together in a coherent way. She set a boundary to contain the fear. Gently yet firmly she encouraged participants to go into their small groups and 'give it a go'. This is similar to mothers encouraging their children to write by putting a pencil in their hand

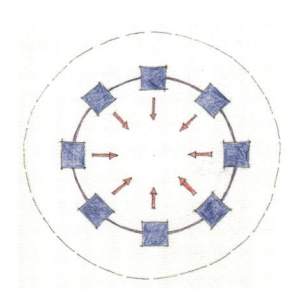

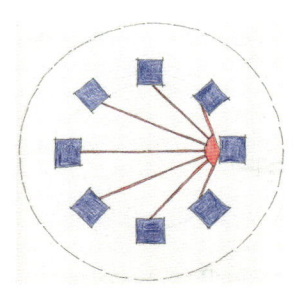

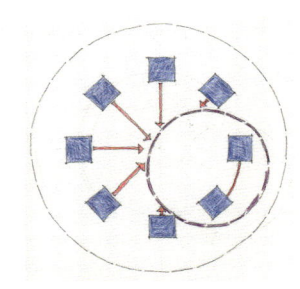

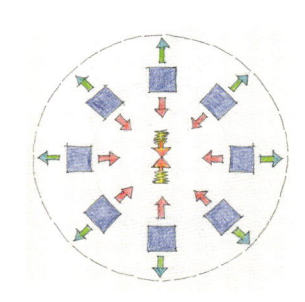

and sitting them down quietly at a table with a piece of paper, saying, 'I know you can do it – just try!'

Michael Pyatok has found that sometimes teams of residents who are about to start developing a site scheme for multifamily housing in their neighbourhood may at first remain 'passive and afraid to touch things'. So a member of his staff 'may have to jump in there and just dump the ingredients on the table and say 'Ok folks you've got to have something here in 40 minutes. The big guy is going to come around and ask "Where is your model?"' Given an hour's time he has never seen a group that did not have a solution or a group that 'fell apart from internal disagreement'.

Attending to Silence

Silence shows itself in many forms and has many meanings. It may be obvious or subtle, almost unnoticed, silent withdrawal or, at its most extreme, non-attendance. Silence can be the result of just needing time to think, to collect one's thoughts, to think about what to say and how to say it. Silence may result from an inability to express strong feelings such as anger or sadness. It can be withholding, like a heavy presence, a smouldering passive anger. Silence, however it shows itself, needs to be noticed and attended to through an appropriate intervention.

At certain times, periods of silence need to be protected so that it feels safe enough for people to think quietly. A period of silence early on is often necessary to enable a group to begin its work. Before Brodie Bain and Bob Mohr of Mithun Architects started working with Lummi Indians on masterplanning the Northwest Indian College, a Native American colleague in the firm described this kind of silence that they would likely encounter: 'You'll do this whole presentation and nobody will have anything to say but they're thinking … the most important thing is to be comfortable with those silences and listen when anybody does speak and don't interrupt anybody.'

Consistent silence, however, from an individual or from part of a group should not be ignored for too long. If not questioned, people may never participate and may eventually leave the group. When individuals leave,

Work group. LEFT When the group is working together on its assigned task, everybody is engaged.

Dependency. CENTRE LEFT When the group is in dependency mode, group members tend to expect the facilitator to provide all the answers. The group members become passengers rather than working together

Pairing. CENTRE RIGHT In pairing mode group members expect the pair to do their work for them.

Fight/flight. RIGHT When group members are engaged in fight/flight mode, they are focusing on whether to stay or leave rather than on the assigned task.

or disappear, the group can feel destabilised, uncomfortable and unsafe. Sometimes people who are silent hold important clues about what direction the conversation could take. They may be thinking about things that are very different from what is being discussed and are not sure how to fit what they are thinking into the ongoing conversation.

Silence itself is a form of communication and requires a meta-conversation to reveal what people have not been able to say. It is always difficult to tell what a silence means and what underlies it but when attention is drawn to the silence, participants' responses often give clues. Tone of voice and body language can indicate what words sometimes leave out.

Finding an appropriate intervention to address silence takes practice as it is always difficult to tell what silence means. One approach is for the facilitator to comment to the group that some participants, possibly a recognisable sub-group, have not spoken and invite them to contribute. Such an intervention, at the level of the group rather than to specific individuals, helps individuals see their silence as part of a pattern, which then usually enables some of them to speak. The responses can free up a stifling silence and may bring in a much-needed perspective. Sometimes it is also helpful to gently direct questions to specific individuals, but such interventions should be made with caution. They can feel exposing.

Silence is Revealing

Silence takes a particularly subtle form when participants engage in interminable discussions that seem to have no purpose or when they return repeatedly to the same topics. Paradoxically, these two patterns emerge as ways of remaining silent on other, more crucial concerns, particularly those that seem likely to generate disagreement. In these situations it is useful to ask participants what is uppermost in their minds or what needs to be said. When participants write their answers, anonymously, on Post-it notes that are posted for everyone to read, the written comments often reveal that participants have similar, or related thoughts. Once revealed, these thoughts and concerns can be discussed, along with the reasons for the silence and so the conversation can flow again.

When Teresa first started working with tenants at Ethelred Estate in Lambeth, south London to determine their priorities for refurbishment of the tower blocks, almost the only people who came to the meetings regularly was a group of vociferous white men. This was a puzzle because black women headed most of the households in these blocks. Sometimes these women would attend but they would remain silent and then disappear again.

The first priority was to find out what concerned the tenants most. Months slipped by and the group seemed stuck on the garage design. The conversations appeared to be focused on the proposals, but Teresa kept wondering what was preventing them from thinking about other areas of

> … no matter how much one might try, one cannot *not* communicate. Activity or inactivity, words or silence all have message value: they influence others and these others, in turn, cannot *not* respond to these communications and are thus themselves communicating.
>
> Paul Watzlawick, Janet Helmick Beavin and Don D Jackson, *Pragmatics of Human Communication*, 1967, p 49

the building. Finally, after listening to yet another explanation about why this design or that design did not work she asked, 'What is really bothering you?' It emerged then that the group of men who were coming to the meeting had quite another agenda that until that moment had remained hidden. They finally admitted that they did not want any development of the underground garages at all because they were using some of them as a workshop for car repairs from which they earned an illicit living.

This confrontation was a key moment. It was as if a dam had been broken. A tenant offered her own flat to meet in instead, away from the formal housing office. Teresa received a letter from another tenant who felt disturbed by the destructive comments that she had heard were consistently being made at the meetings and suggested that a newsletter be started. Not long afterwards, Teresa received another letter asking her if any help was needed with distributing the newsletter. Then another letter came, suggesting that people with disabilities and the elderly be involved in the discussions. From then on the meetings were very energising, full of ideas and dedicated hard work. As a consequence of these meetings, the changes made to the tower blocks went far beyond the original proposal made without any tenant input. The project that emerged included profound changes to the communal environment such as high speed lifts that stop at every floor, provision for a concierge in a welcoming entrance area, and windows and doors to enclose and humanise previously windswept landings. At the time, such changes were almost revolutionary for public sector tower blocks.

In other situations disagreement may arise from participants' frustration over not being able to express their feelings, particularly when the work the group is expected to do focuses exclusively on practical tasks with no space for comments about the tasks or about underlying emotions. Paul Robinson, of Davis Langdon in New Zealand and an expert in value management, was called in to help a community group select an architect for their new church in Auckland.[19] He took the participants through a very logical process based on 'objectively' ascribing and weighting values that they wanted reflected in the new church. They were not able to reach agreement.

After a very frustrating exchange with the group, which was partly Korean, Robinson asked the group members to weight the short-listed architects on their own and to bring their decisions back for discussion. Only four forms from the ten people in the group were returned. The Korean subgroup had completely ignored the entire procedure and wanted to select the only Korean architect on the list, the one who could 'speak their language'. Until then no one in the group had been able to talk openly. What participants felt did not lend itself to the rational procedure they had been asked to follow and could not be expressed in the context of that procedure. This small group of people needed someone to stay with them while they shouted and argued until they discovered their differences and finally understood each other sufficiently to make a joint decision about which architect to select.

Silencing

A prolonged silence from a particular individual or group of individuals may arise from a feeling of being 'silenced' by others in the group. It may be a forced muteness in response to a dominant culture that has been brought into the group through the foundation matrix or that has formed in the group through the dynamic matrix. Those who remain silent may feel that the language being used by the more dominant culture within the group is so different from their own that they cannot find a way to express what they feel. As Patrick de Maré explained, 'It is not the individual who is unconscious but the culture that does not allow the thought to be voiced'.[20] It is important to remember that people come to a group with different perspectives and assumptions and that these differences may lead to silence. Space needs to be made for diverse voices to be heard.

When working across cultures (and sometimes the cultural differences are not evident), it is particularly important to pay attention to the micro-interactions between people that entail a kind of silencing. Very often the 'outsider', however defined, is left without a voice and fades into the background. For those with an 'outsider' perspective, it takes time to develop the ability to stand one's ground, to speak with one's own voice.[21] Most people say nothing in the face of apparent agreement among the 'insider' majority.

When the New Zealand government set out to select a firm of architects for Te Papa, the selection panel included four people from overseas and four people from New Zealand. To establish the bicultural intentions for the building early on, two *Kaumatua* (Māori elders) Kara Puketapu and Apirama Mahuika were included on the selection panel. When Teresa talked to Kara, she learned that he was the initiator of the hugely successful *Te Māori*, Māori Art, exhibition that toured the US from September 1984 to 1986 to great critical acclaim.[22] Despite this experience, Kara felt marginalised and silenced

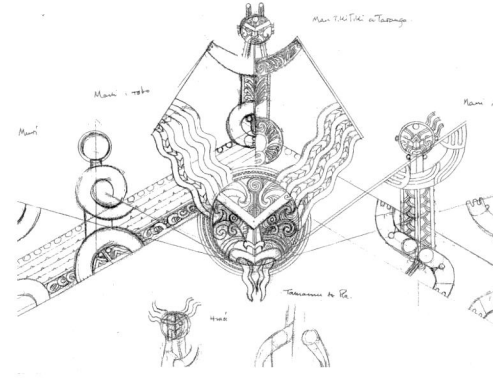

Cliff Whiting, drawings for the design of the *marae*, Te Papa Tongarewa Museum of New Zealand, 1993.
BELOW Front view of the modern *wharenui* (meeting house) from the *marae-atea* (open area in front).
BELOW RIGHT Detail of *tekoteko*, the carved figurehead of Maui above the door to the *wharenui*. Maui is a *tipuna* or ancestor, highly respected throughout the Pacific. He represents creative exploration.

during the selection process. He told Teresa, 'We as Māori were not in command of anything". He had many ideas that he felt unable to contribute, and unlike Apirama, was not included in the group that continued on to work with the designers.

Cultural silencing can be more overt yet still remain unacknowledged. Towards the end of the film *Getting to My Place: The Making of Te Papa* Cliff Whiting, the Māori Joint Chief Executive, is seen presenting and explaining his proposal for the design of the museum's *marae* to Sir Ron Trotter, the chair of the museum's board of directors.[23] This *Pākehā* businessman, used to being in control, adopts a bossy, authoritarian attitude. The *marae* is a Māori institution and the only place in the museum designed in accordance with Māori values and beliefs. Despite this fact, and tapping the table for emphasis, Trotter tells Whiting that the *marae* should not be 'just for Māori'. When Whiting tries to respond softly, Trotter interrupts and tells him that he 'must get that idea that because the museum is bicultural, the *marae* has to satisfy both Māori and Pākehā cultures!' His attitude, expressed both in what he says and how, is culturally silencing.

In that situation Whiting avoided getting into an argument. He simply tried to restate his position without retaliating. He was well aware that he needed to respond thoughtfully as is evident in the comment he makes on film after the exchange. He acknowledges that he had 'to take that sort of crap … in the hope of gaining some ground …'. Cliff Whiting was able to listen to himself in just the way that William Isaacs has recommended from his work with dialogue groups: 'Some of the most powerful contributions come from people who have begun to listen to themselves in the context of the group.'[24]

> The important thing is that such places belong to 'us' and not 'me'. They are places where thoughts and ideas may be exchanged, and joy and sadness may be shared. All of these places need people in order to come alive. Within such places, *wairua* or spirit or soul, is not denied. Any place can become the *marae*, because any area of land can become representative of *Papauanuku*, the Earth Mother.
>
> Hiwi and Pat Turoa, *Te Marae: A Guide to Customs and Protocol*, 1998, p 142

The Words Matter

It is with words that architects and clients communicate. Certainly drawings and models are presented, the project site and other buildings are visited but, always, in addition and surrounding these forms of showing, information is also conveyed through words, written and spoken. In written text and during conversations, in large meetings and small, the specific words and phrases used may carry tremendous importance in shaping design decisions, reverberating throughout the design process and even after the building is completed.

As architects communicate with each other and with the client, language does not just accompany design, it is a constituent of design: '… language is a part of the "doing" (designing) and the thing "done" (the designed work)'.[25] In their observations of staff conversations in an architecture firm, Medway and Clark found that over the course of three days, during the development of one building elevation, the architects referred to a great variety of metaphors by naming them: fridge, boat, crucible, golf club and avocado. The authors

Sketch annotations (top to bottom, left to right):

"David, thanks again for all the drawings — the building starts to make sense now! I was searching for an elevation (external north and south) that somehow makes sense climatically in both directions and not be totally different. The diagram (1) at the bottom has an inclined wall to the south and inclined fins to the north. The fins would cut the glare and the inclined wall will protect the windows."

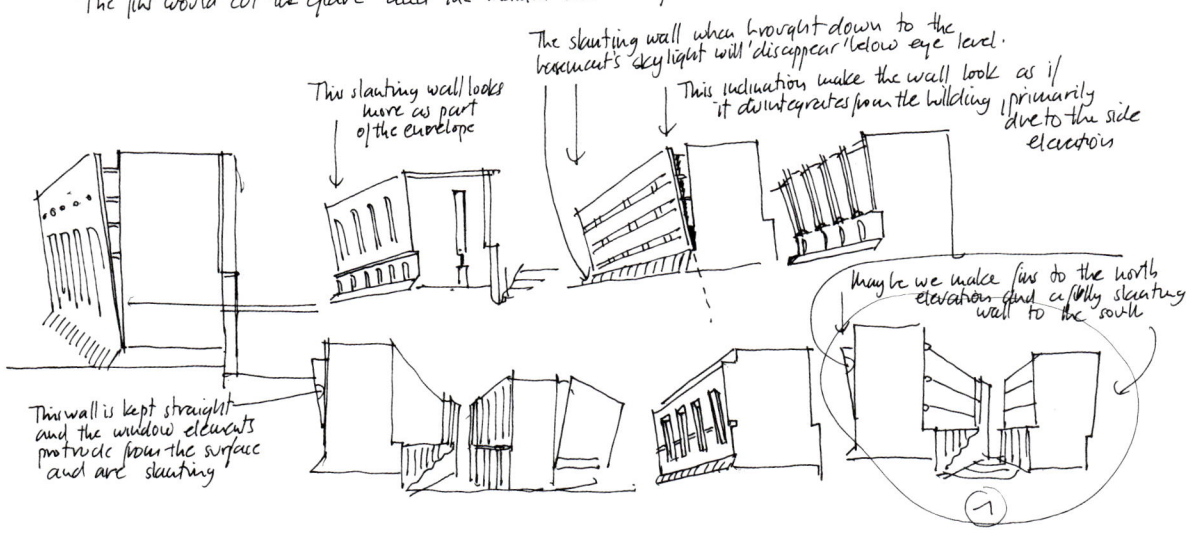

"This slanting wall looks more as part of the envelope"

"The slanting wall when brought down to the basement's skylight will 'disappear' below eye level."

"This inclination make the wall look as if it disintegrates from the building, primarily due to the side elevations"

"This wall is kept straight and the window elements protrude from the surface and are slanting"

"Maybe we make fins to the north elevation and a fully slanting wall to the south"

Ada Karmi-Melamede, Life Sciences Building, Ben Gurion University, Beersheva, 2001. On sketch drawings of the building elevations Ada wrote comments to David S Robins, project architect, giving particular attention to the 'fins' in the last sketch. 'The fins would cut the glare and the inclined wall will protect the window.'

conclude that '… by means of metaphor in language and formal and other associations in the visual mode, things that are not buildings … get into the design for buildings'.[26]

Verbal statements are particularly important in dialogue between the client and architect both because the building does not yet exist physically and because clients, being unfamiliar with the conventions or techniques of drawings and models, rely heavily on language for understanding the proposed design. Architect Joy Siegel realises how important verbal explanations are in conjunction with drawings. After she meets with clients and shows them alternative schemes for the redesign of a house, she leaves the plans with them. Moreover, on each plan she notes the key characteristics of that scheme to help clients recall the differences between the alternatives as they make their choice.

Finding or Creating a Shared Language

The words architects and clients habitually use may not be easily understood by each other since they arise from their different areas of expertise. Frequently, when architects present ideas and proposals they use terms that mean little to their audience. This makes them sound like experts but it does not aid understanding and reduces possibilities for dialogue. After he presented a proposed design for the Northwest Indian College and attempted to explain the architects' thinking behind the design, Bob Mohr of Mithun Architects, realised that 'Everyone heard it but I don't know if I was able translate it in the right way because I was using words like "volume."'

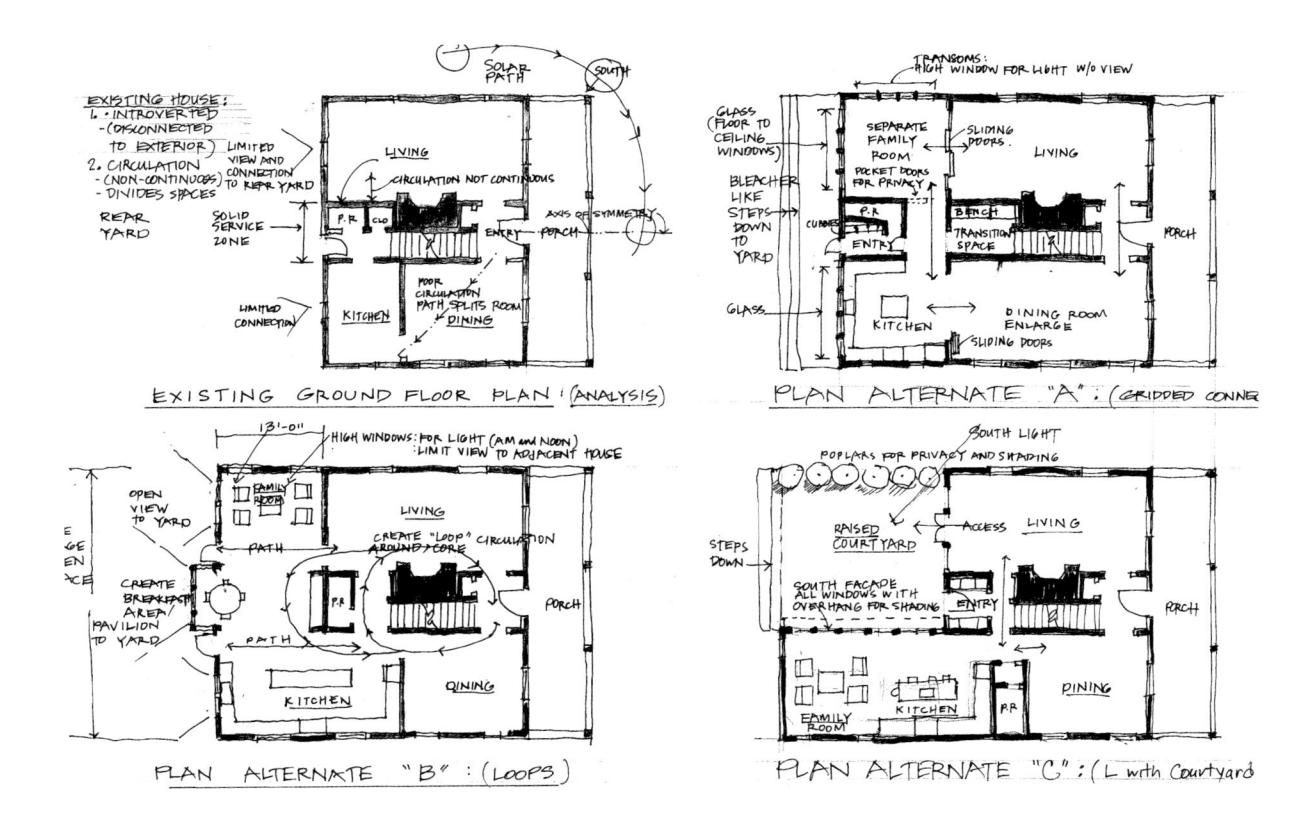

Architects may teach clients some of the language they use, not necessarily architectural terms (like volume) but how to describe their own experiences of buildings. When Rosa Lane is working on the design of an elementary school, she takes groups of clients, teachers and parents to visit other elementary schools so they can learn 'a new language'.

They can observe how one school is different from another and so discover a way to talk about a vision for their school. 'The task is to get them a whole new vocabulary and a whole new experience of what space can be for them. Then you have something you can talk with them about.'

One of Joshua Ramus's objectives for spending the first three months of a project talking and thinking with clients is to *create* a shared language. This 'language' is specific to the project at hand since it involves identifying a series of problems and jointly adopting positions towards those problems, which then become both the basis for design proposals and the means for evaluating them. He told Karen that without a shared language of collectively held positions,

Joy Siegel, Loop House, Millburn, New Jersey, 2007.
After discussing alternatives with her clients, Joy gave them annotated plans to remind them of the differences between the schemes. The clients chose Alternate B that creates 'loop circulation around the core' and a 'breakfast area/pavilion to yard'.

The most effective, and also the simplest techniques to 'grow' a shared language is to make joint trips to as many buildings of similar purpose as possible supplemented by images and descriptions of others.

Sunand Prasad, *Transformations*, 2007, p 18

CHAPTER 4 TALKING • 117

… we're going to get into a struggle because we're not going to be speaking a common conceptual language and we're not going to be speaking a common architectural language. We're going to be like two deaf mutes trying to communicate.

The architect may have to work to understand terms that the client uses. Particular words may inspire additional research and questioning to help the architect understand what the clients do – what their work or living involves. Architect Jenny Ryding, describing the programming process she and her colleagues developed for a new psychiatric clinic at the Academic Hospital in Uppsala, Sweden, explained that they had to learn the meaning of the terms psychosis, depression, schizophrenia. 'We needed to understand all these expressions that people who work in this area of care use.'

When he is working on projects with Native American Indian groups, Johnpaul Jones draws upon a language that he and his client already know, one that captures beliefs common to the American Indian heritage that refer to the natural world, the animal world, the spirit world and the human world. By re-presenting these worlds, Johnpaul describes a shared way of looking at the world that his clients already possess. It becomes a basis for discussion and design. 'As soon as we start talking about these things, then they start sharing with us. What we try to do is convince them through talking about these things, that they are really important. These are the bones that you construct a design on.'

The exact words and phrases clients use to express their ideas and preferences can be very important for the architect to hear (or read). They may be very evocative of particular design approaches. An excellent example is the program for the National Museum of the American Indian in Washington. The Smithsonian Institution required that the programming team meet with tribal groups around the country to discover what participants thought the building should do and be and look like. Denise Scott Brown decided that the programming document should contain direct quotations from the participants in those consultations, without interpretation or analysis. The words and the sentences would speak for themselves, listed in particular categories.

National Museum of the American Indian, entrance, Washington DC, 2004.
Spectrum 8, hanging prisms by artist Charles Ross refract the sunlight over surfaces of the atrium, changing with the quality of sunlight and the time of day.

Native Symbols and Traditions
Adaptability and survival. How can we portray that inner strength?
The circle is almost universal and dominant. It is the shape of Kivas and ceremonial spaces for Pueblos and Hopi.
Kodiak people like informality. They protest having agendas at meetings.[27]

Spatial Character and Interior Spaces
Bring the outside in, avoid all rectangular walls
Simple, elegant lines. Not busy, busy. Our soul is elegant.
A homey feeling, sand, colours of the earth.[28]

Exterior and Entry
This building competes with monuments of the world. It must be compatible, in that setting, as the monument to Native Americans.
Close to nature, not set apart in the universe.
Provide a homelike reception room, with water. Take a few minutes to feel at home.
The Air and Space Museum reminds me of a warehouse – it projects the idea of storage. We want to welcome people; that should be in the entrance[29]

During design members of the design team quoted many of the statements in the program; the statements served both as inspiration and confirmation of their design choices. Later, after the museum opened, comments people made during the consultation meetings were printed in the brief and so served as a way of explaining the building and its origins. According to Justin Estoque, Director of the Executive Planning Office of the museum, these comments remain important in guiding the planning and operation of the museum.

Naming and Framing

In order to convey information, thoughts and ideas both during and after design, all those connected to a project frequently rely on a vocabulary closely associated with that particular project. The nouns used serve to *name* qualities, elements, spaces and types of building and to *frame* and guide design choices. Mostly these are commonly used words but they may also be invented in order to identify new situations and conditions. Sam Miller of LMN Architects explained to Karen how very important language was to the design and construction of the Seattle Central Library. Names had to be given to physical and programmatic elements of the building that had never been created (or named) before. For example, the innovative building skin doubles up in some places, creating an amorphous shape; the team named these 'amoebas', a term that appeared in the contract documents with the builder.

Architects and clients frequently employ the names of types of buildings or other designed places in their conversations with each other. At the beginning, as they are getting acquainted, clients name not just a building but a type of building – a library, a museum, a school, a park, a house. Subsequently, clients and architects may refer to other types both to suggest the characteristics they desire and those they wish to avoid. Existing building types become a rich and shared source of reference, providing architect and client with a common

> When naming a place type we give it meaning by suggesting the formal characteristics and the spatial practices it accommodates; in doing so we also limit the potential for other meanings and practices. The name given to a place type shapes our images of it, how we create or modify an actual place to match the name, and how we occupy it or otherwise interact with it.
>
> Lynda H Schneekloth and Karen A Franck 'Type: prison or promise? in Franck and Schneekloth, eds, *Ordering Space*, 1994, p 25

language to describe what already exists and what they wish to create. With a single word, each participant in the dialogue can convey a tremendous amount of information about the form, image and experience of a place.

The naming of 'types of places' and 'types of things' is extremely important in conversations and decisions about places that do not yet exist. The name of a 'type of place' conveys both a visual image and, also, suggests a range of spatial and social practices and meanings associated with that type. Over and over again in briefing and design, architects and clients refer to buildings and other types to explain what they mean. In describing the school that the Rosa Parks Elementary School was to replace, Kristin Prentice of the Site Committee said, 'it was built like a prison'.

Over and over again participants in the consultations for the National Museum of the American Indian referred to commonly understood types, including warehouse, monument, home. In the first volume of the program, *The Way of the People*, the programming team also employed the names of building types as well as types of objects and landscape to guide design: 'like something else: a billboard, a primordial natural landscape …'[30] The program also draws an analogy between the museum and a nation's embassy in a foreign capital.[31] These examples demonstrate how potent types as metaphors are in capturing and communicating images and how useful that can be in the dialogue between client and architect.

References to types also figured prominently in the program for the Cultural Resources Center, the building to house the entire collection of artefacts for the National Museum of the American Indian (NMAI) in Suitland, Maryland. These references to type were particularly important because the building did not fall into an existing category. It was to house the artefacts in a way that is sympathetic with native beliefs; it would be open and welcoming to visitors; and it would be a place for holding ceremonies involving the artefacts. The program stated:

> It is easier to say what this place is not – *a warehouse, fortress, temple, suburban government office building, high-tech laboratory* – than to say what it is, as it has few successful architectural precedents and must meet apparently contradictory needs.[32]

> The selection of material for the building should respond to the expressed need for the museum to feel profoundly Native and to avoid inappropriate comparisons to *warehouses, hospitals, high-tech laboratories, prisons and vaults*. The interpretation of this goal is central to the architectural design challenge.[33]

As the 'brain and soul' as well as the 'home' of the new museum, NMAI at Suitland will need to be as far removed from the appearance and feeling of a *warehouse* as possible. The design team must understand and provide for the

Polshek Partnership Architects, Cultural Resource Center, Suitland, Maryland, 1998. Native participants in briefing workshops emphasised that the building should not resemble a 'warehouse' in any way, being instead a warm and welcoming place where artefacts were treated as 'living things'. LEFT Entrance BELOW The entrance foyer also serves as a space for ceremonies.

objects as their makers and users did – as living, breathing beings, with spirit and life.[34]

The architectural program for the Cultural Resource Center identified a series of types that should not serve as a model for the building. Such a discussion of appropriate and inappropriate types for guiding design is a frequent topic in the dialogue between client and architect. Another example is the Mary Graham Children's Shelter in San Joaquin County, California that provides housing and counselling for children waiting to be placed in foster care or returned to their own families. For the design of this building the architects and the client agreed that 'home' was not an appropriate metaphor. The client felt that other building types that suggested a shorter stay were more appropriate. Architect Christie Coffin who worked on the project reported, 'It's more like a summer camp or a boarding school. The easy thing to model this place after is a home. We tried not to do that.' (See Chapter 5)

Design language also serves to do what Donald Schön and then Bryan Lawson have called 'framing'.[35] Design projects are too large and too complex to be considered in totality so designers focus on particular features or conditions. Andy Dong recognises the significant role language plays in this framing: 'Embedded in the language is information regarding the design work; the language is attempting to communicate, advance and frame the design work into a conceptual structure …'[36]

One way a project is framed is by naming types to represent a concept that can then guide design. Nigel Cross's observations of a team of industrial designers illustrates the power of this naming of type as a way to frame design. The designers were asked to design a device that would carry a backpack on a mountain bicycle. Early in their discussion team members began to refer to the device as a 'bag'. Then one member suggested that 'maybe it's like a little vacuum formed tray'.[37] The new description, moving from 'bag' to 'tray', generated a breakthrough by suggesting a whole new set of possible physical features the device might have. The team embraced the idea of tray and designed a plastic tray to be placed over the rear wheel, satisfying key problems identified earlier in the process. The tray prevented the straps of the backpack from dangling and protected the backpack from sprays of water or mud from the back bicycle wheel.

Actual types of places and types serving as metaphors are common referents during design. Donald Schön and William Porter observed seven designers working on an assigned design exercise. From the recorded protocols, they identified four 'types of types': functional types (suburban site or branch library); references to particular buildings or kinds of buildings (Richardson libraries, a Japanese entrance); spatial gestalts (end, middle); and experiential archetypes (tongue, entrance like a pair of outstretched arms). They note that types 'hold' knowledge that 'can be read off them' and that types are sources of 'leading ideas'.[38]

Types figured prominently in the dialogue and design of Seattle's Central Library, both in exploring what a library for the 21st century should be and in conceiving and designing interior spaces. The architects invented names that capture significant features of key spaces: Living Room for the main floor sitting area and Mixing Chamber for the main reference area. The concept of 'mixing chamber' captured their intention to 'mix' different disciplines, reference librarians for different departments and electronic media in one space. Sam Miller of LMN Architects remembers that everyone called the space by that name all through design and construction. Then, when it came time to choose names for the floors after the building was completed, City Librarian Deborah Jacobs decided that since people often do not know what 'reference' means, it made sense to stick with 'Mixing Chamber'. The name, which had framed design, was adopted officially to name the space in the completed building.

During the community design workshops for the Rosa Parks Elementary School Kava Massih kept hearing that 'the classroom is like a house, it's sort of a self-contained entity' (see Chapter 2). He then adopted the idea of house for the form of the individual classrooms, each with a pitched roof and windows much like those of a house. The type, 'house', which the workshop participants used as a metaphor for the classroom but not necessarily for how it should look, inspired the architect's choice of form and image as well as pattern of use: each class has its own heating system and shares a patio with the classroom next door. Built, the image of the school is very residential, so much so that many people think the classroom buildings are condominiums, according to Kristin Prentice, chair of the Site Committee. 'All the classrooms do look like little houses, which is the whole idea. We wanted it to blend

OMA with LMN Architects, Central Library, Seattle, 2004. The naming and the inventing of spaces played a significant role in the library's design and the dialogue between architect and client. LEFT The 'legibility section' names spaces and activities. BELOW The Mixing Chamber is for mixing disciplines, reference librarians and electronic media.

CHAPTER 4 TALKING • 123

Ratcliff Architects, Rosa Parks Elementary School, Berkeley, California, 1997.
Comments in the community design workshops inspired architect Kava Massih to design the classrooms to look like houses. The reading centre is in the red tower, modelled after local water towers.

in with the neighbourhood, to look sort of residential.' As the Rosa Parks example illustrates so well, the words exchanged by participants in a design dialogue often open a path to something new, something that meets the client's needs in unexpected ways.

NOTES

1 Jeremy Till, 'The negotiation of hope', in Peter Blundell Jones, Doina Petrescu and Jeremy Till, eds, *Architecture & Participation*, Spon Press (Oxford), 2005, p 38.
2 William Isaacs, *Dialogue and the Art of Thinking Together*, Currency (New York), 1999, p 9.
3 John Forester, 'Designing: Making sense together in practical conversations', *Journal of Architectural Education*, vol 38, 1985, p 14.
4 Jurgen Ruesh and Gregory Bateson, *Communication: The Social Matrix of Psychiatry*, Norton (New York), 1951, pp 179–81.
5 Harlene Anderson, 'The heart and spirit of collaborative therapy', in Harlene Anderson and Diane Gehart, eds, *Collaborative Therapy: Relationships and Conversations that Make a Difference*, Routledge (New York), 2007, p 279.
6 Bryan Lawson, *Design in Mind*, Architectural Press (Oxford), 1994.
7 Bryan Lawson, *What Designers Know*, Architectural Press (Oxford), 2004, p 87.

8   Donald A Schön, *The Reflective Practitioner: How Professionals Think in Action*, Basic Books (New York), 1983.
9   Quoted in Lawson, *What Designers Know*, at p 25.
10 Lynda H Schneekloth and Robert G Shibley, *Placemaking: The Art and Practice of Building Communities*, John Wiley & Sons Inc (New York), 1995.
11 Isaacs, *Dialogue and the Art of Thinking Together*, p 19.
12 David Bohm, *On Dialogue*, Routledge (London), 1996, p ix.
13 SH Foulkes, *Introduction to Group-Analytic Psychotherapy*, Heinemann (London), 1948; reprinted Karnac Books (London), 1983.
14 SH Foulkes, *Therapeutic Group Analysis*, Allen & Unwin (London), 1964; reprinted Karnac Books (London), 1984.
15 Angela Douglas, 'Mapping the matrix: Healing vision and communication', *Group Analysis*, vol 35, 2002, pp 89–103.
16 Wilfred R Bion, *Experiences in Groups and Other Papers*, Tavistock Publications (London), 1961, p 98.
17 Susan A Wheelan has devoted three chapters in *Facilitating Training Groups: A Guide to Leadership and Verbal Intervention Skills* (Praeger (New York), 1990, pp 63–146) to deciding when and how to intervene. Sheila Thompson in *The Group Context* (Jessica Kingsley (London), 1999) also describes the complex ideas integral to group work in a clear and accessible way.
18 *Getting to Our Place*, Gaylene Preston Productions for New Zealand on Air (Wellington, New Zealand), 1999.
19 Value management, as developed by Professor Roy Barton of the University of Canberra, Australia is a structured, analytical process designed to achieve value for money by providing all the necessary functions at the lowest total cost consistent with required levels of quality and performance. See Mark Neasbey, Roy Barton and John Knott, 'Value management' in Rick Best, Gerard de Valance, eds, *Building in Value*, Elsevier (Oxford), 1999.
20 Patrick de Maré, Robin Piper and Sheila Thompson, *Koinonia: From Hate through Dialogue to Culture in the Large Group*, Karnac Books (London), 1991, p 77.
21 Ibid, passim.
22 The Te Māori exhibition was a milestone in the Māori cultural renaissance that began in the 1970s. Featuring traditional Māori artwork, the exhibition toured internationally between 1984 and 1987 starting at the Metropolitan Museum, New York in September 1984. It was a great success and returned to tour New Zealand, again to applause, and a swelling of Māori pride.
23 *Getting to Our Place*.
24 William Isaacs, 'Dialogue', in Peter M Senge, Art Kleiner, Charlotte Roberts, Richard Ross, Bryan Smith, eds, *The Fifth Discipline Fieldbook*, Doubleday (New York), 1994.
25 Andy Dong, 'The enactment of design through language', *Design Studies*, vol 28, January 2007, p 6.
26 P Medway and B Clark, 'Imaging the building: Architectural design as semiotic construction', *Design Studies*, vol 24, May 2003, p 267.

27 Venturi, Scott Brown and Associates, *The Way of the People: National Museum of the American Indian (Master Facilities Programming, Phase 1)*, Office of Design and Construction, Smithsonian Institution (Washington DC), 1991, p 19.
28 Ibid, p 21.
29 Ibid, pp 16–17.
30 Ibid, p 101.
31 Ibid, p 102.
32 Venturi, Scott Brown and Associates *The Way of the People: National Museum of the American Indian (Master Facilities Programming Phase 2)*, Office of Design and Construction, Smithsonian Institution (Washington DC), 1993, p II.21
33 Ibid, p IV.105.
34 Ibid, p V.157.
35 Donald Schön, 'Problems, frames and perspectives on designing', *Design Studies*, vol 5, July 1984, 132–36; Lawson, *What Designers Know*.
36 Dong, 'The enactment of design through language', p 11.
37 Nigel Cross, *Designerly Ways of Knowing*, Birkhäuser (Basel), 2007, p 67.
38 Donald A Schön 'Designing: Rules, types and worlds', *Design Studies*, vol 9, July 1988, p 188.

Chapter 5 — Exploring

At the beginning of a project architect and client embark on a journey together, not knowing for certain what path they will take or what the final destination will be. Even though they may have clear expectations at the start, these often change as new needs and new possibilities are discovered along the way. Many architects relish the uncertainty of this journey, finding it stimulating. Denise Scott Brown commented to Karen that architect and client 'are starting out on an adventure and we can't be sure what will happen'. Architect Louise Braverman observed, 'It is an exciting process. It's like going on a trip where you don't have a planned itinerary. There's a sense of adventure.'

For the journey to be one of exploring and discovering, the architect and preferably the client as well, needs to be inquisitive, ready to learn. They are not colonisers who impose their own assumptions and preconceptions upon the unknown but explorers who, despite any expectations they may have, remain open-minded enough to find what is new or different. Even though many parameters appear fixed and the client may feel certain about what is needed or desired, often it is precisely within what appears to be immutable that new possibilities are revealed. Remaining flexible and keeping options open for as long as possible requires considerable tolerance for uncertainty, which many architects possess. Clients are more likely to long for certitude but tolerating uncertainty is well worth the effort. In her research Dana Cuff found that clients whose projects turned out to be of exceptional quality were both 'flexible' and 'open minded' and 'accepted the inherent uncertainty of the design process'.[1]

Antar Dayal, Flat Earth, 1993. Despite evidence to the contrary, people once believed the earth was flat. Eventually, following recognition that the world was round, new maps were drawn.

… even when problem goals and constraints are known or defined, they are not sacrosanct and designers exercise freedom to change goals and constraints as understanding of the problem develops and definition of the solution proceeds.

Nigel Cross, *Designerly Ways of Knowing*, 2004, p 20

Denise Ho, brothers' houses, San Shui, China, 2010. Each house has a pitched roof above a single open space and sleeping loft. The roof is made of traditional ceramic tiles supported by untreated timber. Traditionally wood trusses would support the roof. Instead, two steel channels are used to open up the space below for a mezzanine. The tiny openings at the top of the brick wall, used during construction, become sources of light.

Exploring as an Attitude

When architects explore, they draw ideas and insights from both current and expected patterns of use, from the site and the client's needs and desires. They refrain from projecting their own prior beliefs and personal preferences upon the project. In a previous book written with Bianca Lepori, Karen called this approach 'architecture from the inside out' to refer to design that is generated *from* an understanding of body, site and community rather than being imposed *upon* them.[2] Such an approach has a rich history in the work of Alvar Aalto, Eileen Gray, Hans Scharoun and Aldo van Eyck.

The difference between architecture from the outside in and architecture from the inside out is evident in architect Denise Ho's experience developing a design for a vacation house for her brothers in San Shui, a small village in rural China. When she began the project, Denise envisioned a single, modern form built exclusively with modern building techniques and materials but, as she told Karen, something 'felt wrong'. Denise realised she needed to forget her own preconceptions so she visited the village several more times. She observed the local customs, noted how the houses were sited and learned about traditional building methods. From her new understanding of what was already there in San Shui, she developed a design.

Being Open and Inquisitive

Denise believes that she fell into the trap of projecting her own concept upon the site in San Shui because she was not 'open' initially. She started the project with her own image of what the house should be, already knowing, already moving ahead with a particular orientation. This is not her usual approach. Denise normally starts a project taking the stance of *not* knowing, of being fully attentive to what she may see and hear.

One custom Denise noticed in San Shui was the gathering of villagers in the forecourt in front of the village's ancestral hall. From that observation Denise developed the idea of three small houses, arranged in an L-formation, defining their own forecourt. Each faces south, as do all houses in the village, to capture the summer breezes and winter sun. In the design, each house is brick built using traditional methods. However, unlike traditional houses, the facades facing the forecourt are completely glazed, giving views of the landscape, with doors that open generously on to the forecourt to make it an extension of the homes, ideal for large family gatherings.

Being open to the new and unexpected requires an inquisitive mind, an interest in asking questions and devoting time and energy to learn. This is the approach that architect Mark Gillem of Eugene, Oregon uses.

> It's almost like you're an ethnographer going in and learning as much as you can about that client and spending as much time as you can. My relation to the clients is a long-term commitment to learn about the culture of an organization, to learn how that organization does its work, and how their needs can be transformed into built form.

When Mark finds that the client's goals conflict with the aspirations of other groups in the community, the first step he takes is to meet with each group to find out its particular goals. His purpose is to understand, not to persuade. He then explores how design can meet those different and, at first, apparently conflicting goals. In one case – the expansion of the educational and social facilities in a new building for the First Presbyterian Church in Berkeley, California – the first architect the church hired had proposed tearing down an existing historic building on the site. This raised the ire of the community and local preservation groups.

During his meetings with all concerned groups, Mark discovered that church members wanted the historic building either to be demolished or to become part of the church's new and expanded educational campus. The preservationists wanted the building preserved but did not insist that it continue to face the street. Mark proposed rotating the building 180 degrees,

My philosophy about design is that we never have a fixed image of what we are going to produce … If you have an agenda, you are looking for something from the client to fit into a solution. The creativity is about starting from nothing and then generating with the client.

Denise Ho, Hong Kong, March 2004

Mark Gillem and ELS Architecture and Urban Design, First Presbyterian Church, Berkeley, California, 2005. The courtyard can be used for outdoor events. Geneva Hall, the new building for educational activities, is to the left; McKinley Hall, the retained historic building used for counselling, is to the right.

CHAPTER 5 EXPLORING • 131

so it would face the interior of the site and form a larger plaza to provide needed, enclosed outdoor space. With the additional floor area provided by the now retained historic building, he was able to make the new building, Geneva Hall, only three storeys high rather than the previously proposed four storeys. With this creative response Mark was able to address the concerns of other community groups that the church follow the rules in place for other buildings in the community concerning height limitations.

Questioning Assumptions

Treating what appears to be fixed, such as stated requirements or implicit beliefs, as mutable can open a path to new possibilities. One telling example is the stated requirement in the brief for the Seattle Central Library that four levels of nonfiction books were needed. This prescription became an opening for the architects to think about other ways of spatially organising the collection, leading eventually to a gradually rising book ramp rather than separate levels.

One could easily assume that the renovation of a library requires the replacement of the shelves. That could be a mistake. Adopting this assumption during the renovation of the Highlawn Branch Library in Brooklyn would have left insufficient funds for a true re-design of the library. Louise Braverman recognised this key problem in the project immediately and found a way to keep the bookshelves. She proposed that the shelves be cleaned and covered. The material she chose was a type of fibreglass typically used as siding for long-distance transport trucks. Louise designed an efficient system for cutting and applying pre-cut panels to cover the tops and ends of the shelves. This new covering is durable, easy to maintain and gives the library a clean, contemporary look. The cost saving allowed the remaining funds to be used for significant reorganisation and refurbishment of the interior, improving circulation and image.

Assumptions may be so deeply embedded in conventional ways of thinking that they can be difficult to uncover and question. For the Seattle Central Library, the architects and the clients agreed it would make sense and be cost effective to place all the meeting rooms on one floor, with easy access to the street. While using a computer program to determine the best way to meet building code requirements for exiting the seven different meeting rooms, the architects assumed the rooms would be square but, with square spaces, the results from the computer program were not satisfactory. Fortunately, as architect Joshua Ramus recounted to Karen,

> A young person on the team said 'Why do we have to make meeting rooms square? We don't sit in them square. We sit in them kind of round.' So we made them all round and it worked and we presented it nicely. The library board consulted the maintenance staff who said, 'Fantastic. It's a nightmare to vacuum and sweep in squares.'

Finding Opportunities within Constraints

Surprisingly enough, what may seem to be constraints on design can become opportunities. After determining the basis for the conflict among stakeholders in the First Presbyterian Church project, Mark Gillem found both a way to meet their differing goals and, also, a design opportunity. Keeping the historic building and re-orienting it created more outdoor space within a campus-like setting and provided more indoor space for the church's counselling services. A limited budget can also feel like a restriction but Louise Braverman treated the budgetary constraints for the Highlawn Branch Library renovation as an opening to further thinking and research.

Clients' programmatic requirements may also feel restrictive to architects but they need not be. The architecture and urban design firm Interboro received the commission to design a temporary space for sculpture on a vacant site in Tribeca in Manhattan. The owner of the site, who plans to develop it as luxury housing in the future, required that a fence enclose the future park. For Interboro 'fence', rather than being a limitation to design, became a source of inspiration. How could this feature serve as a physical boundary enclosing the site as well as supporting other activities and experiences? What appeared to be the answer to an implicit question became, instead, another question: What can a fence also be?

Site restrictions offer opportunities for design, as illustrated by the shape and orientation of the site for Diana Gordon's house, which inspired Hideaki Ariizumi of studio a/b architects. On a 166-foot long 50-foot wide (51 x 15.2 metres) lot, he designed a linear house of 2,440 square feet (227 square metres), open to the south and its view and covered to the north, with a spacious, open feeling inside. What he calls the 'diagonal wall' runs from the south-west to the north-east and divides the site into a dwelling and a garden, making the interior of the house widest at its western end.

studio a/b architects, Gordon Residence, Greenport, New York, 2008.
The long narrow site served as an inspiration rather than a constraint to design.

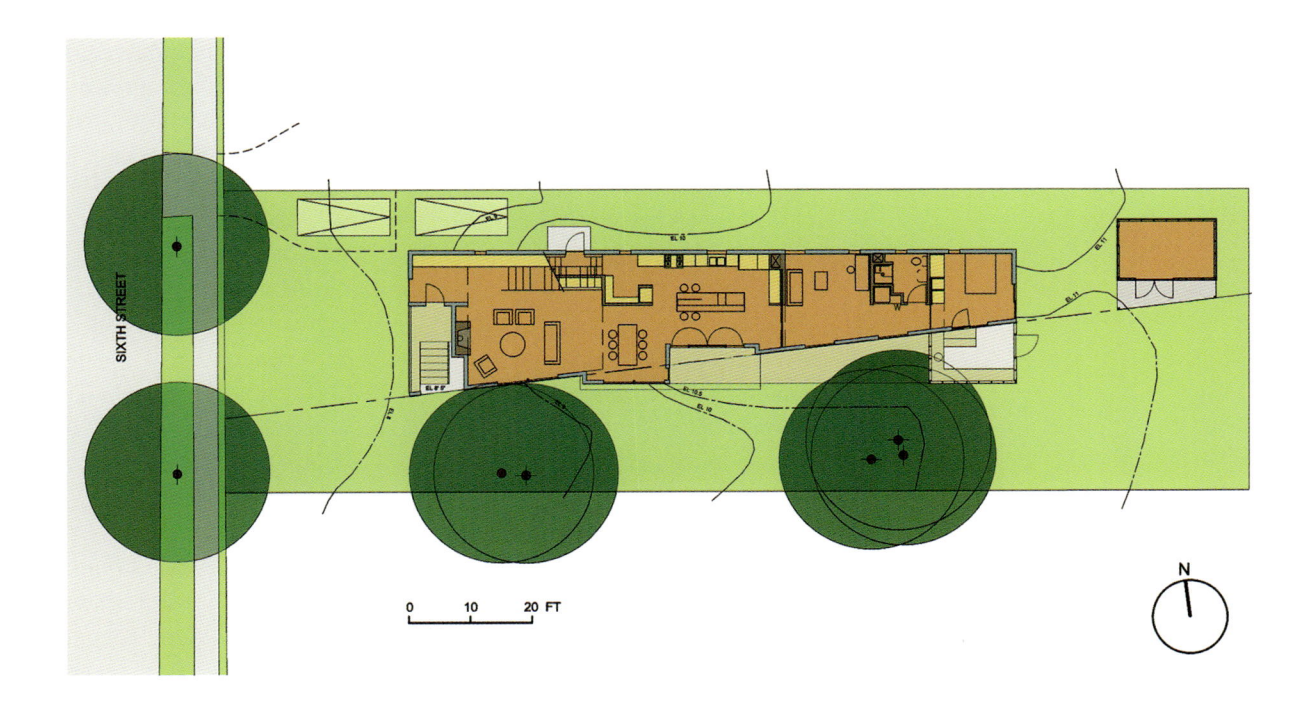

CHAPTER 5 EXPLORING • 133

Time constraints can lead to new possibilities as well. In their winning submission for the design of the Chelsea and Westminster Hospital in London architects Sheppard Robson successfully addressed a number of constraints that included designing and building all the required facilities of a 665-bed teaching hospital with 70 departments and other ancillary facilities in the shortest possible time. To do that the architects borrowed a procurement approach from the commercial world – shell, core and fit out – that relied on prefabrication and dry construction techniques. Not only was the speed of construction increased, but the contractor was provided with a quick-dry envelope creating a warm, rain-free environment to work in, making it possible to maintain a high standard of finishing and to reduce the time usually spent waiting for wet materials to dry.

This construction approach made it possible for the client to brief from the top down enabling decisions about accommodation to be made as the building was being built and thus speeding up design and construction time. The steel frame, composite metal floors and stud partition walls, with as many elements as possible prefabricated off site to simplify construction, were not only quick to erect but, like a kit of parts, easy to dismantle and reassemble. This built-in flexibility has since facilitated adaptations as medical and operating techniques have changed.

Sheppard Robson Architects, Chelsea and Westminster Hospital, London, 1993. Steel frame, composite metal floors and many prefabricated elements simplified construction and create built in flexibility as needs change. Views of open walkways and stairs help people orient themselves in a complex building.

By National Health Service standards the speed of design and construction of the hospital was breathtaking: five years from inception to completion compared with the usual 12 to 15 years. While the time period was radically reduced, development costs were higher than the NHS norm, which over time it is hoped will be offset by significantly reduced operating costs. The physical environment in this hospital has also enabled it to fulfil its function as a place of healing in remarkable ways. Not only have patients responded positively to the environment, so have staff.[3] (See Chapter 6)

Taking the Other's Standpoint

While designing the interior of the Highlawn Branch Library Louise Braverman imagined what it would be like for one of the Korean neighbourhood residents on her first visit to the library:

I'm there. I'm Korean. I don't speak English. How do I get to books very quickly, without being embarrassed? How do I get to the Korean section quickly?

I guess I think in a humanistic way – how a person feels in that space or how can I help that person. If you hang around there long enough you start to see who's there and then what they would feel like – when they're feeling good or when they're unsure of themselves.

Following this line of thinking, Louise designed a much clearer system of circulation, one that leads patrons directly to a 'hub' in the centre of the library. There they can find information from the librarian and can be easily directed to the correct shelf since the shelves radiate out from this hub. Louise often pursues this kind of exploration – taking the standpoint of the future occupant. In designing Chelsea Court, housing for formerly homeless people in Manhattan, she imagined what she would want if she were to live in a single room.

I thought, what do I want? I don't want to cook in a microwave. I want a real stove so I got it in. I found a 20-inch stove that was really inexpensive. I want a room you could have guests come into. So we found this collapsible furniture that is both a couch and bed.

While designing the kitchen for the community and education building on the campus of the First Presbyterian Church in Berkeley, Mark Gillem adopted the viewpoint of one particular occupant who often washes the

Louise Braverman, Highlawn Branch Library, Brooklyn, New York 2006. Upon entering the library visitors immediately see the central hub and can be easily directed from there to the correct shelf.

CHAPTER 5 EXPLORING • 135

dishes. The architect commissioned to develop working drawings and oversee construction argued that the small window Mark had placed above the kitchen sink on the second floor, beneath the larger window of the pastor's office, would spoil the building elevation and should be omitted. Mark, who had designed the elevation, remembers replying,

> 'I think it looks good in the elevation but that is purely subjective and what matters is Barbara who has been on the kitchen committee for 20 years. Am I going to be able to sleep at night knowing Barbara is in that kitchen without a window?' The window stayed.

Early in the design process, or even before the architect is hired, clients may sense whether architects will be sympathetic to their needs and aspirations and have some insight into their project. It helps if the architect can see the project from the client's perspective. This was very likely one reason OMA was chosen to design the Seattle Central Library. Alex Harris, Director of Capital Fund, recalls that the firm's research on libraries was apparent in their presentation during the selection process. Members of the library board were impressed by the 'kind of intellectual rigour with which they thought about libraries and this library in particular'. John Young of the Richard Rogers Partnership believes that the firm won the competition for Lloyds of London because their submission 'proved to Lloyds through patient analysis that we understood their problems of growth and change in a volatile market better than Lloyds themselves did'.[4] The submission presented no design but showed 21 different ways their two sites could be developed in phases.

Even without prior, in-depth research architects can take the client's point of view early on simply by placing importance on what the client is likely to value. Of all the architects being considered for the De Young Museum in San Francisco, Herzog & de Meuron were the only ones who talked about the museum's collection in their presentation. They received the commission.

Exploring as Actions

During their initial conversations and as the project proceeds, architects and clients learn about each other and the new territory that is the project. A wide variety of actions facilitates this process of exploring and discovering.

Noticing

Observing the client's current environment and patterns of action and visiting buildings similar to the project at hand can generate significant information and insights. With their training and experience architects are able to notice important connections between the design of a space and everyday activities and relationships. While the client may take certain arrangements for

---

The problem with architects and planners isn't so much that they always think they have the answer, it's that they always think they know the problem. We have to listen more and talk less. You know, like detectives do.

The Architectural League of New York 'Interboro', *Young Architects 7: Situating*, 2006, p 151

granted, the architect is able to detect how features of the space constrain or support what the client does, or might like to do.

In his very precise written brief for the design of a new apartment in Hong Kong, Julien Grudzien did not mention his children. Yet, while visiting Julien and his family in their old apartment, Denise Ho noticed how important the children were in the lives of the parents and the nature of the relationship between the parents and the children.

> We asked to look at each room and we asked him questions. The children's books were very high up on the shelf so we asked him 'Why are the books so high up and the children cannot reach them?' He said 'I take the book and read it with them.' So we began to see some kind of activity between him and the kids. It must be happening very often.

Denise also noted how Julien talked with the children as if they were adults. 'He doesn't want the kids to be silly, like babies.' So in her design she gave the children more independence by placing their books and videos at their level in the living room, making them easily accessible, as are the shoes they remove when they enter the apartment.

Architect Christie Coffin of The Design Partnership spends extended periods of time watching the daily operations at clients' current facilities.

> Usually I like to just sit there and kind of do 'a day in the life'. Just be there and watch people and chat with people as they're doing what they're doing and just do field work. It can't be as rigorous as in a full anthropological study but you can begin to understand and know a little more and know what questions to ask them when you're together designing things.

While spending time in this way at the Mary Graham Children's Shelter in San Joaquin County, California, a shelter for children who have been removed temporarily from their homes because their parents are in jail or in drug treatment programs, Christie had a chance to talk with the children and watch them interact with their counsellors informally. 'One counsellor was talking with a teenage girl about which boys in her movie magazine were cute.' Christie noticed that such a conversation was possible because they had

Denise Ho, Grudzien Apartment, Hong Kong, 2003, graffiti wall in children's bedroom. The children's liveliness and their close relationship with their parents, which Denise observed, inspired many aspects of her design.

an informal place to sit. This insight led to a particular design feature in the new facility: a 'kitchen counter counsellor station' with a locking drawer for storing files.

Christie also noticed that sometimes children were moved from one room to another. In talking to the staff, she discovered that when the staff felt that certain children required more supervision, they moved them to bedrooms that were visible from the counsellor station. This system caused a lot of disruption, which Christie wanted to help avoid in the new building. 'And so we came up with a cottage with a kitchen counter counsellor's station from where you could see the doors of all the bedrooms.' Christie also noticed that the boundary between indoors and outdoors was very distinct and that it was 'a real expedition to go outdoors. We set up a situation where cottages have porches opening to an outdoor area and it is very easy to make that transition between indoors and outdoors and you can still have responsibility for the children.'

Sometimes architects join the client's world as participants to gain as much understanding as they can. In preparing to design Woodlands Nursing Home in New Cross, south London architect Sunand Prasad actually worked a few shifts in a hospital ward to observe the future patients and staff of the new nursing home. He became acutely aware of the pungent smells of urine and disinfectant and the thudding sounds zimmer frames (walkers) made on the linoleum floors, sometimes loud enough to frighten other patients. These sensory experiences led him to specific design decisions. In early design stages for a school for autistic children, three members of the architecture team from Penoyre & Prasad conducted this same kind of 'participant observation' in the existing school.

The Design Partnership, Mary Graham Children's Shelter, San Joaquin County, California, 2003. Architect Christie Coffin noticed how children and counsellors often interact informally and recommended a 'kitchen counter counselling station' where this could happen in the new facility.

Sunand Prasad calls this early part of the design process 'immersion'. 'By this we mean getting absorbed in the world of the client and the users of the buildings in order to gain a deep understanding of how they work and what it is that they are after, even if they have not (yet) articulated it.'[5]

To design the Uluru-Kata Tjuta Cultural Centre with the Anangu, an Aboriginal group in Australia, architect Greg Burgess took the idea of 'immersion' further. Both to gain their trust and to understand how he might best engage them in design, he lived with the Anangu for a month, camping, hunting, collecting wood, talking and hearing their stories.[6] From his previous work with Aboriginal groups Burgess also knew that direct questioning was not a method they would respond to well. He began without a fixed idea of what he would do, instead 'remaining open-minded and relaxed, letting the Anangu take the lead'.[7]

Asking Questions

During her visits with Julien and his family, Denise Ho watched the children and their parents interacting and also asked questions to clarify or confirm what she was seeing and to learn more. Similarly, Christie Coffin's observations at Mary Graham Children's Shelter generated certain questions for the staff, such as how bedrooms were assigned. Noticing leads to questions and answers to those questions may lead to more questions and to more observing.

Glynis Berry of studio a/b holds a number of questions in mind when she visits clients in their current homes; usually she finds answers to them through informal conversation. Her partner Hideaki Ariizumi also seems to have a number of questions he often asks. Diana Gordon recalls that early in the design process he asked where she planned to put the bed in the master bedroom. Only when the house was finished did she grasp the significance of his question. When the sun comes up, she can see 'the shapes of the trees emerge behind the solar blinds. The mysterious look of the trees is just wonderful. And I had never thought about what it would be like from the bed.'

Some architects start with questions. Mark Gillem has a standard set of questions he often uses in initial meetings with clients. Louise Braverman follows a particular, sequential process. Before meeting with all the staff of a facility she will design, she asks each person to provide her with a wish list of what they would like to have and a list of practical needs. She studies these lists carefully before meeting with the clients. 'So in the group discussion I can raise my own questions – so you want x, y and z. Do you really mean this or that? We're having a conversation. Always they start it and then I ask questions to understand it better.'

The method of asking questions can be formal and organised, informal and spontaneous, or a combination of both. This question and answer exchange may take place with one or a few individuals, in larger meetings, focus groups and design workshops or through standardised questionnaires. Recommendations for particular methods of asking questions of clients and future occupants during the design process abound in books about architectural programming and other works. Notable among these is John Zeisel's *Inquiry by Design* and the presentation of more projective techniques in Clare Cooper Marcus's *House as a Mirror of Self* and Toby Israel's *Some Place Like Home*. Toby describes a sequence of exercises constituting a 'design psychology toolbox' to be used to discover a group's vision for a new building as well as to explore practical needs, the setting and individual and group associations with past places.

> Ordinary people, including you and me when we are not practicing our specialties, package their descriptions and explanations in stories.
>
> Charles Tilly, *Why?* Princeton University Press, 2006, p 119

Asking direct questions is not always the best way to find things out, particularly with clients who prefer, less direct ways of exchanging information. Johnpaul Jones, one of the architects for the National Museum of the Native American Indian, describes how information can emerge when different worldviews are given space (see Chapter 2). As an American Indian, he was already alert to possible contributions that come from participatory thinking. He described to Karen how he brought a group of elders to the site of the National Museum of the American Indian to see how they would think about how the building should be sited. They walked about, they dug, they buried something and then they said:

> 'Well this is the centre of the site'. They didn't use mathematics like we do. Then Douglas [Cardinal] figured out the same centre spot with geometry. You get that in participation with the people and listening. I see that happen all the time in our Indian work. We get the elders telling us things that you can't really get them to talk about in a program so much.

Collecting Stories

Through telling stories people can explain what is important to them about a site or a community, providing rich and detailed information to designers that comes directly from their own experiences and their own memories. Story telling allows people to speak in their own voices, without direction or censoring; it is also an easy way to describe, to explain and to convey complex thoughts. Some clients may be more comfortable telling stories than answering a series of direct and focused questions. When many different people participate, the stories they tell can reveal quite different perspectives. 'When the telling of stories is opened up to a wider range of perspectives, the meanings of place do not cohere into a unified view but branch off and overlap with each association.'[8]

In studying the site to develop a master plan for the Northwest Indian College campus in Washington state the architectural team from Mithun met with faculty, staff and students and heard the stories the native Lummi elders told. Brodie Bain recalls, 'We did find out a lot of things. They talked about Big Foot living on the site and sighting Big Foot. Even walking through the site you see evidence – pieces of bark and all kinds of interesting things you wouldn't normally see.' This endeavour of collecting stories proved to be particularly important to the project since the previous architects had, unknowingly, chosen a site that had been the location of several murders (see Chapter 2).

When Teresa was helping community members in Spitalfields in London think about the new design of Bishops Square, she encouraged workshop participants to tell the histories they knew. Together they pieced together a shared understanding of what was important about Spitalfields as a place. Participants recounted that the neighbourhood, originally outside London's city wall, had always been a place where alternatives to the mainstream flourished. Many immigrant groups had come to live there: French Huguenots, Jews and, most recently, people from Bangladesh. It had always been a place of contrasts: open spaces and narrow streets, riches and poverty, frenetic activity and quiet contemplation. This shared memory work set the framework for how the scheme should be developed.

In developing the design for a multi-services community centre in Pine Bluff, Arkansas, architect Rosa Lane asked participants in a large workshop to tell the histories of their community and, as importantly, to rewrite the history they wanted but never had. These were also stories. When asked what distinguishes her approach from that of other architects, Rosa replied: 'I would say that I get very energized by the clients telling their stories whether it be referencing their past or referencing their future. I absolutely love it. I'm not afraid of it. I seek it.'

Stories are a good way for clients to convey rich and detailed information to the architect, they are also a good way for architects to communicate with a larger public. Sometimes architects and planners present individual cases of people or households, capturing illuminating detail of each case and indicating a variety of possibilities across cases. Interboro used this method of exploration and presentation in their research about the grassroots efforts of Detroit residents to expand and improve their properties. Each case is the story of a homeowner who bought or appropriated an adjacent empty lot (or more than one). Two sisters buy the vacant lot between their houses and create a shared yard. Over a period of years an extended family buys six contiguous lots, making a large walled garden. Together the stories illustrate a variety of ways homeowners have reconfigured and reused abandoned properties, creating what the architects have called 'blots'.

Researching, Experimenting

Clients and architects conduct research in a variety of ways. In large projects the briefing process may include personal interviews, surveys questionnaires, and field observations with standardised forms and inventories. These methods, drawn from the social sciences, are outlined in many guides to architectural research and briefing. Architects also conduct research in

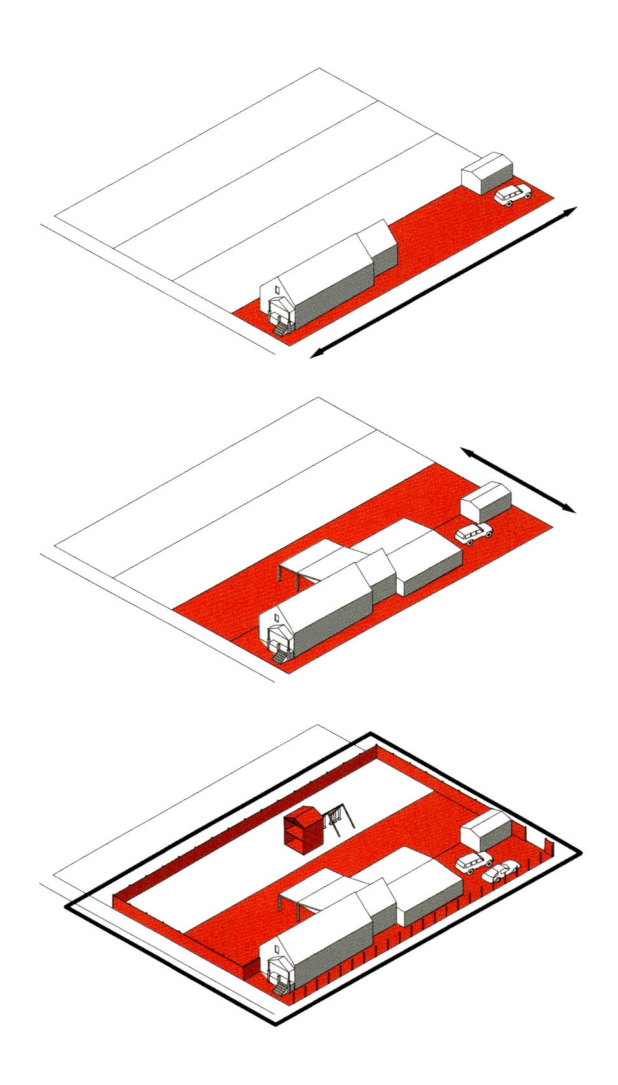

Interboro, Courtyard Blot, from 'Improve Your Lot!', Detroit, 2006. Originally Victor Toral owned one lot. After buying the adjacent empty lot, he built two additions, extending the house laterally. Then he enclosed his land and the city-owned lot next door with a fence, transforming his property into a courtyard house.

Freecell, Verb Media, New York, 2003. The architects measured each item of equipment and then designed and built a counter/room divider that would accommodate the use and storage of each one. RIGHT Shop drawing BELOW Completed counter/divider.

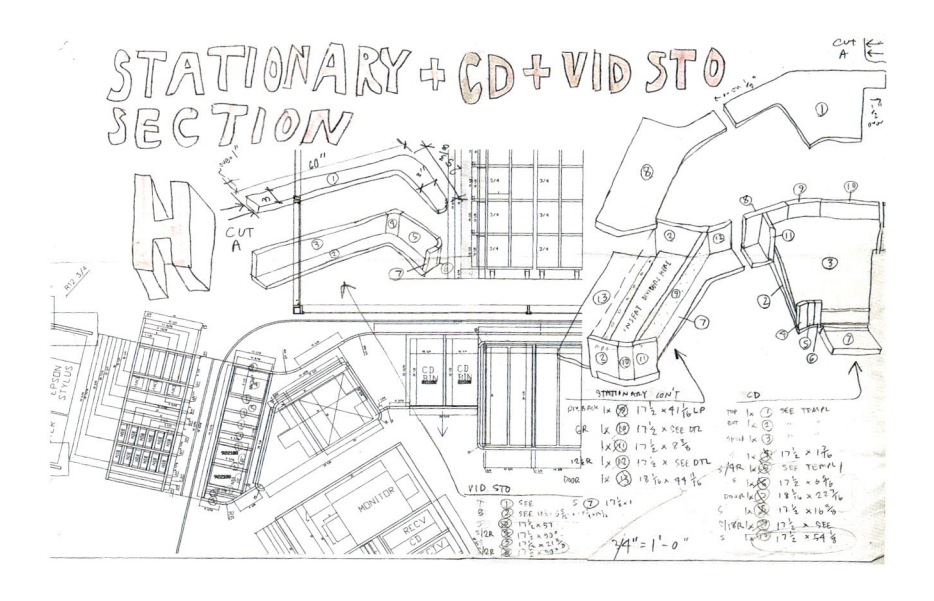

other ways by seeking information from published sources, other building professionals, local authorities, zoning boards, historical preservation groups, construction and fabrication companies. They also make detailed analyses of site conditions and create mock-ups of proposed designs.

For the branch library in Brooklyn, Louise Braverman researched materials and methods for covering the existing bookshelves. She reads a variety of catalogues regularly, including ones on farm equipment, collecting possibilities she might use in future projects. Architect Lauren Crahan of Freecell reports that she also looks to other fields, including agriculture, for possible materials to use. In the workspace Freecell designed for Verb Media, curtains screening the conference room and the editing bay hang from tracks usually used in hospital rooms. The curtains on the windows are made from plastic-coated agricultural screening, commonly used to cover greenhouses.

With their attention to storage and display, Freecell takes careful measurements and often builds prototypes to test and compare. For the Verb Media project, the clients took digital photographs and made lists of all the equipment they depend upon in their video graphics design business and asked the architects to triple the amount of storage space they already had. Freecell then measured the dimensions of each item of equipment and studied its use and requirements for accessibility. As a result, the winding counter/storage unit has a 'home' designed precisely for each piece of equipment allowing for its easy accessibility and use. Likewise when designing shelving for the wine store SIP in Brooklyn, Freecell purchased and measured the 12 sizes of wine bottles that would be sold in the store to develop a storage/display system that would accommodate each type, either horizontally or vertically.

Research for the Central Library in Seattle was extensive, even after the architects had been selected. The architects joined members of the client team in three months of research about the future of libraries, which included joint visits to recently completed libraries in Europe and the US and holding seminars with a variety of specialists in technology. From this research OMA and LMN Architects derived two main ideas to be addressed in the design: that the provision of books would remain a key function of libraries and that libraries were taking on new responsibilities as public places. Both these discoveries informed their design in significant ways: providing ample space for the collection of books to expand in the future and incorporating a variety of social spaces. Additional, extensive research was undertaken with engineers and other consultants to design the exterior cladding of the building.

To test the proposed, highly unusual book ramp, designed to replace conventional floors of books, three different full-scale mock-ups of the ramp were built in an empty warehouse. Staff and the public, particularly people with disabilities, tried out and evaluated the mock-ups. Key problems resolved were the way to get from the ramp to the book aisles and the best slope for the ramp (finally determined to be two degrees, with landings at each end).[9]

Freecell, SIP, Brooklyn, 2005. To determine the best shelving to accommodate a variety of types of wine bottle, vertically and horizontally, the architects built a full-scale mock up.

… the Seattle Public Library is the first project explicitly begun in the way OMA's partners had always wanted to work: research the needs of the client and, based on that research, build a conceptual platform that includes a set of core principles and a list of programmatic requirements upon which the eventual design of the building will stand.

Jacob Ward, 'The making of a library: The research', *Metropolis*, October 2004, p 98

Unless you draw something, you do not understand it. It is a mistake to believe that now I understand the problem and now I draw it. Rather, right at the time you draw you realize what the problem is and than you can rethink it.

Renzo Piano in Edward Robbins, *Why Architects Draw*, 1994, p 127

Sketching and Drawing

Architects draw for a variety of reasons: to record, to visualise, to communicate, to persuade and, as importantly, to explore and gain further understanding. Sketching to quickly outline an idea graphically is particularly useful for exploring and discovering. Commentators frequently use the words 'explore', 'examine' and 'discover' to describe this kind of drawing. Bryan Lawson has written:

> The process here seems to be one in which the designer externalizes some features of the design situation in order to examine them in a more focused way … Designers describe this also as temporarily freezing something in order to explore the implications of it.[10]

Drawing in this fashion is a visual form of thinking: the graphic depiction of certain features allows them to be literally seen and studied. Architects can then discover consequences, possibly problems, arising from configurations of features that, without the sketch, would have remained hidden. For example, early ground floor sketches of the National Museum of the American Indian allowed the architects to explore the consequences of different locations (and sizes) of the entry space and the major gathering/performing space.

Drawing as a means of exploring is also revealed in Donald Schön and Glenn Wiggins' observations of the design process in action, in conversations between a first year design student and her critic. They point to a series of 'move experiments' the student makes that constitute a series of discoveries. The acts of drawing and then studying and talking about the drawing (which the authors call 'designing') enable her to make 'discoveries'. 'She discovers to design and designs to discover.'[11]

In their argument for the value of integrating briefing with designing, Julia Robinson and Stephen Weeks recognise the significance of drawing as a means of exploring. Regarding the exercises they give to students, they write:

> The combination of verbal and graphic exploration is intended to allow students to explore physical forms (graphic) and their

studio a/b, Gordon House, Greenport, New York, 2008.
In his first sketches Hideaki Ariizumi explored ideas for the form and the interior of the house.

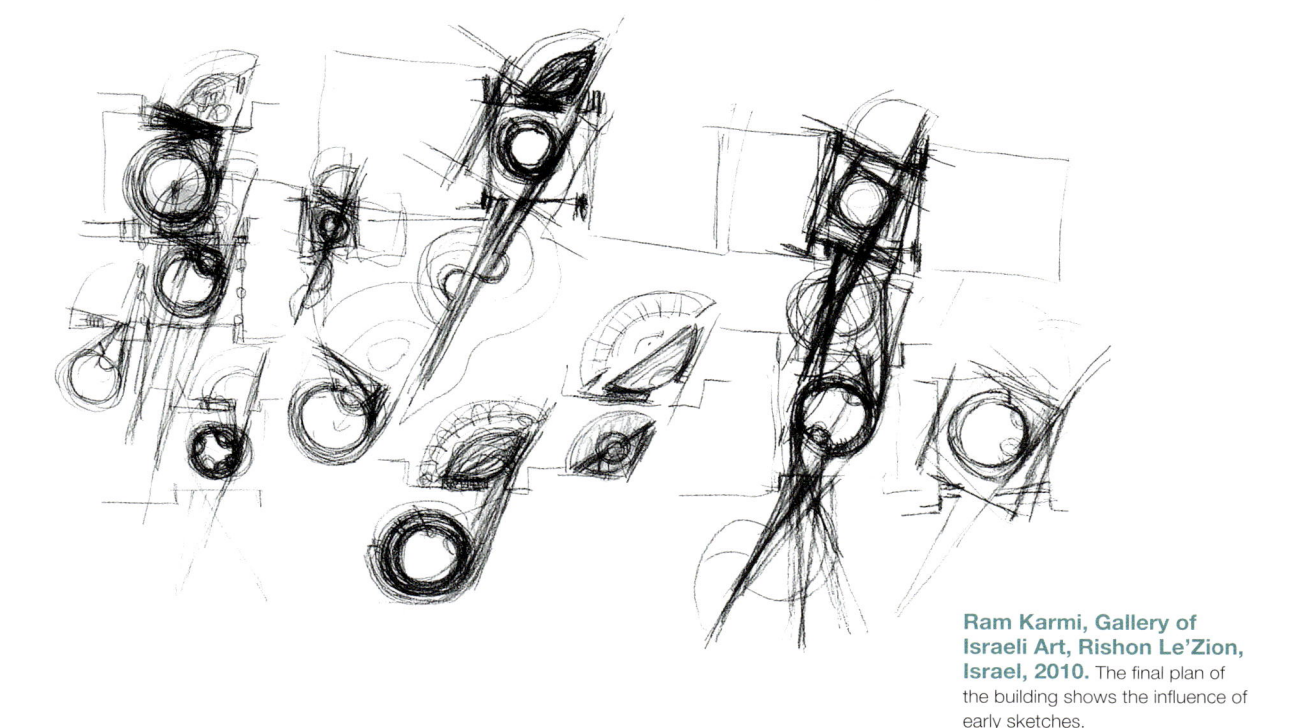

Ram Karmi, Gallery of Israeli Art, Rishon Le'Zion, Israel, 2010. The final plan of the building shows the influence of early sketches.

implications (verbal), so that the students become conscious of what they are doing and why. This may be the most important intended outcome of this process: that designers become conscious of the implications of their designs.[12]

Architects also use drawings and sketches in their conversations with clients to help explain the ongoing design process, to represent different options and to elicit more information from the client. The series of schematic site plans Hideaki Ariizumi generated for the design of the Gordon House served this dual purpose: he and his partner Glynis Berry could think through the options themselves and could present and explain these options to the client. Edward Cullinan sketches what he calls 'three-dimensional doodles' on the spot during meetings with clients. 'I am quite happy to sketch possible schemes … in front of clients, sometimes at the first meeting. But we always explain to them that this isn't a scheme, it is just a reaction to what they have been talking about.'[13] He finds these sketches a very useful way to get immediate feedback from the client even when meeting with large groups.

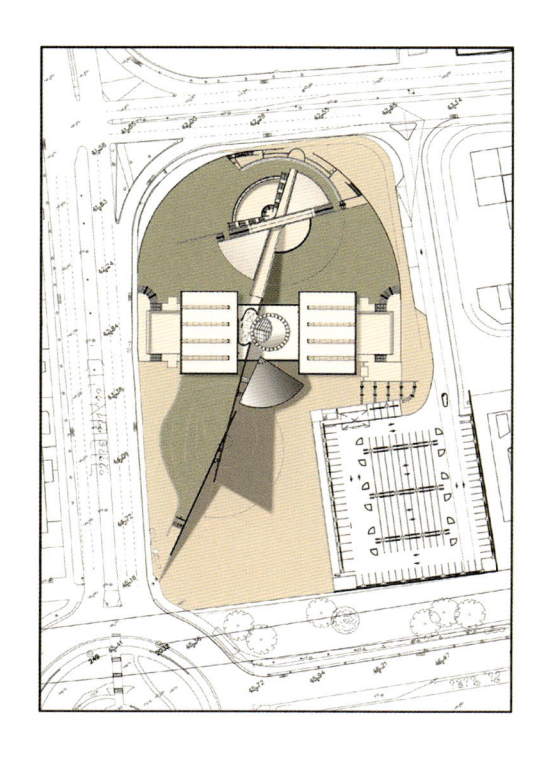

CHAPTER 5 EXPLORING • 145

Douglas Cardinal and GBQC Architects, Johnpaul Jones, Ramona Sakiestewa, Donna House (project designers); Jones & Jones, Smith Group with Lou Weller and the Native American Design Collaborative, Polshek Partnership Architects and EDAW (project architects), National Museum of the American Indian, Washington DC, 2004.
The brief and the architects emphasised the importance of a variety of sensory experiences, including taste. The cafeteria serves Native American food from four different regions.

Deciding What to Explore

During their initial conversations and throughout the development of a design, architects and clients explore a great variety of subjects and issues to ensure that the final design addresses client needs and fulfils possibilities unforeseen at the outset of the project.

Mission

Frequently architects start their work by seeking to understand the client's goals and, with organisations, by studying mission statements and talking with staff. Mark Gillem loves the discovery of mission, goals and needs.

> I don't see my role as the artist coming in to provide a monument to architecture. What I love about architecture is that we can really find out what someone's real needs are, what their mission is, what their goals are and we can help them meet that in a way that enhances what they can do.

The mission of the client organisation and related purposes of the building are key elements in the written briefs for projects. Right at the beginning of *The Way of the People*, the program for the National Museum of the American Indian, Venturi, Scott Brown and Associates quote the full mission statement adopted by the museum's board:

> The National Museum of the American Indian shall recognize and affirm to Native Communities and the non-Native public the historical and contemporary culture and cultural achievements of the Natives of the Western Hemisphere by advancing, in consultation, collaboration and cooperation with Natives, knowledge and understanding of Native cultures, including art, history, and language, and by recognizing the Museum's special responsibility, through innovative public programming, research and collections, to protect, support, and enhance the development, maintenance and perpetuation of Native culture and community.[14]

The program states that the Cultural Resource Center in Suitland, Maryland is to be the 'brain and soul' of the new museum while the museum building on the Mall in Washington is to be the 'Indian community's outreach to the international public' that 'communicates with a Native voice, Indian stories, values and culture to millions of individual visitors through a multi-sensory experience that reaches people, not only through visual media, but through smells, sounds, touch and, for some, taste as well'.[15]

Brodie Bain of Seattle practice Mithun puts great importance on an organisation's mission, describing architectural projects for institutions as 'mission-driven work' since they have 'specific missions that you're helping to express and support'. In her work she has focused on institutions of higher education and finds that every one is a little bit different. The Northwest Indian College's mission is: 'self determination, to empower the students to decide how much they want to integrate into the western world vs keeping their culture, to give them the skills to have the choice and not to lose their own culture'. Brodie explained to Karen that the Northwest Indian College was looking for a 'a place that had a sense of community that made students who were coming off the reservation for the first time feel at home and comfortable'. She contrasts that mission with that of another project – a liberal arts college – where the mission is 'to create responsible citizens and open thinkers and people that accept diversity'.

Needs and Aspirations

In their conversations with clients architects discover everyday needs and constraints. Louise Braverman and Bob Allies both see determining these basic requirements as the easier part of their work. The harder part is finding out what is different, special to this client organisation, including how it functions now and how it will function in the future. Here architects have an opportunity to discover and propose possibilities for the organisation to modify its manner of working. Bob Allies describes the difference between being a 'mirror' and a 'critic':

> I do think architects have to be very clear about how responsible they are for fixing how organizations function. It is always difficult to know whether you are a mirror for the organization – to give them what they want – rather than to have another role where you question and become a kind of critic. If we are just a mirror, we are not really giving them the benefit of what is possible or to help people to realise dreams that they didn't even know they had …

During the design of an extension to the Horniman Museum in London, the client decided to continue some patterns of use and to change others. Since education is a significant aspect of the museum's mission, many large groups of children visit. The client was keen to continue to keep a separate entrance for these groups so as not to overwhelm other visitors. As Bob Allies reported, 'They were used to that way of doing things,' but the client did accept other changes including the addition of a café with a separate entrance and a much more open relationship to the adjacent garden.

For the design of a new building for Sarum Hall School in London, then located in a house, Allies and Morrison proposed several alternatives that included courtyards and classrooms around a garden, all quite different from the original building. The head teacher could not accept these proposals because in each one her office would have been much further from the rest of the school than she was accustomed to. So the architects explored ways to 'draw everything much tighter', developing a different design that more closely approximated the layout of the original school.

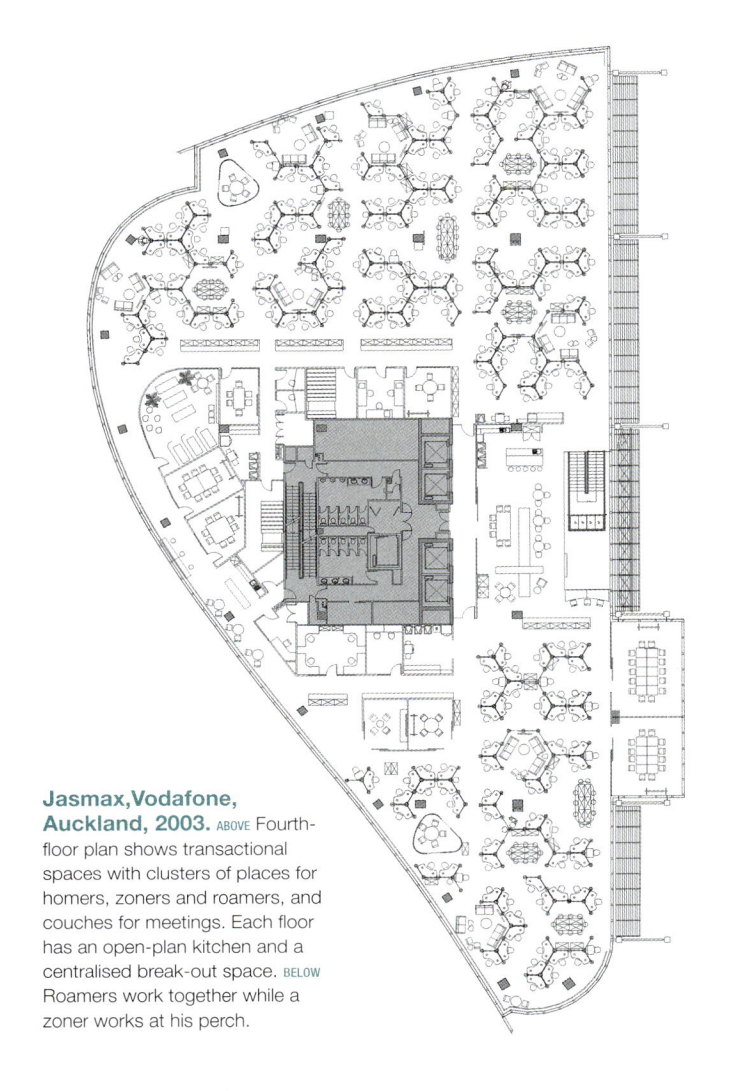

Jasmax, Vodafone, Auckland, 2003. ABOVE Fourth-floor plan shows transactional spaces with clusters of places for homers, zoners and roamers, and couches for meetings. Each floor has an open-plan kitchen and a centralised break-out space. BELOW Roamers work together while a zoner works at his perch.

As the example of the Horniman Museum illustrates, architects often discover needs that the client may not have expressed or recognised. Design that responds to these needs can take the project beyond the minimum – sometimes in small and subtle ways, sometimes in quite dramatic ways. Tim Hooson of Jasmax in New Zealand is very enthusiastic about enabling corporate clients to rethink their aspirations, including their approach to management and their working methods, before deciding what form their new space should take. Sometimes what is needed is not a new building but a rethinking of what is already there. Other times the architects help the client develop a new mode of working. One example is Jasmax's work for Vodafone in Auckland.

Vodafone assumed that everyone should have a desk in a fixed location. Through their workshops with Vodafone staff, Jasmax discovered different work styles, related to the staff member's role and task or skill base, which were often aligned with individual characteristics (eg sales people tend to be extroverts and analytical staff are usually introverts). After determining three different work roles and styles (zoners, homers and roamers), Jasmax designed an environment with a variety of work points that accommodated those differences, offering more choice and fewer formal workspaces.

Their design broke traditional facilities and property rules: a building with different kinds of work points for 1,530 people but only 850 formalised workstations, with break-out areas providing more work points. There are also high tables where zoners can work standing up, together in a group or just co-occupying the space as in an airport lounge. Vodafone New Zealand provides less formal work space than is the norm for the company worldwide: 1.7

148 • EXPLORING CHAPTER 5

people per formal workspace versus 1.1 or 1.2 elsewhere. But in Auckland, with the increased range of options, workers have more choice.

Ways of Operating

Jasmax is keenly attuned to the idea that buildings are frameworks for activities that can support or constrain particular ways of pursuing those activities. For Vodafone the firm investigated in detail the different work styles of staff and then designed distinct settings to support and enhance those different ways of working. During briefing and design architects and clients have the opportunity to explore the client's present ways of operating and relating and how these might be supported or changed in a new building. This is exactly what Christie Coffin of The Design Partnership did during her observations of daily life at the original Mary Graham shelter in San Joaquin County, California. She noted the informal conversations that occurred between counsellors and children and discovered the system for assigning children to bedrooms that was causing unnecessary disruption.

During the community design workshops for the Rosa Parks Elementary School in Berkeley teachers talked about their philosophy of education and what they did not like about many schools, including the usual separation of classrooms from each other and the lack of a heart. To support closer relationships between classrooms and to create a ' heart' in the new school, classrooms are grouped around small courtyards and the entire school shares one larger open space. Two classrooms share an outdoor patio that is accessible only from the classrooms. Teachers, parents and students were all opposed to single large toilets because they tend to be dirty and dangerous so in the new school smaller bathrooms are located in each courtyard. Teachers described how helpful it would be to have private spaces where they could store materials and meet with individual students. The result was an office/resource room shared by two classrooms (see Chapter 4).

Additional features of the classrooms support each teacher's autonomy. The classrooms are quite remote from the principal's office that is located in a separate building near the school's entrance. Each class has its own high-end residential heating and the teacher can override the school district's heating system. Architect Kava Massih noted, 'It's almost like these autonomous

Ratcliff Architects, Rosa Parks Elementary School, Berkeley, California, 1997.
Classrooms are grouped around two small courtyards, each with its own bathrooms.

Allies and Morrison Architects, The Place, London School of Contemporary Dance, 2001. Dancers warm up on the extended landing.

kingdoms or queendoms. Years later, I went back. They had their third or fourth principal and that was one of her main criticisms: "They're out there on their own and I don't know what they're doing, I'm not in control of this place.'" Since the members of the school administration did not participate as fully in the design workshops as the teachers did, it is not surprising that the ways of operating and relating in the new school address the teachers' concerns more than the administration's.

During the design of Seattle's Central Library architects and clients together explored what role books may play in the future. Through examining the client's brief the architects discovered that the library was already operating a new way – not as a gatekeeper of information but as a curator of information – a change that the client had not recognised. Joshua Ramus describes this kind of exploring as providing a mirror: 'Here's a mirror. You are doing your job differently and you have already changed and the problem is that you don't know it.' Once the client agreed on the importance of this new way of operating, the challenge was to design space that 'can encourage and enhance what they're doing'.

In each of these examples, architects discovered not only the particular kinds of actions that the new building should house but also, as importantly, the *manner* in which occupants could pursue those actions in the future and the kinds of relationships they could have with each other. Something quite tangible in design, a patio shared by two classrooms or a courtyard shared by four, supports both certain kinds of activities and certain kinds of relationships between people. Bob Allies commented that for the renovation of the London School of Contemporary Dance determining what was 'desperately needed, like proper size dance studios – higher and wider' were the 'easy bits of the project'. The harder part was finding the right relationships; one of those relationships was the opportunity to warm up in the circulation space outside the dance studios.

Movement

It is surprising how often the design of public buildings makes it difficult for people to find their way from one place to another or even to locate the entrance. Studies of occupant satisfaction in recently designed schools of architecture in the US revealed that in most of the schools studied, being able to find one's way through the building was a problem, a consequence of both the design of circulation and the system of numbering rooms.[16] The informal, directional signs hung by staff at Seattle's Central Library indicate that way finding is a problem there as well. While the book collection served by the book spiral is a central feature of the building, many visitors ask librarians, 'Where are the books?'

Anticipated paths of movement and their legibility to occupants can shape a project's spatial organisation from the beginning, both indoors and outdoors. Early on architect Johnpaul Jones realised that the brief for the National Museum of the American Indian listed so many different spaces for specific activities that one or more large central spaces were required to make the spatial organisation of the building legible to visitors. For the library renovation in Brooklyn Louise Braverman also thought about legibility of circulation and the importance of orienting patrons immediately upon entering. Regarding the library's previous design Louise commented, 'You walked in and it was a kind of cloud. What do I do next? How do I know, when I walk in the door, where I'm supposed to go? So I knew they needed a central hub and that had to be architecturally defined to draw people to it.'

Louise Braverman, Highlawn Branch Library, Brookyn, New York 2006.
In the redesigned library, when people enter they immediately see the central 'hub' and can easily be directed to one of the radiating shelves.

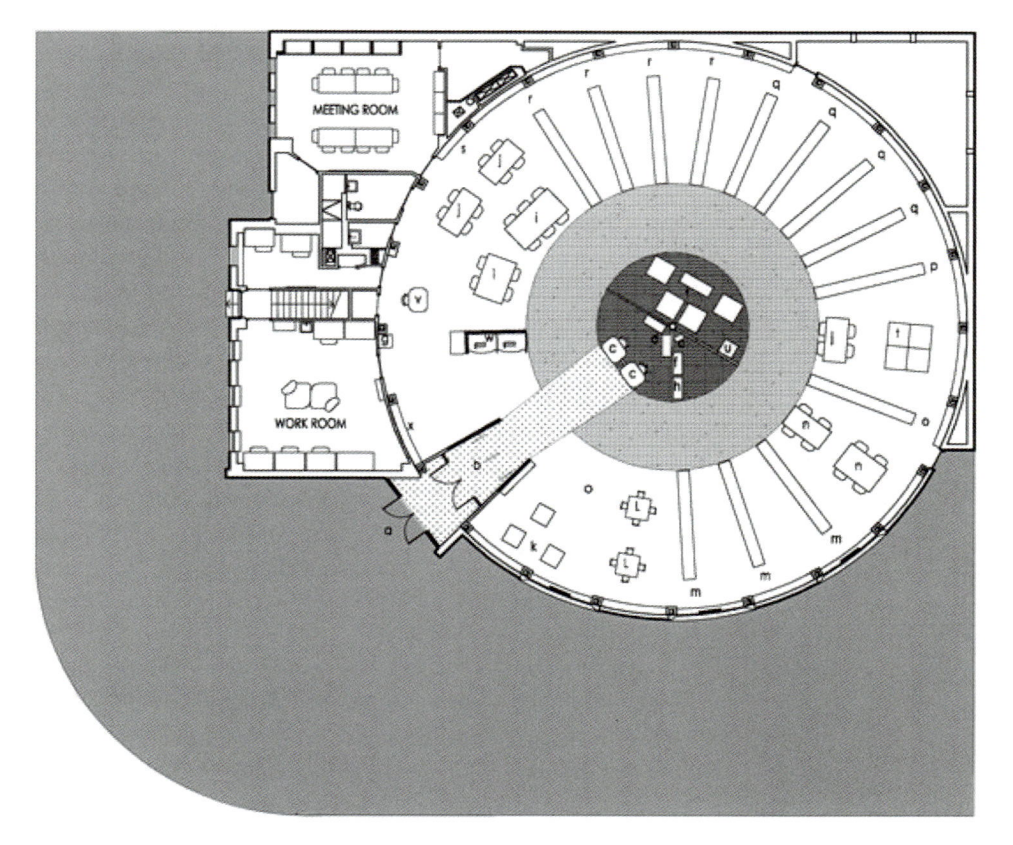

a. Entry
b. Security
c. Information Desk
d. Reference Books
e. Queue Monitor
f. Reservation, Print, Release Station
g. Kiosk (ABC Machine)
h. Copier
i. Adult Computer Stations (10)
j. Adult Reading Tables
k. Children's Floor Seating
L. Children's Reading Desks
m. Children's Stacks
n. Young Adult Computer Stations (4)
o. Young Adult Stacks
p. English as a Second Language Stack
q. Foreign Language Stacks
r. Adult Stacks
s. New Articles Stacks
t. Lounge
u. Soda Machine
v. Transaction Desk
w. Express Checkout
x. Book Drop

Another circulation issue to explore is whether different routes are needed for different groups of occupants. For the Supreme Court building in Jerusalem Israeli architects Ada Karmi-Melamede and Ram Karmi designed distinct routes to the courtroom for the judges, the public, and the prisoners so they do not encounter each other until they meet in the courtroom. For the design of Chic's Chinese Clinic in Hong Kong architect Denise Ho paid careful attention to the movement patterns of doctor and patients. In her design the doctor can pass directly back and forth from one cubicle to another without entering the shared space of the clinic while patients enter the cubicles from that shared space.

For the redesign of existing buildings for the Walworth Surgery in south London, Penoyre & Prasad interviewed doctors and staff very carefully and devised a system of circulation that gave careful attention to the legibility of circulation to patients and the relationships the doctors desired to have with them. A new addition to the existing buildings creates, for patients, a two-storey, glass-fronted reception area and view of the internal vertical circulation. Physicians and staff enter the building through a separate, more discreet doorway that leads to stairs to all levels of the building. While circulation from the reception area to the consulting rooms is clearly visible, doctors nonetheless often come to the reception area to escort patients to their consulting rooms.

Together, Apart

The coming together of people in shared spaces and possibilities for being alone in more private ones are always important considerations in briefing and design. In his Hong Kong apartment Julien Grudzien wanted his work station to be in the master bedroom so the children would not disturb him while he worked or while his wife was lying on the bed. But Denise Ho imagined how the children, whose bedroom and playroom were on the same floor, would run into the bedroom to join their mother on the bed and how Julien would then have to make them leave. Gradually Denise persuaded Julien to have his work station on the lower level of the apartment, spatially distant from the area where the children could play. She gave careful thought and then design support to how members of this family could be alone at certain times and together at others.

The space for Chic's Chinese Clinic in Hong Kong was only 1,000 square feet (93 square metres) but had to accommodate three private cubicles for acupuncture as well as a space large enough for yoga classes and group meditation, a doctor's work station and a work area for preparing herbal

Denise Ho, Chic's Chinese Clinic, Hong Kong, 2003. The doctor takes this route from one acupuncture cubicle to the next. Clients enter cubicles through the doors on the right. Shelves provide storage for pillows. Cubicles can be wheeled back to the outside wall on the left to create open space for yoga and meditation sessions.

treatments. To address this array of requirements, Denise Ho designed three 6½ x 6½ feet (2 x 2 metres) cubicles that can be wheeled back against the outside wall, along with treatment beds, storage shelves and hinged doors folded inwards to hide them. With little effort the space is converted from a group of private spaces to an open, shared group space for yoga and meditation sessions.

The opportunity for people to come together in generously sized, pleasurable spaces is often successfully achieved in the design of public buildings, as in the Supreme Court Building in Jerusalem, the National Museum of the American Indian, and Seattle's Central Library. It is not surprising that in studies of occupant satisfaction in nine recently completed architecture school buildings in the US many occupants gave positive evaluations of the large, open public areas which often serve as gathering spaces.[17] Such spaces can be both indoors and out, usually with seating and often with views and direct access to the main routes of circulation. It is not always desirable, however, for gathering spaces to be easily accessible to all visitors. Sometimes the spaces need to provide some privacy and seclusion. This is true of the outdoor ceremonial spaces at the National Museum of the American Indian and at the Cultural Resources Center in Suitland, where separation from the main public spaces, visually and physically, gives some privacy and quiet for the performance of sacred ceremonies.

Spaces where people can be alone or in small groups need the same kind of careful attention as the public spaces, particularly when visual or acoustic privacy is needed to facilitate concentration, as in patient examining rooms, architectural studios and offices.

Spaces for private contemplation or relief from the crowd are essential for individuals to maintain a capacity to engage with the family or the community. Without such spaces, individuals can lose a sense of self and the capacity to think. The National Museum of the American Indian has such spaces that offer a welcome relief from the throng of visitors.

The Five Senses

People experience their surroundings through all their senses. Often only sight receives full attention in design decisions as Juhani Pallasmaa describes in *Eyes of the Skin* and as Karen and Bianca Lepori discuss in *Architecture from the Inside Out*. Yet it is in the near environment of feeling, smelling, touching and tasting as well as seeing that people live. The conditions and qualities of the near environment can make everyday tasks easier and more pleasurable.

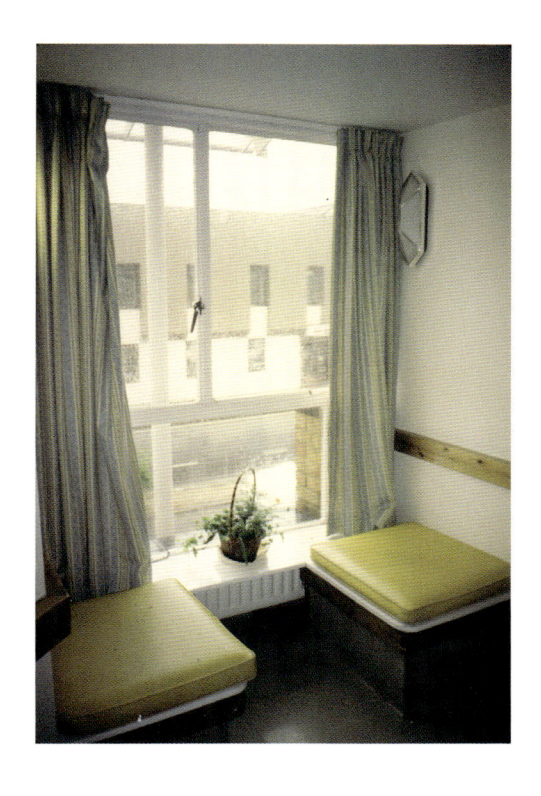

Edward Cullinan Architects, Lambeth Community Care Centre, London, 1985.
Seating outside patient rooms offers privacy and intimacy.

Instead of detaching us from the physical and sensuous realities of the world, such as gravity, temperature, materiality, texture and the interplay of shadow and light, architecture needs to invigorate and heighten sensory experience. It should not project a dream world of unreality but reenchant, reeroticize, and repoeticize the experiential world.

Juhani Pallasmaa, 'From an archipelago of authenticity' in G Caicco, ed, *Architecture, Ethics the Personhhood of Place*, 2007, p 44

Sound, ambient temperature, light and shade all need to be explored during design to facilitate intended activities and to make life enjoyable.

As intended, a visit to the National Museum of the American Indian is sensory rich. Visitors may experience gentle sounds of water moving and falling, the scent of newly tilled earth, a sweet fragrance of flowering trees, the call of a lone bird, a flute playing, strong sun and then deep shade, a rainbow of light on the atrium wall. Even taste was a consideration in the insistence on a cafeteria that offers a choice of Native foods from five different regions.

For the design of the Health Garden in Stockholm, Project Leader Yvonne Westerberg and architect Ulf Nordfjëll carefully considered possibilities for rich sensory experiences (see Chapter 6). Spaces in the garden can be organised into five 'stations' to stimulate an increased awareness of each of the five senses as a form of nature-guided therapy.[18] For those who come for support, the healing journey starts with a period of meditation followed by a slow walk around the garden stopping at each of the stations for five minutes. The first station by the entrance stimulates the sense of smell. Here hundreds of pelargonium plants grow. Their leaves emit a citrus smell. A peeled skin of a lemon is placed in the same area and participants are invited to compare the smells.

Ulf Nordfjëll, Health Garden, Haga Park, Stockholm, 2004. A stream runs between the rows of flowers creating the calming sound of running water.

The next station focuses on touch. Here the invitation is to lie down and relax on the hammock or one of the reclining beds and to reflect on how it feels to lie down and stroke the soft leaf of lamb's ear. (Lamb's ears are popular plants in gardens because of their soft, inviting texture.) In the third station sitting and holding a big platter full of different flowers and leaves inspires the sense of sight. Taste is stimulated in the fourth station by eating slices of pineapple. The fifth station, in one of the corridors, for sitting and listening to the trickling stream, stimulates the sense of sound. After the journey around the garden participants are invited to talk about their experiences. On one occasion, a senior executive dressed in a pin-stripe suit recounted how lying down and touching a leaf of lamb's ear brought back a forgotten memory from his childhood stroking his teddy bear. Thus his journey to health began.

In designing the Woodlands Nursing Home in London that would house many patients with dementia the architecture firm Prasad & Penroye considered experiences of sound, smell, light, colour and texture. Carpeted floors muffle the sounds of zimmer frames (walkers), good ventilation and plantings in the four gardens are intended to mute the smells of urine and disinfectant. Light and colour create lively spaces and changes in the texture of handrails and doorknobs along with changes in wall colour offer cues to location for these elderly patients.

Some sounds are welcome. Others are intrusive. Intrusive and uncontrollable noise can be stressful, reducing comfort and the ability to concentrate and, when excessive, threatening one's emotional stability. Too often, however, sound quality and the possible intrusion of sound are ignored. While concert halls and other performance spaces are designed to achieve appropriate sound quality, many other settings do not receive sufficient attention regarding acoustics and sound insulation. Studies of occupant satisfaction in recently completed architecture school buildings demonstrated that noise was consistently a problem in studios and review spaces designed with open plans. While the noise may not be loud, it is unpredictable and reduces the ability of students to concentrate, to engage in conversation with teachers and other students and to hear commentary during reviews.[19] For these reasons students and faculty consistently preferred private studios and review spaces to those that are open plan. The same study revealed that heating, ventilation and air conditioning were frequent problems, sometimes resulting from the design ignoring the solar orientation of spaces or possibilities of heat gain and glare resulting from glazing in the facade. These findings illustrate how important it is to explore and address conditions that affect everyday, embodied comfort.

Light and shadow seem to receive more attention in design and seem to be more successfully addressed than sound, temperature control and ventilation. Ada Karmi-Melamede is particularly aware of the potential of designing with natural light; she refers to it as the 'material that costs nothing', particularly in Israel where she works. At the Arison School of Management, the Lauder School of Government in Herzliya and the Life Sciences Building in Beersheva, she drew light into below ground spaces by excavating a lower ground floor that extends beyond the building walls.

When designing the National Museum of the American Indian, Johnpaul Jones, one of the project designers, noticed that visitors standing at the entrance to the Air and Space Museum were exposed to the heat of

Ada Karmi-Melamede, Arison School of Management and the Lauder School of Government, Herzliya, 2005. Tall windows bring light into a below ground corridor.

the midday sun. So he ensured that the overhang at the entrance to the new museum provided shade and that the building cast a shadow, cooling the north side where visitors might sit. Inside the museum, the oculus in the dome casts a soft diffuse light across the inner atrium and, as the sun moves across the sky, sunlight is refracted by the glass prisms hanging in the windows, reminding people of the passage of the day when they are inside.

Light is at a premium in the north-western US but even on grey days the reading and gathering spaces in Seattle's Central Library are bright since the building is clad completely in glass. Those glass panels that regularly receive direct sunlight have been embedded with wire mesh to filter the sunlight while the building surfaces that are in shade are clad in clear glass.

Stuff

Daily life at home, in institutions, at places of work and recreation depends on being able to view, select and use a great variety of objects. The objects may be hidden away or on display; they may be intended only to view or to use. The presence of these items, the roles they serve and the requirements that follow are all subjects for architects and clients to explore.

Freecell is particularly adept at studying the use and storage of objects and finding in the particular features of the objects inspiration for design. For the firm Verb Media Lauren Crahan and John Hartmann of Freecell measured each piece of equipment the company used. They then designed a counter/divider to accommodate the size, shape and use of each item and, in doing so elegantly, gave each item pride of place. Over and over again

Freecell, NYC Velo, New York, 2005. Ascending and descending ramps activate the bicycles on display.

these architects discover the particular functional and aesthetic qualities of objects and address them ingeniously. The resultant design reveals the defining qualities of the objects, making them special in a way that is reflective of their use and meaning. For the NYC Velo bike store in Manhattan, the architects designed and built ascending and descending ramps, or rubber walkways, attached to the wall that display the bicycles on them as if they were in motion, allowing customers to imagine riding them. John Hartmann recalls, 'We didn't want to stack them, we wanted to activate them.'

Freecell's skill in enriching the viewer's experience of displayed objects is evident in their exhibit design for Le Corbusier's section drawings of a Baghdad stadium at the Henry Urbach Gallery in Manhattan. The architects placed each drawing between two glass panels and hung the series of ten from the ceiling, allowing visitors to walk around each panel and to see through the openings Corbusier had made in each drawing. Moreover, section drawings through the right side of the stadium were hung in a row on the right side of the room facing front, while sections through the left side of the stadium were hung in a row on the left side facing the back of the gallery. The strong diagonal line of the stadium seating always descended from upper right to lower left, down to the aisle between the two rows of drawings, in effect down to the floor of the stadium. Through the design of the exhibit the architects were able to dramatise the special features of the drawings and to give an embodied sense of 'stadium'.

Both the presence of particular objects and the manner in which they are stored or displayed are so ingrained in a building type that their arrangement may not be questioned. That was not the case, however, for Seattle's Central Library or the National Museum of the American Indian: in each case basic assumptions about what libraries and museums are and how they work were questioned and revised and, accordingly, the display and accessibility of items in them. Rem Koolhaas of OMA was concerned about the lack of coherence in the appearance of the books in the library. He also raised the possibility of devising a new cataloguing system. The client rejected these suggestions but did accept what was first seen as a risky way of storing and accessing the nonfiction collection in a 'spiral' rather than on separate and distinct floors. With empty shelf space provided, this arrangement allows departments to expand without having to move books from one section to another. The user's ease in finding books, without having to go from one floor to another, and the librarian's ease in adding volumes, are both addressed.

At the National Museum of the American Indian tribal members and leaders made it clear throughout the briefing process that it should not be a traditional museum in the European-American sense since institutions in that mould run counter to Indian beliefs that material objects are 'living' and should not be separated from their context.

> Indians see objects as living and a part of the larger environment, and museums as places that separate things which ought to be seen as part of ongoing life. Indian objects derive their importance from use, contact with natural elements and their relationships to people.[20]

During briefing workshops participants also voiced their desire to portray their culture as active and alive through performances, craft demonstrations and outreach programs and not primarily through the display of objects. The museum as built does offer many possibilities for the expression of a living culture through: generously sized spaces for live performances (both

Polshek Partnership Architects, Cultural Resources Center, Suitland, Maryland, 1998. Storage space is spacious, airy and light to 'house' rather than to 'store' Indian artefacts.

indoors and out), a secluded ceremonial space, two theatres, a resource centre, two museum shops and a cafeteria with regional varieties of Native American food. The exhibition spaces display only a very limited number of objects from the museum's vast collection and members of tribal communities curate these exhibits.

As planned, the museum's full collection of 8,000 artefacts is housed in the Cultural Resources Center in Suitland, a suburb of Washington. The briefing and designing of this building addressed very carefully the meanings and required care of objects in American Indian culture. The objects, stored in rooms that are filled with daylight, are accessible to researchers, native communities and spiritual leaders who can come to the centre both to see or one might say 'visit' the objects and to give them special ceremonial care. Sometimes tribal leaders leave water and traditional foods for the objects and the museum also accommodates ceremonies that involve the burning of sage. The centre houses rather than stores these special things and in doing so it creates a welcoming and pleasing environment for visitors and staff.

The architects for both the National Museum of the American Indian on the Mall in the US and Te Papa in New Zealand were commissioned to design the buildings but not the exhibition spaces or the means of displaying objects. This task was given to exhibition designers, thus severing the design of spaces for display from the design of the rest of the museum. In both buildings the exhibit spaces are 'black boxes' that seem largely independent of the rest of the building.

The competition submission for Te Papa that won Jasmax the commission had to be significantly changed to accommodate the Exhibition Conceptual Plan that had already been developed by the time the competition winner was announced (see Chapter 6). Tom Dixon, who had served as Architecture Advisor to the Museum of New Zealand, commented to Teresa that 'There's a kind of split between the shell of the building and its contents and while the two teams [architects and exhibition designers] worked very closely together inevitably there was a point where the building as a whole had to go down one track and the exhibition areas had to go down another.' Even after the architects modified the design in response to the exhibition concept, their proposal to glaze over the mediating three-storey wedge-shaped space between the Māori and Pākehā exhibition spaces was overridden by the exhibition designers, leading architectural graduate Giles Reid to comment that the space 'is now dark and loses its power as a place of vivid contact between cultures, and earth, sea and sky'.[21]

Site

In adopting the attitude of an explorer, architects examine the full range of characteristics of a building site with care: topography, climate, trees, views, orientation as well as current uses and historical, social and cultural context. Unfortunately, even the most basic features of a site are sometimes overlooked. The site for Helen Hitman's house is a steep hillside overlooking the Bay of Islands in northern New Zealand. Yet the schemes submitted by two architecture firms placed the house on a platform, ignoring the rugged steepness below, the views to the south and the sun coming over the hill to the north. Fortunately, the third scheme made full use of all these site assets (see Chapter 3).

While others weaved narratives of sickness and death out of abandoned storefronts, overgrown parking lots and weathered murals we learned – by hanging out, talking to people and watching what was going on – that the very same phenomena can be conditions for new and exciting kinds of life.

The Architectural League of New York 'Interboro', *Young Architects 7: Situating*, 2006, p 151

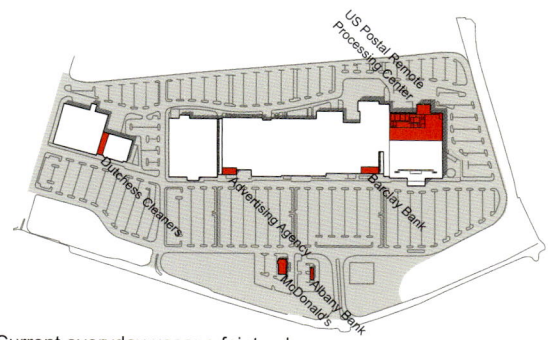

Current everyday uses: a faint pulse

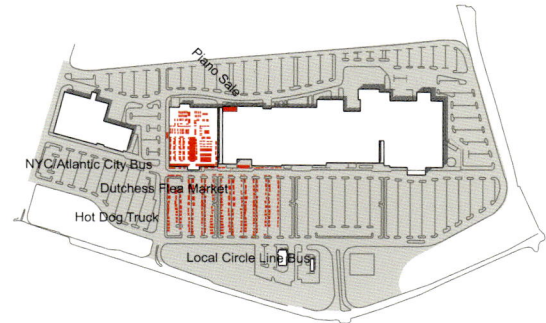

Current temporary programs

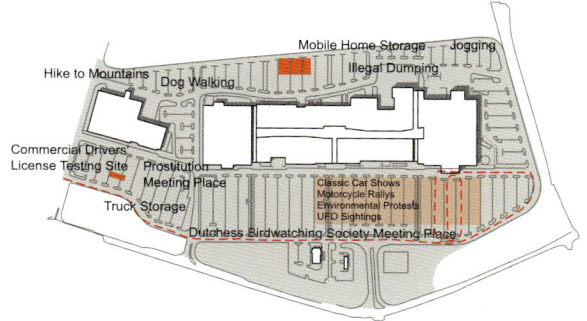

Illicit and unpredictable events: arrhythmia

Interboro, 'In the Meantime, Life with Landbanking'. Dead Malls Competition winning entry, Los Angeles Forum for Architecture and Urban Design, 2003. Interboro's observations revealed that Dutchess Mall in New York State, officially closed, still hosts a range of activities: ongoing uses, intermittent events and illicit, unpredictable events. These they represented through the metaphor of a beating heart.

Exploring also means approaching a site and its context as potentially full and alive, even when no buildings are present and no ongoing uses appear to exist. This approach often reveals what is in fact present but not immediately evident, as illustrated by Interboro's winning entry for the Dead Malls competition. The competition, sponsored by the Los Angeles Forum for Architecture and Urban Design, invited projects that proposed a future for a 'dead' shopping mall.

Interboro chose the Dutchess Mall in Fishkill, New York that closed, at least officially, in 1998. However, by spending time at the site at different times of the day and week, Interboro discovered that the old Service Merchandise anchor store and parking lot was still home to one legitimate business (a dry cleaners) and many other uses: a popular weekend flea market, drivers licence testing and practice, food carts, prostitution, carpool meetings and motorcycle rallies. Rather than imposing an entirely new set of uses upon the site, as colonisers might do, they suggested programs that drew upon the uses that were already there:

> … our programs are ones that can be imagined being developed out of cultures that have already started to grow around the site. The result is not a master plan but a collection of small, cheap, feasible moves that can come in over time and lead to many possible features.[22]

Over the short term 'to incubate healing cultures', Interboro suggested a nightclub, a beer garden, a summer stage, a sculpture garden, a car wash and a recycling centre. Over the longer term, additional uses could include a day care centre, recreation area, a bus stop and a monument

What is present on a site may only be the remnants, both physical and cultural, of the past but these remnants can be extremely important to the local community and to the client as a living connection to their history. In

Mithun, Northwest Indian College Masterplan, Washington, 1933 site conditions. An analysis of the site's history, including aerial photographs, identified the former location of important social and environmental features. St. Joachim Church remains; the barns, shed, farmhouse and outbuildings are no longer standing. Remaining trees from the apple orchard are the only remnants of the former farm.

KEY
1 St. Joachim Church
2 Hay or wheatfield
3 Established forest
4 Driveway
5 Barn/shed
6 Farmhouse and outbuilding
7 Vegetable garden
8 Apple orchard
9 Lummi Day School
Areas of blue indicate wetlands

their meetings with tribal elders Brodie Bain, Bob Mohr, Dakota Keene and Ron Van der Veen of Mithun toured the site for the Northwest Indian College on the Lummi reservation and heard the stories the elders told. They also analysed historical aerial photographs showing site conditions in 1933. Some site features were still present in 2004, including trees from an apple orchard that tribal elders fondly remembered walking through on their way to school. One important aspect of the final masterplan was the preservation of those trees.

During the early stages of design of the National Museum of the American Indian, Johnpaul Jones discovered that Tiger Creek still runs under the site, 20 feet (6.1 metres) below ground. The water that now runs along the northern side of the museum alludes to this hidden creek. Understanding the site within the larger context of tribal traditions was also crucial to the design. While most visitors would be approaching the building from the west, from other museums on the Mall, it was important to Indian traditions to have visitors enter the building from the east. The site design draws people in from the west, along the water to the entrance that faces east. As Johnpaul Jones says about Washington DC, 'There's a lot of Greeks and Romans here. Trees are lined up in straight lines' but 'that's not where Indian people come from'. Both the building's form and the design of the landscape emerged from an understanding of Indian traditions, not from the designed context of Washington.

Cultural traditions were also part of Denise Ho's exploration of the village in San Shui. She visited the village's ancestral hall and its forecourt where villagers sit around the banyan tree. She noted that the houses face south to catch the summer breezes and winter sun. Her design drew directly from those observations: three small houses to define their own forecourt that faces south.

In pursuing design as a journey and, like an explorer, remaining open and inquisitive, architects and clients can discover what was previously unknown or unexpected. Such discoveries, about the site and its context as well as about many other aspects of a project, generate important opportunities for design.

NOTES

1 Dana Cuff, 'The social production of built form', *Environment and Planning D: Society and Space*, vol 7, 1989, p 443.
2 Karen A Franck and R Bianca Lepori, *Architecture from the Inside Out: From the Body, the Senses, the Site and the Community*, Wiley-Academy (London), 2007.
3 A study at Chelsea and Westminster Hospital found that 75 per cent of patients, staff and visitors said that observing and watching the visual and performing arts greatly diminished their stress levels, changed their mood for the better and helped take their minds off immediate worries or medical problems. Of nurses and doctors, 50 per cent reported that the quality of the hospital environment is a very important factor in why they chose to work there. Among the findings on treatment, labour during birth was reduced by two hours on the obstetric wards. 'Chelsea and Westminster Hospital Arts for the Kings Fund: A study on the effects of the visual and performing arts in health care' reported in *Investing in Design: Developing a Business Case for Good Design in Health*, The NHS Confederation Briefing (London), June 2003, p 2.

4 Quoted in Edward Robbins, *Why Architects Draw*, MIT Press (Cambridge, MA), 1994, p 184.
5 Sunand Prasad, *Transformations: The Architecture of Penoyre & Prasad*, Black Dog (London), 2007, p 18.
6 Lisa Findley, *Building Change: Architecture, Politics and Cultural Agency*, Routledge (London), 2005.
7 Ibid, p 196.
8 Matthew Potteiger and Jamie Purinton, *Landscape Narrative: Design Practices for Telling Stories*, John Wiley & sons Inc (New York), 1998, p 193.
9 Fred Moody, 'The spiral', *Metropolis*, October 2004, pp 108–11.
10 Bryan Lawson, *What Designers Know*, Architectural Press (Oxford), 2004, p 46.
11 Donald A Schön and Glenn Wiggins, 'Kinds of seeing and their functions in designing', *Design Studies*, vol 13, April 1992, p 154.
12 Julia Williams Robinson and J Stephen Weeks, 'Programming as design', *Journal of Architectural Education*, vol 37, 1983, p 6.
13 Robbins, *Why Architects Draw*, p 60.
14 Venturi, Scott Brown and Associates, *The Way of the People: National Museum of the American Indian (Master Facilities Programming, Phase 1)*, Office of Design and Construction, Smithsonian Institution (Washington DC), 1991, p 2.
15 Ibid, p 8.
16 Jack L Nasar, Wolfgang FE Preiser and Thomas Fisher, *Designing for Designers: Lessons Learned from Schools of Architecture*, Fairchild Publications (New York), 2007.
17 Ibid.
18 George W Burns, *Nature-Guided Therapy: Brief Integrative Therapies for Health and Well-Being*, Psychology Press (London), 1998.
19 Franck and Lepori, *Architecture from the Inside Out*.
20 Venturi, Scott Brown and Associates, *The Way of the People, (Phase 1)*, p 35.
21 Giles Reid, 'Museo-logic', *Architect New Zealand, Special Edition on the Design of Te Papa*, February 1998, p 37.
22 The Architectural League of New York, 'Interboro' in *Young Architects 7: Situating*, Princeton Architectural Press (New York), 2006, p 153.

Chapter 6

Transforming

The Turbine Hall at the Tate Modern in London is an imposing space, immensely tall and long. People wander through and gaze up, possibly at a large sculpture that towers overhead, or they sit on the raised walkway to the side. But they have no close contact with the space or with one another. That changed dramatically in 2007 with the insertion of a ragged chasm in the concrete floor, sometimes a metre deep, extending the full length of the hall. This intervention not only attracted and held visitors' rapt attention, it also engaged their bodily participation, inviting exploration, play and risky gymnastics. Children and adults followed its jagged path to the end; they peered into it, sometimes from a kneeling position, sometimes lying down on the floor and reaching their arms inside. They jumped over the crack, sometimes back and forth; they balanced at its edge and even lay down across it. They posed in playful positions for photographs. They talked with one another.

According to the Tate's brochure, this project by the Colombian artist Doris Salcedo entitled *Shibboleth* was intended to draw attention to the history of racism and colonialism. The crack symbolised this fissure in modernity. It is hard to know if visitors grasped this intention. What the crack did do was stimulate an amazing array of imaginative physical responses from both adults and children, making the floor of the Turbine Hall a kind of playground; a large, impersonal space became lively and even intimate.

For a few months the Turbine Hall was not only changed but transformed. While change creates an apparent difference, transformation alters an underlying composition or structure. The first has been called 'first order change' where the overall system remains the same; 'second order change' occurs when the system itself is altered.[1] A metamorphosis. One thing becomes another. The caterpillar turns into a butterfly.

Transforming occurs at many points in the design process. Architects transform their understanding of what is written and spoken into drawings and models that eventually guide the construction of a building. In the best

Doris Salcedo, Shibboleth, Tate Modern, London, 2007.
A long, deep crack in the floor of the Turbine Hall engaged visitors, stimulating exploration and play and transforming the space.

… second-order change is ordinarily viewed as something uncontrollable … a quantum jump, a sudden illumination which unpredictably comes at the end of long, often frustrating mental and emotional labor, sometimes in a dream, sometimes almost as an act of grace in the theological sense.

Paul W Watzlawick, John Weakland and Richard Fisch, *Change*, 1974, p 23

of cases, architects not only design a change of state but a state that exceeds their clients' expectations. In the hands of a good designer architecture can transform occupants' ways of doing things, either by encouraging new kinds of actions, routines and relationships or by enhancing those that already exist. New York architect Joshua Ramus suggests that, at first, clients may be unaware of this ability that architects and architecture possess. 'They don't understand that architecture can actually solve problems. It can DO things. It doesn't have to just represent.'

Like new experiences in life, new or redesigned spaces create new possibilities in quite unexpected but welcome ways. This can happen at the scale of a floor surface, a garden, a sidewalk, a workspace, or an entire building. The significant effects even small-scale interventions can have on people's actions and perceptions reveal the potential power design always holds as a transformative tool.

Transforming at the Human Scale

The greatest power of architecture, for people, is how it affects their interactions with their surroundings and other people. Good design can transform everyday experiences and actions from the mundane to the special. When they focus exclusively on making large-scale, visually arresting statements, architects overlook this potential for architecture to be transformative at the scale of the human body and everyday life. 'Transforming at the human scale' also suggests that ideas for transforming places come from insights into what is needed and what is possible, from the experiences and inventions of both clients and architects.

Work Architecture Company, Lee Angel, New York, 2005. The wall of beads, serving as both display and storage, enlivens what was previously a dreary space.

To develop a design for the Lee Angel jewellery showroom in Manhattan, Amale Andraos and Dan Wood of Work Architecture Company interviewed everyone who worked there. The architects heard numerous comments about the 'cramped, rigid nature' of the space. When visitors entered they 'were immediately shunted off to the showroom' with no opportunity to learn about the jewellery-making process.[2] The architects noted the repeated references to the 8,000 jars of beads the designers use; eventually these jars inspired the architects' design. Now, upon entering, visitors immediately catch sight of an L-shaped wall stretching the full length of the corridor that leads from the reception area to the showroom. This wall of beads holds the

8,000 jars organised by colour, lit from both the back and the front, creating a glorious display of texture and colour for visitors and easily accessible for staff. Storage is transformed into display while still maintaining its role as storage; a cramped, uninformative space becomes both tantalising and illuminating, giving visitors a glimpse of the jeweller's creative process.

Starting out initially without a client, landscape architect Steve Rasmussen-Cancian noticed a need in Oakland, California for sidewalks that are places to be, not just to walk along. From that recognition and with inventiveness and eventual collaboration with local organisations, he has transformed sidewalks in Los Angeles and West Oakland, California. With the placement of movable tables and chairs built of plywood, sections of public sidewalks become 'outdoor living rooms' at locations where residents already tended to gather or where gathering would improve the pedestrian environment. These are not simply benches for sitting; even at a bus stop the furniture is designed and installed to foster interaction between people. These modest, movable interventions not only give people places to sit and talk and watch the passing scene; their simple presence legitimates the use of the sidewalk for those activities. The sponsorship, participation in design and construction and ongoing maintenance of the living rooms by neighbourhood organisations further strengthen and enhance the transformation of a sidewalk in to a public, outdoor living room.

Clients may also notice a need not previously met and to respond to that need they may invent a new type of place. When Yvonne Westerberg was a young occupational therapist in training in Stockholm, an elderly patient showed her how to make rhododendron cuttings. Yvonne drew upon that early experience when she began gardening with elderly patients in the early 1990s. Her first step was to collect stones and moss from the forest to make a 'landscape'. Yvonne remembers how one elderly patient with dementia who had not spoken for many months, started stroking one of these stones. The patient smiled, saying 'Ronneby. It's Ronneby.' Ronneby is a small town in the south of Sweden where she had lived as a child. Yvonne then understood that:

> Nature and the garden landscape can help people communicate. You don't need the cognitive as much because nature talks for itself. It talks to you, with you, it's a part of yourself, with your memory but also, I think, because you *are* from nature. You are born *in* nature from the start.

Steve Rasmussen-Cancian for Venice Community Housing Corporation, Outdoor Living Room, Venice, California, 2008.
Movable plywood furniture on a neighbourhood sidewalk invites sitting and talking.

Ulf Nordfjëll, Garden of Senses, Sabbatsberg Hospital, Stockholm, 1998.
TOP Gardening helps people communicate with each other.
ABOVE A clothesline for towels evokes memories of childhood.

As Yvonne continued to garden with this group of elderly patients with dementia, she realised how many people could benefit from such contact with nature (see Chapter 2). She began to write about her vision of a Garden of the Senses that would be a place for memories, culture and Swedish traditions, both for meeting and to be alone. After six years of hard work explaining her ideas and raising funds, Yvonne invited the landscape architect Ulf Nordfjëll to design the garden she had dreamed of at the Sabbatsberg Hospital in Stockholm.

Yvonne explained to Teresa that communication is difficult for people with mental disease. They lack memory and words. So the garden was designed to increase their capacity to remember, to recall things from their own childhoods. Flowers planted are familiar to patients. Vegetables and berries offer the taste and the scent of different kinds of foods over the course of the year. A clothesline for hanging towels out to dry gives the impression of being at home. An old teahouse, built in 1783 and integrated into the garden, became an indoor space, outside, with the security of an 'old building smell'. Senile hospital patients who came to the garden started to become active, interested and enthusiastic, engaged in remembering and talking.

As a result of creating the Garden of Senses, Yvonne Westerberg won a prize that took her to the US where she read the early research of Roger Ulrich who reported the benefits of contact with nature for hospital patients.[3] He also described the value of gardens to relieve stress in patients and staff. Yvonne was inspired to create a Health Garden to give people suffering from burnout, a crisis or chronic pain an existential healing experience (see Chapter 5). She found a large abandoned glasshouse in Haga Park in Stockholm and set about creating a therapeutic garden with Ulf Nordfjëll, drawing on findings from horticultural therapy and other research connected with evolutionary theory.[4]

Even though the Health Garden is a single glasshouse, within it very different 'rooms' have been created to follow a progression from rest to activity. At one end is the activity of gardening, at the other, stillness. This space of stillness fits the theory of evolution. Civilisation began in the savannah, in Africa. When people rest in the hammock or sit in the resting chair with the sound of the water and the 'green fields' around them, they begin to feel they will survive. In the centre of the glasshouse is a 'meeting room' with a big table for discussion or drinking coffee. Following the theory that often the most difficult thing to deal with is other people, the table is surrounded by the fortifying quality of nature: the calming sound of streams of running water can be heard all the time. Everywhere one looks one sees things that have been selected with love and care. The candelabra hanging over the table is made of cut glass to reflect the light of the candles below. The entire environment communicates that it is okay to rest, to be at peace without anyone having to say anything. People who are disabled, ill or exhausted need an oasis. This kind of garden is one way that society can show them that it is important to rest.

Ulf Nordfjëll, Health Garden, Haga Park, Stockholm, 2004. ABOVE LEFT The First Room, a place of rest and relaxation, evokes memories of the beginning of civilisation in the African savannah. ABOVE The Meeting Room, a place for conversation and drinking tea or coffee.

Looking Beneath the Surface

By looking beyond or beneath the problems that seem to be most pressing architects can uncover problems the client has not recognised and thereby realise a more complete transformation.

Initially Allies and Morrison, the architects for the extension of the Horniman Museum in southeast London, followed their client's lead and focused on the problems of the existing building and what it lacked: poor quality educational facilities, an inability to stage proper temporary exhibitions and no café. At first they did not consider the adjacent garden as it had no visual connection to the museum (see Chapter 5). As design proposals were made over a period of time, the architects realised something extremely important: that the relationship of the building to the garden could be changed. Bob Allies recalled:

Allies and Morrison Architects, The Horniman Museum, London, 2002.

TOP View to the outdoors from the café. ABOVE In the redesign the museum was opened to the adjacent garden.

Doing a renovation is not about putting on an external coat. It's not about going to a party. 'What do you fancy tonight?' It's about understanding the problem and the building.

Denise Ho, Hong Kong, March 2005

It was like a nerve. Once you touched it, then of course they were terribly sad that all those people would go to the garden and never get to the museum and people would go to the museum and never go to the gardens yet they were responsible for them both.

The realization that you could somehow join the two together was a bit of a breakthrough for everybody. There was a moment when we said, 'If you knock a hole in that wall there, you will see the garden and if you walk in a straight line, you can get out.' And that is exactly what happened.

It was not a redefinition of what the museum was. 'It was more changing the fabric of what they had, rethinking ways in which they could use it.'

The board of Villa Monte Rosa, a condominium in Hong Kong, was seeking an architect for the renovation of the complex of 20-storey buildings. It is likely that board members expected proposals, so common in Hong Kong, for an immediate paint job to the exterior, in bright colours. But when architect Denise Ho met with the board, she did not make such a proposal. She told them instead, 'I can't bring in a design. I don't even know you.' She then described several problems she had observed during a previous visit to the complex when she had spent several hours observing and taking pictures. Key among those problems was the haphazard location of air conditioners on the outside of the buildings and the discoloration and deterioration of the building facades caused by the method of installing and repairing them. All households install their own air conditioning systems in whatever location they choose and with whatever exterior pipes that are required. Temporary scaffolding for the installation is necessary. It is erected by whichever company the apartment owner hires. The scaffolding is dangerous and, over time, damages the building facade.

Denise got the job. With input from both the residents and a company that installs air-conditioning units, Denise designed a permanent metal frame to be fixed to the building facades that would standardise the placement of air conditioners, conceal them and make their installation simpler and safer without defacing the building. The result was a practical solution that eases the lives of both residents and installers and, through this new method of installing air conditioning units, radically improves the appearance of the buildings both immediately and over the long term.

By looking beneath the surface Denise employed systems thinking, a way of recognising that what appears to be the 'problem' (the discoloured and deteriorated facades) is usually a symptom of a larger set of interacting forces

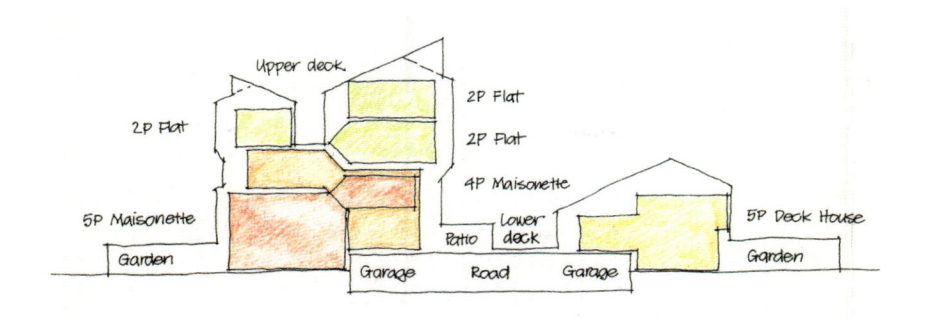

Borough Architect's Department, Myatt's Fields North, London Borough of Lambeth. TOP LEFT Cross section of original. Each dwelling has two floors. BOTTOM LEFT Cross section of rebuilt street. BELOW View of rebuilt street.

KEY P: Person

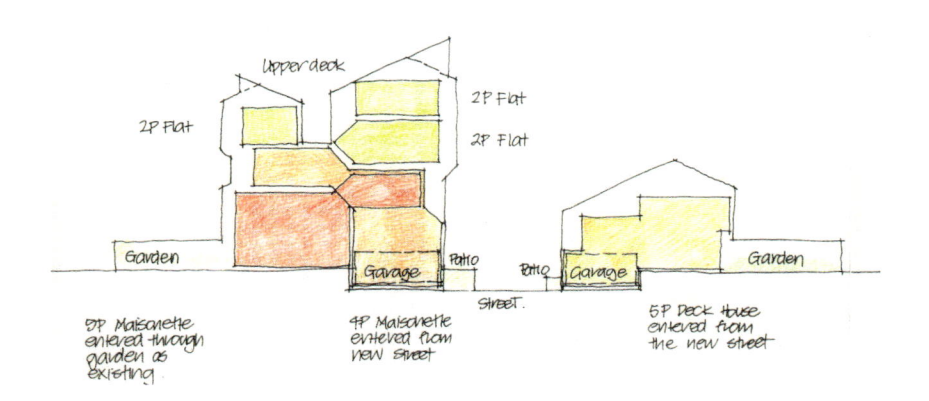

that remain hidden until brought into focus (the method of installing and repairing air conditioners). A pattern of relationships is found between what initially appeared to be disconnected problems. By breaking the original pattern and replacing it with a new pattern, not only can the problem be resolved but the situation itself can be transformed.[5] Then instead of treating what was a symptom of the problem, the problem itself is resolved.

Teresa employed this approach when she was asked to solve the problem of illegal access to restricted areas on Myatt's Fields North, a housing estate in Lambeth, London. Although designed in the 1970s to

CHAPTER 6 TRANSFORMING • 171

provide a pleasant car-free environment where children could play safely and people could walk about and talk to their neighbours on car-free decks, by the late 1980s it had turned into a living nightmare for residents. The pedestrian decks, which provided the only means of access to many of the houses, had been built over the ground-level streets, which were the only route to individual garages under the houses. The garages were never used and the streets under the deck became dark, dank and frightening. Eventually the housing management locked them with steel gates. Nevertheless people managed to gain access for illicit activity including drug use and illegal diversion of telephone and electricity services.

The same solution of fitting increasingly stronger steel gates and corrugated iron walls across the entrances had been applied repeatedly over several years but the problems did not abate. Residents who wanted to gain access simply grew smarter in their methods of breaking into this forbidden zone. It was then that the housing management office asked Teresa to solve the 'problem', assuming that the illicit use of space under the decks was the problem and that she would design stronger gates and provide stronger locks.

Teresa recognised that many professionals had already tried this 'solution' to address what she sensed was a symptom of an underlying problem. She decided to resist what Paul Watzlawick refers to as 'more of the same' and decided to engage with the problem in a new way, enabling her to see that the physical structure of the estate was generating the problem.[6] The presence of the decks and the split means of access to the garages and the houses created a dark underbelly to the estate that invited illicit activity. While musing about what to do, she remembered that the pedestrian deck had been constructed in pre-stressed, pre-cast concrete and could be removed to reveal the ground level street below. Each garage could be connected to each house with direct circulation between them and with an entrance to the house from the new street. Although this proposal was overtaken by more radical forms of demolition and rebuilding, one street was reconstructed according to Teresa's proposal.

Treating Type as a Question

Libraries, schools, museums, churches, theatres and hospitals are just a few examples of building types that organise the ways people make, occupy and think about the world.[7] Each type serves particular purposes, supports and encourages certain kinds of actions and relationships and is expected to look a certain way. Types guide what people do in particular places; they also guide what architects design since clients always come to architects with particular types in mind.

All of us live in a world of types that was already here when we were born. At some point in time, however, these types were *invented* and they remain in a kind of flux as they are continuously critiqued, modified and even discarded and as new ones are invented. Questioning the conventional social and physical characteristics of a given type, rather than simply accepting and reproducing them, is one important way architects and clients generate innovative design proposals. This is precisely what happened during the briefing and designing of Te Papa Tongerewa Museum of New Zealand in Wellington, the National Museum of the American Indian in Washington DC and the Seattle Central Library.

In each of these cases architect and client approached the type as a question, not as an answer. They explored in depth how the project at hand was and was not a 'museum' or a 'library' as defined by mainstream and, for the museums, Eurocentric understandings of that type. And in each case, answering the question led to innovative architectural and social characteristics for the new building, significantly modifying 'museum' and 'library'. Through the hard work of thinking, talking, exploring and designing a type was transformed. Transforming type requires belief and determination: a strong and clear vision for the new building and the willingness and capacity to stand up to the controversy a transformed type often provokes. Members of the public may be disappointed or angry when the new building is not the kind of museum or library they envisioned or are accustomed to.

A given type is defined by a complex and closely interconnected set of features. One way to identify the different kinds of features that constitute a type is according to characteristics of *form*, *use* and *meaning*.[8] These three characteristics are so closely interdependent that a change in one will lead to changes in the others. When architects and clients question a given building type during the briefing and design process, they are likely to question all three characteristics together. Thus, architects and clients working on Te Papa Tongarewa Museum of New Zealand, the National Museum of the American Indian and the Seattle Central Library explored what the new building should do (its use) and what it should represent (its meaning). Decisions about its design (its form) evolved from all these considerations.

A Museum of Two Cultures?

Te Papa Tongarewa was to be a new type museum for New Zealand and possibly for the world: one that no longer relied on a European definition of 'museum' as a place for collections, scholarship and formal education. Instead it would be 'a lively, dynamic and exciting place' where learning would be fun. A state-funded institution, it was to replace and integrate the treasures from two existing museums: the National Museum that presented both Māori history and culture and the country's natural history and the National Gallery that housed Pākehā art, much of which had been imported. The building was not to be a monument. The challenge, as the brief presented it, was 'to tell the story of New Zealand with richness, life, excitement and feeling'.[9] Architects were instructed that the new building should seek to reduce 'threshold anxiety' so that visitors would be welcomed rather than intimidated.[10] (See Chapter 4)

This vision required that people change their thinking about museums. Many New Zealanders remember their school trips to museums, such as the imposing Auckland War Memorial Museum, where they were expected to speak in whispers and listen quietly as teachers and museum staff taught them history from the colonists' perspective. The new museum would change all this: it would no longer privilege the Pākehā worldview. To tell the story

---

Although humans are born into communities of people who have established patterns of spatial types, the uses and meanings of types and the distinctions between them were, and are, invented, passed on, modified, and discarded by cultures.

Lynda H Schneekloth and Karen A Franck 'Type: prison or promise?', in Franck and Schneekloth, eds, *Ordering Space*, 1994, p 27

… because the building types that we take for granted are not fixed, but change over time, their nature cannot be assumed to be fully understood, but remains a constant question.

Julia W Robinson, 'The question of types', in Frank and Schneekloth, eds, *Ordering Space* 1994, p 179

Too often Museum buildings convey messages of exclusion because of their architectural form. This has resulted in the term, threshold fear – the fear many people have of passing through the door of an institution, which in subtle, and not so subtle ways, has raised cultural barriers.

Tom Dixon, *The Museum of New Zealand Te Papa Tongarewa Building Design Brief*, 1990, p 18

of New Zealand in all its fullness meant that the new museum would represent 'the *mana* (power, authority, prestige) and importance of each of the two main streams of tradition and cultural heritage': that of Māori or first peoples and that of Pākehā or those who came later.[11] The museum was to represent a profound shift in the country's identity from New Zealand to Aotearoa New Zealand that is from an identity that had silently subjected Māori to the Pākehā worldview to an identity where all peoples of New Zealand could express the richness of their cultures. The museum's name would be in both English and Māori: The Museum of New Zealand Te Papa Tongarewa with the Māori title understood to mean 'Our Place'.

The museum would have two directors, one Māori and one Pākehā, and the stories it would tell would be those of both first and second peoples, told for the first time in the same place. As a 'house of biculturalism', Te Papa would reflect a national culture that encourages mutual encounter, enrichment and fluency in both cultures.[12] As Cheryl Sotheran, the founding Joint Chief Executive of Te Papa, told Teresa, the museum might not exhibit '"imported works" but it would definitely respond to the lives of *Tangatawhenua*, those who are there by right of first discovery, as well as *Tangatatiriti*, those who came afterwards by right of the Treaty of Waitangi … It would be a place where everyone could recognise their shared and different histories.'

This concept evolved out of considerable debate over a period of nearly ten years starting in 1984 with the election in New Zealand of a new Labour government under David Lange. From then until 1989, an intricate dance of negotiation took place between the government and the Te Papa Development Board. Funding was always in short supply and at risk of evaporating. In 1989 an international competition was held with a selection panel of representatives from different interest groups.[13] From the 147 designs submitted, the panel chose the submission by the Auckland-based practice Jasmad, as it was known then, Jasmax now. To develop the design Jasmax worked with the museum board's Design Panel: Tom Dixon, architectural advisor to the government, and Richard Thorp, an Australian architect who had been on the selection panel.

The architects for Te Papa faced a daunting task: to design a museum that was bicultural in all respects and that engaged visitors in a lively experience of the bicultural richness of Aotearoa New Zealand. According to John Hunt, Jasmax architects were careful to avoid culturally significant forms borrowed from either Māori or European heritage as a strategy for depicting the national expression of identity, seeing the expression of identity as a more subtle and complex issue.[14] Instead they designed a building that, inside and out, reflects two distinct and sharply different cultures that meet in an in-between internal space described as the 'wedge'.

One part of the building faces the car park and the city beyond with a solid and largely blank wall; this part, mostly rectangular in shape, contains the Pākehā exhibition areas. These are laid out in a grid following European settlement patterns. The other part of the building, which faces the sea and is oriented toward the rising sun, is more porous, and seeks to replicate the Māori relationship to the land and sea. This part that is almost a triangle in form contains Māori exhibition areas and the *marae*, which opens to a deck looking out to the sea.

The open, wedge-shaped space placed between the two parts of the museum extends vertically through the building, becoming a void on levels three and four where it is crossed

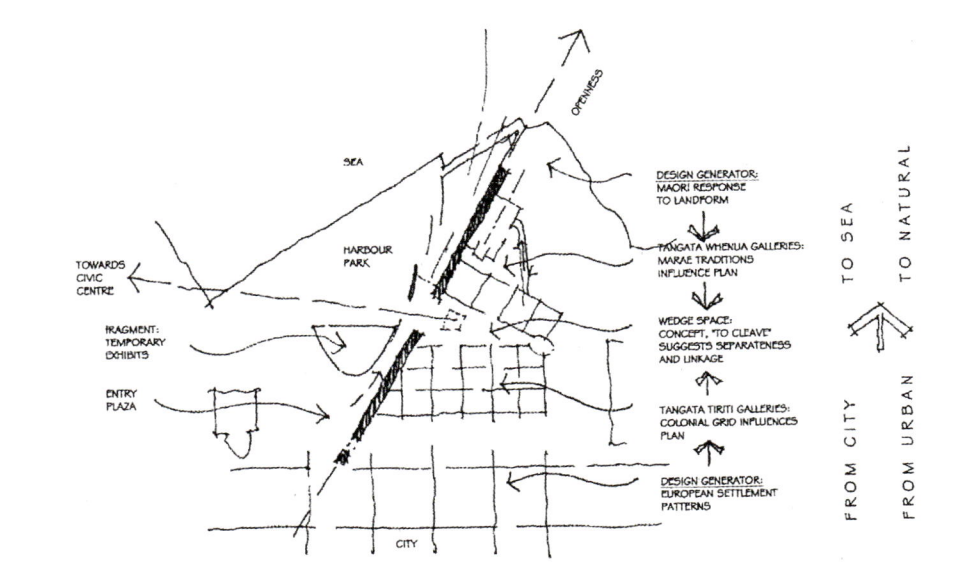

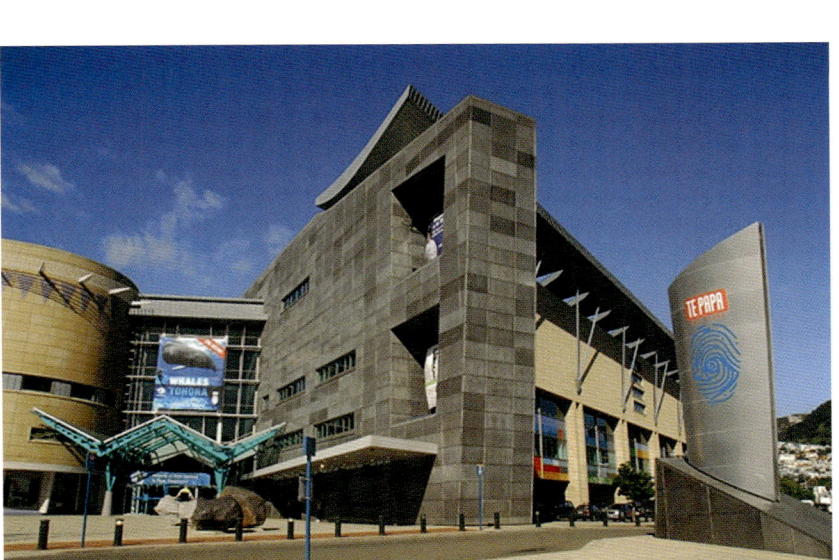

Jasmax, Te Papa Tongarewa Museum of New Zealand, Wellington, 1993. TOP The museum's internal grid reflects the transition from the city to the land and sea and the different settlement patterns of Māori and Pākehā. LEFT At the harbour's edge the museum faces the ocean beyond with the city grid behind. BELOW A basalt wall slices through the building alongside the museum entrance.

CHAPTER 6 TRANSFORMING • 175

... the very earth which we share is an intimate and deep-seated grinding-together of two peoples, an architectonic fault-line of pressures and upheavals, a seismic folding-together of stratified languages, forged in the intense heat of a fault ... The fault-line metaphor at Te Papa powerfully and unambiguously indicates and expresses these meanings of *Papatuanuku*, the earth on which we live.

Michael Linzey, 'A fault-line at Te Papa: the use of a metaphor', *Fabrications*, BNET UK, June, 2007, p 7

by a bridge. This is a triangular meeting and dividing space, that represents 'encounter and dialogue' between the two cultures. Architect Pete Bossley of Jasmax has explained that a wedge is 'associated with the idea to "cleave", which ... means both to separate and to adhere' and expresses 'the shifting nature of the relationships between the sub-cultures, in a process of ongoing re-definition'.[15]

A 13-foot (4-metre) thick basalt wall runs diagonally through the north-western edge of the building from the entrance to the sea, parallel to an earthquake fault line nearby. The wall serves as an actual fault line as well as a metaphor for the cultural divide in Aotearoa, New Zealand and cuts through an imaginary rectangle to form the triangular Māori exhibition area. The wall forms a hard edge to the building and encloses the long, ramped ceremonial walk to the Level Four promontory with its breathtaking views of sea and sky in front of the *marae*.

Te Papa has the first ever 'living' *marae* inside a museum: a communal meeting place to be used following Māori protocol, not just a cultural artefact to be viewed by tourists. Cliff Whiting, after 20 years of restoring old *marae* and designing and carving new ones, was asked to lead the design of this *marae*. He was also Joint Chief Executive of the museum and Director of Māori and Bicultural Development. According to Cliff the challenge was how to meet the museum's intention of creating 'a *marae* for all the people', not just for Māori. During construction Cliff took the unusual step of not making the site *tapu*, or sacred, so that he could invite visitors on to the *marae* to talk with him. To help visitors understand and begin to identify with the *marae* he compared its role in Māori society to that of the church in Pākehā society. He feels that the visitors who 'came through the place all the time ... were important as this thing evolved because it was their reactions and their confirmation of the ideas that really helped'.[16]

Jasmax, Te Papa Tongarewa Museum of New Zealand, Wellington, 1993.
The gates to the *marae* at the top of the ceremonial walk open for the *whaka,* a replica of the canoe that Māori seafarers used to cross the Pacific hundreds of years ago.

The *marae* was designed to be a place for all cultures to feel at home. All museum visitors have a 'right to stand' on this *marae* and will find carved ancestral images that reflect their origins, whether they are first people or second people from all over the world. Te Papa as a forum for the nation is actively embodied in this authentic yet inclusive and welcoming *marae*. The *wharenui* or meeting-house on the *marae* is not carved in the traditional polished timber but cut out from medium density fibre-board and painted in beautiful colours. The *marae* is now a lively part of the museum hosting the annual Matariki Festival of traditional and contemporary music and dance and Kaumātua Kapa Haka performances featuring senior Māori musicians and dancers from around the country.

In a country of four million 'Our Place' has proved to be an enormous success. Before the museum opened in 1998, staff predicted a peak audience of 2,000 a day was expected but the number multiplied to between 20,000 and 30,000. In its first ten years 15 million visited, quite a transformation from the embarrassing emptiness of the two museums it replaced. The museum continues to be a busy place, hosting fixed exhibitions, regular events and touring exhibitions that focus on what it means to live in Aotearoa New Zealand. The latest fixed exhibit to be added was 'Our Space' where visitors are given the opportunity to create their own vision of New Zealand using state-of-the-art interactive technology.

The evolution of Te Papa relied on an extended and often difficult dialogue within the Te Papa team and in the public domain. Biculturalism was neither well defined nor well understood. According to Cliff Whiting, the question was how to achieve it. 'It was an uncertain process that would take more than making biculturalism a corporate principle and then watching it happen.'[17] He, in particular, found himself constantly caught between the two worlds and their distinct ways of working, having to facilitate between them.[18] In reference to Māori, Cliff told Teresa, 'we had to really work at that bicultural thing after having been ignored … We were working to have voice. We are not after dollars but status and *mana* [authority, power, prestige] after not being recognised for over 100 years.'

Many Pākehā had a different perspective, expressing outrage that the origins of New Zealand would be a generator for the museum. Traditional museum lovers saw the replacement of artefacts with experience as a betrayal.

Cliff Whiting, designer and carver of the marae, Te Papa Tongarewa Museum of New Zealand. LEFT Hirini Melbourne and Richard Nunns play in front of the *wharenui* in the *marae*. RIGHT Figurehead above the door to the *wharenui* shows Maui, a highly respected *tipuna* or Pacific ancestor, and now a superhero for New Zealand children.

Continuing resistance to the bicultural agenda from the traditional art-going public finally forced additional building to incorporate more gallery space for Pākehā art. Cheryl Sotheran told Teresa that 'The engagement with Māori continues to be profound ... the harder battle was the one about "the art". What it stands for is the challenge that Te Papa posed to the dominant culture of New Zealand in terms of the value of its narratives and stories.'

Ten years after the museum's opening, Mike Linzey, Senior Lecturer at the School of Architecture, Auckland University, suggests that attitudes of many New Zealanders have changed to greater acceptance of once-contested differences and that perhaps 'the fault-line metaphor at Te Papa actually contributed to this change in the cultural landscape and the attitudes of most New Zealanders'.[19]

A Museum that is not a 'Museum'?

From the very beginning, the National Museum of the American Indian on the Mall in Washington was envisioned as radically different from other museums. The most fundamental difference was – and is – that it would both present and enact a 'living' culture, rather than only presenting 'dead' objects from a past culture. The mission statement adopted by the museum's board in 1990 touches on these intentions, repeatedly using the word 'culture' and suggesting the museum's responsibility to house a range of activities in relation to an ongoing culture: '... through innovative public programming, research and collections, to protect, support, and enhance the development, maintenance and perpetuation of Native culture and community'.[20]

In the briefing consultations held with Native groups in the US and in Canada, participants were adamant that the building should not be a typical museum with collections of inert objects completely separated from their context and use. One participant, Raymond Apodaca, Governor of Ysleta del Sur Pueblo, said:

> It is not for the museum to preserve culture. That is our job. The museum is an instrument to teach our views of ourselves, our understanding of what we are, that which we are willing to share with the world outside. [21]

The brief, based largely on input from these consultations, states clearly that through conducting traditional museum activities in new ways and introducing new activities, the building would change the definition of what a museum is. The changes would be great enough that the brief suggested that 'museum' might not be used in the name of the building. A different name would better capture the mission of this building, beyond the typical display of objects, to include performances and demonstrations with a strong sense of context. 'It must have exhibition and presentation spaces that allow for the mixing of media and activities that are important to the presentation of context and values.'[22]

Everyone also thought it was essential for the museum to show that Native cultures are very much alive today, to help sustain Native languages and to cultivate strong relationships with contemporary Native communities.

Duane Blue Spruce, 'An honour and a privilege', in Blue Spruce, ed, *Spirit of a Native Place*, 2004, p 19

The founding director of the museum Richard West lists three messages that emerged very clearly from the consultations with Native groups during the briefing of the building.

> First, while acknowledging our deep past, Native peoples want to be seen as communities and cultures that are very much alive today. Second we want the opportunity to speak directly to museum visitors through our exhibitions and public programs and to describe in our own voices and through our own eyes the meaning of the objects ... And third, we want the museum to act in direct support of contemporary Native communities.[23]

The completed building and surrounding landscape successfully fulfil this vision and express Native values regarding the importance of hospitality, the natural world and a living culture. Outdoors the landscape recreates a variety of local micro-ecologies. There is a secluded, circular space for ceremonies and an outdoor theatre; performances are also held in front of the entrance. Indoors the central atrium space, called the Potomac, hosts live performances and demonstrations. There is a theatre on the first level and a conference centre on the fourth level. The Lelawi Theatre on the fourth level presents a multimedia film on Native life. From large windows in the spacious resource centre on the third level one has direct views of the Mall and the Capitol. A warm and welcoming cafeteria on the first level serves meals from five different Native communities. Exhibition galleries are limited to enclosed spaces on the third and fourth levels. Members of Native communities, not professional art historians, curate the changing exhibitions (see Chapter 2).

Participants in the meetings with tribal groups during the briefing process recognised that actual museum buildings, no matter how well planned and designed, were not sufficient to meet the purposes they envisioned. They noted

Douglas Cardinal and GBQC Architects, Johnpaul Jones, Ramona Sakiestewa, Donna House (project designers); Jones & Jones, Smith Group with Lou Weller and the Native American Design Collaborative, Polshek Partnership Architects and EDAW (project architects), National Museum of the American Indian, Washington DC, 2004. Inside and out the building, the activities it supports and the experiences it offers communicate Native values and practices. LEFT The Potomac is the central welcoming and performing space. RIGHT Along the building's north side visitors hear the sounds of water cascading over rocks (see Chapter 2 pp 46-47).

that a 'fourth' or 'virtual museum' was also needed since only a small proportion of indigenous populations of the Americas would be able to visit any of the National Museum of the American Indian's three sites (the museum on the Mall, the Heye Center in New York and the Suitland Cultural Resource Center in Maryland). This virtual museum now includes outreach programs that connect the museum's resources to Native communities: an Internship Program for students, a Native Arts Program, a Visiting Professional Program. The museum also develops curricular materials for schools and produces radio programming.[24]

A new type, still called 'museum', can be disconcerting and even discomforting. When the National Museum of the American Indian opened, it sparked criticisms similar to those levelled at Te Papa. Many visitors expected a conventional museum with more historical information on display and many more of the treasured objects from the collection of George Heye (which were moved from New York to the new NMAI Cultural Resource Center in Suitland, Maryland). Some also expected 'more Western-style scholarship, the authoritative voice of academically trained curators'.[25] But that is precisely the opposite of what all those connected to the development of the musuem's brief and design set out to achieve and were able to do with great success.

A Library for the 21st Century?

When the Office of Metropolitan Architects and LMN Architects accepted the commission for Seattle's Central Library, they recognised the challenge the library board faced. The new library had received tremendous public support (a bond for $200 million had been passed by a large margin of the votes) but there was no commonly held opinion about what a library for the 21st century should be. Joshua Ramus, architect at OMA at the time, explained to Karen

OMA with LMN Architects, Central Library, Seattle, 2004. The library supports the continuing importance of books as one of several forms of technology and, as part of meeting its social responsibility, offers a variety of spacious sitting areas. LEFT Living Room RIGHT Reading Room

that 'very vocal groups in Seattle expressed a wide range of conflicting opinions from favouring a new version of the Carnegie library to a technologically oriented library with no books at all'.

The importance of taking a very clear stand on what the new library should in fact be, was one reason the architects and the client team engaged in three months of joint research that included visiting libraries in different countries and holding a series of seminars with a range of experts. From this period of research, the teams of clients and architects agreed that books were, in fact, a 'technology' and would remain important but likely not the 'preeminent form of technology'. Consequently, the architects stated in their Concept Book that their first objective or 'ambition' was:

> To redefine/reinvent the Library as an institution no longer exclusively dedicated to the book, but as an information store, where all media – new and old – is presented under a regime of new equalities. In an age where information can be accessed anywhere, it is the simultaneity of all media and the professionalism of their presentation and interaction, that makes the Library new.[26]

The architects also recognised that libraries are undergoing an evolution. With the explosion of information, people need help in accessing and evaluating it so, as Joshua Ramus commented, libraries are moving from 'being gatekeepers of information to curators, or mentors'. This means that the social responsibility of libraries is increasing. The client team easily understood and accepted the explosion of media but members of the team were doubtful about the explosion of the library's social responsibility. The architects were able to demonstrate clearly how many of the space requirements listed in the original program were dedicated to that responsibility. The board was persuaded and subsequently the architects stated their second objective in their Concept Book:

> The library as designed and built recognizes and supports the continuing importance of books and also accommodates current and expanding information technologies. It provides significant amounts of space to sitting. The largest and most welcoming spaces are lounges, with some of the ambiance of light-filled airport lounges; the first space one enters from 5th Avenue is the 'Living Room.'[27]

The two ambitions – that books are understood as part of an array of technologies and that the library now has a curatorial role – generated several inventions. In the new building library staff no longer sit at reference desks spread out throughout the library. Instead they are centralised, along with many computer terminals, in a space named The Mixing Chamber that, with its circular reference desk and its location one flight up from the main entrance level, has some of the atmosphere of a reception area in a boutique hotel. The reading and sitting spaces throughout the library do indeed possess the ambiance of airport lounges, with one containing a café. These areas are spacious, light-filled, welcoming and informal in feeling. They have little of the furniture, furnishings or ambiance of traditional library 'reading rooms' panelled in wood, with their rows of desks and chairs.

The stated ambitions and the many subsequent design choices including the book ramp transformed the form, use and meaning of 'library' as traditionally understood, making it one that would address the needs and role of a 21st century library. The design of the library's form emerged directly from careful examination of what the library should do and not vice versa. Since the form of the building is so striking and unusual, critics who were not aware of the process behind the design or of how fully the building met client needs were quick to assume that the design resulted only from concerns over form. Joshua Ramus remembers the response of some journalists to the photograph of the model of the building, journalists who had not attended the architect's public presentation of the thinking behind the design, 'When they saw the picture they came to the conclusion, "This is just fancy pants architecture. Our money is getting wasted. It's all about the architect's ego".' But in their interviews with journalists the librarians disagreed, saying, 'No, it's everything we need.' The journalists did not realise that once needs are addressed to the client's full satisfaction, there is an opportunity for the form to be surprising and unexpected (see Chapter 2).

Scrutinising Form and Use

Transformation of a building type can result from questioning the purpose of a type and of the roles it fulfils, as Te Papa, the Seattle Central Library and the National Museum of the American Indian illustrate. A transformed type also arises from close scrutiny of a type's conventional physical and spatial characteristics or its patterns of use. The designers of Chelsea and Westminster Hospital in London transformed the conventional physical and spatial features of a hospital in response to very demanding requirements: to design a hospital that could be built very quickly, on a tight urban site and that would not rely completely on air conditioning. These constraints stimulated a rethinking of what a hospital could be like physically. Similarly, when starting their work with the Dallas Theater Center, architects from REX did not ask the general question 'What should a theatre be?' Unlike the architects for Chelsea and Westminster, however, they did not start by analysing how the form of the new building should be different. Instead, they started with issues of use: what should the new theatre be able to do?

A Hospital with a Heart

We walked into a tall glass atrium filled with light. The air felt fresh. A colourful mobile moved ever so gently above us. 'This isn't a hospital,' Karen exclaimed to Teresa, 'this is an art gallery with some beds added!' But Chelsea and Westminster is a hospital, of 1 million square feet (4,290 sqaure metres), with 665 beds and 70 departments, built completely to the edges of its tight site. The cathedral-like naturally lit atrium, the exposed elevator landings and open walkways radically changed the conventional form of a hospital. These innovations arose from the architects' initial response to requirements in the competition brief: that there be thermal efficiency, economical use of services particularly a reduced dependency on air-conditioning and that town

Sian Tucker, Falling Leaves, Chelsea and Westminster Hospital, London. The building is filled with art, even in the operating theatres. The Ethylene-tetra-fluoro-ethylene (ETFE) foil roof fills the atrium with light.

planning height limitations apply on the already small site. Then, once the building opened, the new form invited activities highly unusual for a hospital setting (see Chapter 5).

As Anthony Furlong of Sheppard Robson explained to Teresa, hospitals are usually solid, enclosed buildings, which therefore contain many dark spaces and endless corridors and depend on air conditioning throughout. In preparing their competition entry, Sheppard Robson acknowledged that some spaces required air conditioning, such as the operating theatre but they asked, 'Why do you need to air-condition wards?' Having operable windows in the wards would reduce running costs and would give patients both light and air. So the architects said, 'Rather than making it all solid, let's open it up.' Wards, departments and outpatient services are located around the periphery of the building. Circulation rings the atrium on each floor with bridges, open landings to the glass elevators and open walkways that replace conventional enclosed corridors. Moving along these routes, patients, staff and visitors always have a view of the atrium and contact with the light, air and vista it offers.

Designing and building the atrium generated multiple innovations in the choice of materials and systems. Sheppard Robson chose ETFE (ethylene-tetra-fluoro-ethylene) foil for the roof, formed into air-filled cushions that have insulating qualities equivalent to triple glazing, supported on a light-weight aluminium structure. Up to then ETFE, had been used exclusively in theme parks and zoos. It is chemically inert, does not degrade… and allows ultra violet rays through which kill bacteria – a great advantage for hospitals.[28] In winter heat from the sun is collected in the atrium to heat the wards, which is supplemented by a combined heat and power system that is connected to that national electricity grid. Electricity can either be put into the grid or taken out depending on the hospital's requirements.[29] Ventilation is controlled through louvres at roof level; dampers at ground level supply fresh air from the outside. In summer, the air in the atrium and in the wards is cooled by natural ventilation through high louvres, but laboratories and operating theatres are kept at a constant temperature with filtered air conditioning.

The built form of the hospital set the stage for transformations in use and image. Before it opened, Allen Jones's sculpture *The Acrobat*, was placed in the atrium and 2,000 original works of art were hung throughout the building – in the atrium, on operating theatre ceilings, in treatment and changing rooms. Susan Loppert, director of the hospital's arts programme after the hospital opened, advocated for art that would not only be a diversion to patients but would also challenge and engage them. And she expanded the programme to include the performing

Clean Break Company dancers perform for patients, staff and the public in the atrium of Chelsea and Westminster Hospital, London.

CHAPTER 6 TRANSFORMING • 183

arts. Performances held in the atrium now range from traditional jazz, folk and world music to full-scale operas, chamber music concerts, poetry readings, and dance. These events, two or three every week, are free and open to the public. Chairs are provided for a seated audience but patients and staff also watch and listen from the stairs, landings and walkways. The entire atrium becomes a place of performance.

With its seating areas, café, creche, shops, works of art and performances, the atrium relieves the monotony of hospital life. Naturally-lit, heated and ventilated and occupying a third of the building, it breathes life into the hospital. As the sun rises and sets and as clouds pass high above, the whole interior changes. At night the atrium is a special place. Teresa remembers passing from a ward through the atrium on her way to the operating theatre:

> It was one o'clock in the morning and dark. I just lay on my bed, which they rolled on to the lift. I could see out from the glass lift and then from that great high bridge. As we moved along, I could see the beautiful things hanging down and the lights sparkling. I felt like I was moving through the star-lit heavens. It was the most beautiful experience. Exquisite. Compare that with going along the usual hospital corridor – narrow, enclosed, with its glare of electric light.

Sheppard Robson designed the lighting standards for the bridges and balconies to continue the indoor outdoor theme of the atrium; they do have a twinkling, star-like quality at night.

The magic world of the bridge at night, Chelsea and Westminster Hospital, London.

Building requirements that might have been treated as restricting design possibilities instead opened a path to discovery and the trans-*form*-ation of a building type. Although the conventional design of wards and departments was not modified, the radically different overall form of the building offers myriad opportunities for activities and experiences not usually found in hospitals. Chelsea and Westminster set a precedent for other hospitals. The Royal Alexandra Children's Hospital in Brighton, designed by the Building Design Partnership, and the Evelina Children's Hospital at St Thomas's in London, designed by Hopkins Architects, are both organised around a central atrium that provides natural light and ventilation. In both, the atrium is the site of a café, art exhibitions and live performances.

A Theatre as a Tool

When the Dallas Theater Center was located in a building designed as a steel shed, all kinds of physical interventions were routinely made to the building to stage productions. Joshua Ramus of REX explained to Karen that for a production of *The Cherry Orchard*:

> They wanted a well in the middle of the stage. They brought in a backhoe through the back and dug a 20-foot well right through the centre of the stage. That kind of physical manipulation is exciting to the best artistic directors and the best stage actors in the US so they got them all.

Indeed, as the architects discovered, it was that capacity to make radical physical manipulations to the building that had helped generate the theatre's national reputation. It was also possible in the steel shed to stage proscenium, thrust and flat-floor productions, until rising labour costs made that difficult. These qualities of the former building, key to its reputation, made designing a new one risky. A new building could make the flexibility of the old one far more difficult, if not impossible, to achieve. As Joshua put it, 'Our role is to show up and build you guys a wonderful building that sends you back in to the dark ages?' So one of the key positions the architects and client took at the beginning of the project was to design a 'new, beautiful, exciting and pristine' building that would be so physically flexible that it could offer all the freedoms of the old building, quickly and without the costs incurred by extensive and expensive union labour.

To meet this challenge the architects questioned the most fundamental assumptions about the organisation of space in theatres: that the entrance, ticketing and lobby are located in the 'front of house' and that the fly tower, shop, costume fabrication and all backstage functions are located in the 'back of house' with the 'house' – stage and seating – in between the two (called 'chamber' in the architects' diagram). In their proposal, back of house functions are moved to be above the chamber (performing area and seating) and front of house functions are placed below. With sophisticated built-in equipment, radical changes in the arrangement of seating and stage are possible with the touch of a button to stage thrust, proscenium and flat-floor productions. As importantly, the perimeter of the house is now open to a wide variety of possibilities.

> If you want to bring in elephants for the last act of *Aida*, you can do that. If you want to see downtown in the last act of *Hamlet* but not hear it, you can do that … And if someday you want to do Beckett and have no walls at all and have birds flying into the stage, you can do that too.

SUPERFLY STAGE

As Joshua puts it, 'We made a tool. Our architectural statement was a tool that gives the artistic director and the managing director freedom to invent.' The theatre is also a tool for earning additional revenue. With the configuration of a completely flat floor and no seating, the theatre can lease out the space for events such a s car shows or corporate Christmas parties in the afternoon and still do a show in the evening.

REX, Dee and Charles Wyly Theater, Dallas, 2010. ABOVE The design transforms the traditional theatre by placing all support spaces above or below the performing/seating area and exposing that area on all sides.

REX, Dee and Charles Wyly Theater, Dallas, 2010. Seating and performance space can be easily changed mechanically to create different configurations. Enclosing walls can be closed or open. RIGHT No seating at all. With wall open, the theatre can be used for a car show. BELOW Tiered seating arrangement at intermission.

By understanding how the theatre company used its previous venue as a *tool* for productions, the architects were able to identify what the new theatre had to do, that is, what the company needs to accomplish through their manipulations of space. By designing a new arrangement of spaces and a new kind of perimeter 'wall' for the seating/performing areas, and by specifying the necessary equipment, the designers accommodated the flexibility of the previous building and dramatically extended the possibilities. They transformed both the form and the use of a theatre together, integrating what the theatre *is* physically, spatially and technologically with what it can *do*. Use and form are intertwined to create a new type of theatre.

> I have an agenda. It just so happens that my personal agenda is that we really like inventing and transforming type.
>
> Joshua Ramus, New York, November 2008

Transforming through Dialogue

Dialogue has the power to transform individuals, groups, ideas and designs. As people talk to each other 'on the level' sometimes for hours, weeks or months, they may feel as if nothing is being achieved. But something is: a context is being prepared or repaired, a shared mind is invisibly growing. Patrick de Maré, the British group analyst who developed the original theory of large dialogue groups, often said, 'Just talking is what is important'.[30]

Significant shifts occur through just talking. When Teresa is developing an initial design proposal she often discovers conflicting requirements. To relieve the pressure of an apparently insoluble conflict, she talks about these inconsistencies with the client. The clients, feeling their needs are being taken seriously, make suggestions. Even though their comments may not contribute directly to resolving the conflict, something is clarified. Then Teresa starts the process again, with less confusion; frequently something emerges that resolves the contradictions and holds the practical and dream qualities together.

While working on this book Teresa and Karen encountered many of the situations they were writing about. Karen recalls that:

> At one point each of us withdrew from the project and each other for several months. Then, luckily, we talked about our feelings of anxiety and discovered that both of us were afraid of the same thing – that whatever we wrote the other would reject. This simple airing of our fears relieved the tension and words began to flow again.

Teresa notes that when the flow of conversation is blocked, ideas and thoughts often seem stuck. This dynamic occurs in any working partnership from time to time, including that of client and architect. People may begin to feel upset or angry, unable to describe what is happening. The unexpressed feelings can contribute to extreme fatigue and limit creativity.

These key moments feel lifeless yet are also full of potential and need to be noticed. When working with groups, Teresa will ask a question to shift awareness or she will invite participants to write their thoughts and feelings

> [Transformation] is a free play of the mind, an invention outside the logical processes.
>
> Jacob Bronowski, 'The logic of the mind', *American Scientist*, vol 54, 1966, p 6

down on slips of papers and post them anonymously for all to read. From her noticing and asking a strategic question, something usually shifts. Intervening in this way takes thoughtful attention and skill. Timing is also important and demands the capacity to 'contain' difficult feelings for long periods of time. Containing means taking in what is said – both the words and the feelings that accompany them – metabolising the feelings and waiting for the right moment to talk about what appears to be happening.

Meetings of tenants at Ethelred Estate in Lambeth, London started out as consultations to discuss the proposed refurbishment but, after the unspoken conflicts in the community were revealed and challenged, the meetings rapidly became community gatherings that provided much more (see Chapter 4 p 108). For the first time tenants slowly built themselves into a community and the meetings were a focus for this shift. Before long, tenants took over producing the community newsletter, which had been an outcome of one of the early meetings, and added their own news, recipes and tips. At every key stage of the design and building process, they organised celebration parties and invited everybody involved, including children.

Through talking people build relationships with one another; a context is created that reduces anxiety and makes creative work possible. Confidence grows, ideas begin to flow and the relationships generated form a crucible for change; it is a recursive process, a dance that continues. Group analysts call the environment that surrounds a relationship, a project or a workshop the 'matrix'. For the matrix to become a generative crucible, often painful differences and conflicts need to be faced, talked about and worked with to liberate the people involved from a tense and restricting atmosphere.

Dialogue Generates Possibilities

Ongoing dialogue creates a fertile ground for ideas. By talking and respecting the thoughts of others an arid desert becomes a rich garden of possibilities. In architectural projects individuals and groups as well as the designed environment can change as a result. *Design through Dialogue* presents myriad examples of this alchemy of dialogue with small projects for houses and schools and larger ones for museums and libraries.

At Ethelred Estate the physical changes were not particularly revolutionary. What was significant was that the people who became involved could express their concerns, be heard and be taken seriously and, as a result, something profound happened. The process of paying attention to people as individuals, engaging them in ongoing dialogue and helping them find meaning changes both the design of the building and the community around it. Through sensitive involvement, tenants at Ethelred changed not only their outer physical world but their inner emotional worlds as well.

There is movement, but it is not brought about by force … The movement is natural, arising spontaneously. For this reason the transformation of the old becomes easy. The old is discarded and the new is introduced. Both measures accord with time; therefore no harm results.

I Ching quoted in Fritjof Capra, *The Turning Point*, 1983, p 5

Swedish architect Mats Fahlander's original commission was to design a small inexpensive timber house at Vemdalen, a ski resort 500 miles north of Stockholm. Mats put far more work into this project than an architect normally would, but from his efforts and his client's a joint partnership developed and they generated a creative spirit that transformed the design and construction process. The time he and the client spent talking and getting to know each other created the context for an innovative design and a more ambitious project.

The client was initially open with Mats about the limits of his budget and Mats was able to respond with 'Let's go for it' and made an agreement with the client that his fee would be based on the initial budget. As a result of this agreement, they both felt secure in what rapidly became a joint venture. The client worked with Mats to save money by finding materials and components from all over Europe. Many disappointments occurred along the way but client and architect were able to tackle the difficulties together because 'they had become a really good team'. As Mats said, 'When you are able to struggle together it's not so hard. That takes a lot of the stress out! I enjoyed it very much. He was brave to dare. He always listened to my opinions and now he is getting something back.' Mats explained to Teresa,

> I think there were times when I felt I was crazy. I thought 'I shouldn't be here designing these things in the middle of the night. There's no way he is going to pay me for this.' But I did it anyway as far as I had the energy for it. In this case it did work because now he is presenting me to other clients, and he bought another site up there, and most likely I will design that house as well.

Mats Falander, House at ski resort, Vemdalen, Sweden, 2005. Much of the natural timber for the structure and furniture was sourced by the client.

Dialogue Reveals and Respects Difference

While working on this book Teresa recognised what different languages she and Karen speak:

> We had to negotiate not just American English versus UK and NZ English but two different professional languages as well and consequently two different ways of thinking and writing. My experience of the difficulty of bridging them put me in touch with how an architect must feel when a client meets 'my beautiful design' without a word of appreciation or how a client, who has been very clear about what she wants, is faced with a design that includes nothing that is important to her.

Differences of opinion between client and architect or within client groups are nearly inevitable. The question is not how to avoid them but how to respond to them. Most people prefer not to disagree or to notice when others disagree, hoping that differences will resolve themselves or just evaporate. But if differences are not revealed and respected, fresh thinking becomes impossible. In order to draw differences out and transform them, participants need to be willing to voice their thoughts.

Because the architecture firm Bohlin Cywinski Jackson in Seattle appreciates the value of revealing and respecting difference, the firm always requests that members of couples who seek its design services for a new house fill out separate questionnaires, independently of each other, to describe how they live, how they use space and what they seek in a new house. This way, if there are differences, they are revealed and can become opportunities for design. If the couple were to fill out a single joint questionnaire, these differences would disappear into what could be a consensus or a compromise. According to Robert Miller, one of the architects from Bohlin Cywinski Jackson who designed a weekend house in Steamboat Springs, Colorado, the wife envisioned a tranquil place, with quiet sleeping places for their children. In contrast the husband imagined a lively, social space where the children might stay up all night playing board games. As Robert explained, the couple described conventional bedrooms but 'emotionally they had very different conceptions'. He suggests, 'It's important not to jump to conclusions but to sit back and listen and understand what the problem really is.'

After the architects discovered that husband and wife held opposite views for their new house, they developed a design that addressed both visions. Two small bunkrooms for quiet, introspective time open on to a shared and possibly noisy space for group activities. Each small room, 9 x 10 feet (2.7 x 3 metres), offers a bed, a closet, shelving, pin-up space and drawers under the bed with additional platform space for a sleeping bag for a sleepover. A swing door can be closed, revealing the pin-up space and drawings on the inside surface. When open to the common play space, the bunkrooms, called 'pods', look neat and tidy.

Bohlin, Cywinski Jackson, Threshold House, Steamboat Springs, Colorado, 2010. With the design of two flexible bunkrooms, a weekend house accommodates both the need for quiet, introspective time and the possibility of noisier group activities.

Although many people understand that the outcome of difference and even conflict can be creative, most avoid it. Architect Mark Gillem, however, realises that conflict among stakeholders in a project needs to be respected and explored.

> It's like the *Wizard of Oz*. They all have different goals. One wants to go back to Kansas. The scarecrow wants a brain. They have different goals but their one objective

is to get to the wizard. I tell these groups that it's OK to have different goals. You want to have 50,000 square feet. Fine. And you want to save the historic building. So let's figure out how all these can be met in one objective. And it usually works. And the personal allegations and attacks – let's just put that aside.

How architects respond to disagreements with clients is equally important. Architect Edward Cullinan is not only open to criticism from clients, he actually seeks it with his initial design proposals, particularly when the client consists of a group of people.

> I've discovered that much the best thing when a large number of people are going to be involved is to go public straight away with your first thoughts and let them express their ideas – draw their fire and let everybody have their say and their howl. Then you develop the schemes or do other schemes as a result of that so-called debate … it is very painful at times because you always get hacked to bits in the first round. So you go public, get hacked to bits in round one and only after that do you start piecing together a scheme.[31]

Edward Cullinan Architects, St Mary's Church, Barnes, London, 1984. In designing the new church after a fire, Cullinan listened carefully to the parishioners' differing views about how the church should be rebuilt and took strong criticism from them of his initial design. BELOW, FROM LEFT: Plan of original medieval church; plan and axon of Victorian church. BOTTOM FROM LEFT: Elements retained in 1980s' redesign; elements added; as built (see also Chapter 3 p 82).

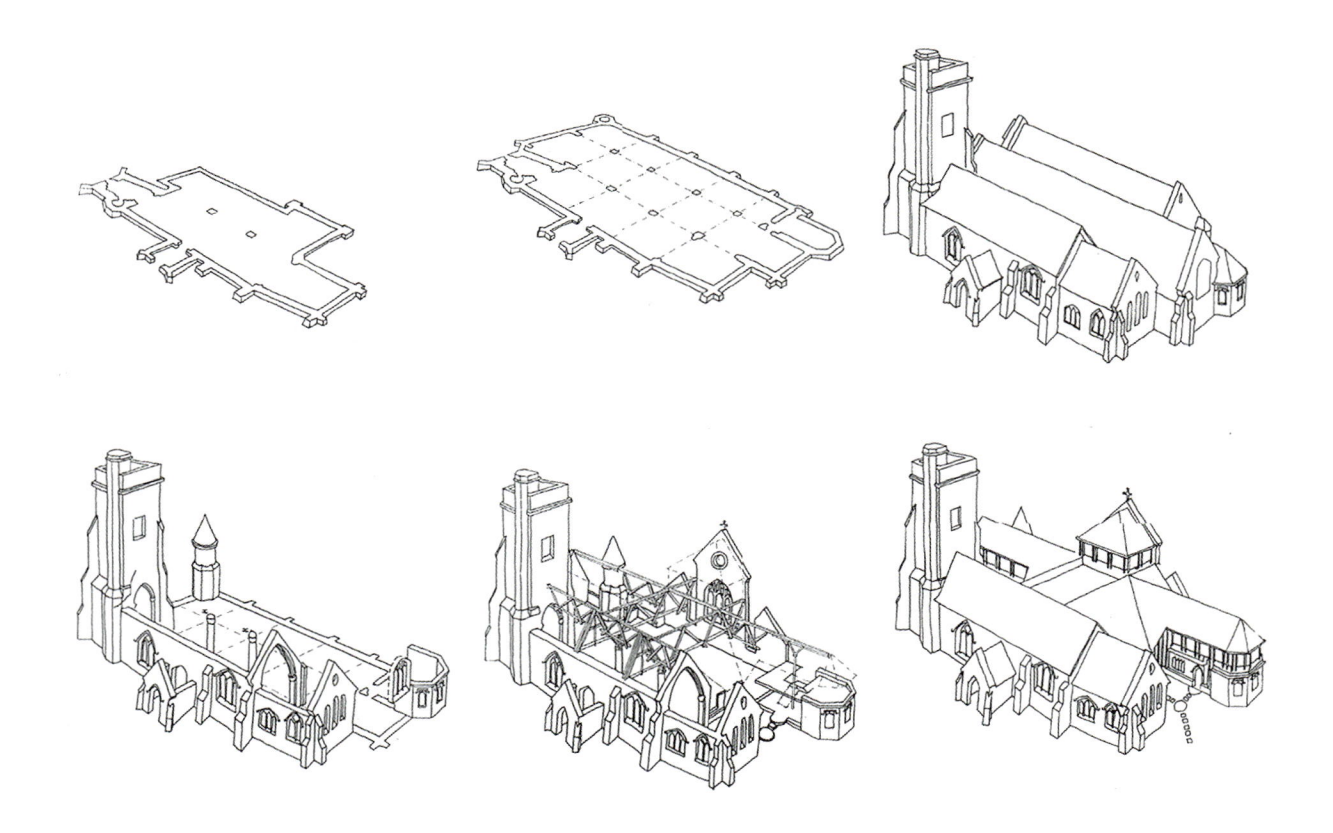

CHAPTER 6 TRANSFORMING • 191

Many architects, however, view objections as a threat, as something they need to defend against, and consequently try to persuade the other party of their (correct) point of view. To add to the natural propensity to avoid conflict, most architectural students are taught to defend ideas rather than to enquire or to listen. Adversarial approaches to practice already built into our culture are reinforced in architectural education in student design reviews. In these sessions, often called 'juries', there is an implied and sometimes not so implied judgement of right or wrong and guilty or not guilty. Through these 'courts of judgement' students learn to be defensive and protective not only of their designs but of themselves as well, learning skills that close down the possibilities that a respect for difference can engender.

Difference as a Path to Something New

Transformation comes from accepting tension as inevitable to the creative process and working with the tension until something shifts and the creative product slots into place. To engage in this process requires that the designer, or the writer, step back and watch the entire picture, holding the tension of not reacting immediately or jumping in to relieve the pressure. This holding allows something new to emerge – new insights, new possibilities.

The differences Karen and Teresa discovered and struggled with during the creation of this book also became paths to something new, as long as they could bear the tensions with patience. Karen remembers that at first she found the importance Teresa placed on the nature of the relationship between client and architect excessive.

> Every time I drafted any text, Teresa would add material to it, usually at the beginning, describing the importance of the relationship. I was a bit resistant. Finally, I got the point and 'Relating' became its own chapter, towards the beginning of the book. And then, from that decision, we realized that the other chapters could explore other angles of the designing and briefing process, overlapping but different, all active. As we have emphasized throughout the book, from a difference something quite unexpected emerged – an unusual way of structuring the book.

A design requirement or a site constraint may also stimulate creative tension. An empty lot in lower Manhattan will eventually be a luxury residential tower but for the three to five year period before construction begins, the landowner is willing to provide the space to display sculpture, with two caveats. The new space should not look 'too permanent' or have a name that implies it is permanent (like park or garden) and it must be completely enclosed by a fence. With input from their two clients, the landowner and the Lower Manhattan Cultural Council, the firm Interboro transformed what a 'fence' can be. On the east side of what will be called 'Lent Space', which faces a city park, the fence will consist of 8-foot (2.4 metre) high panels of marine-grade plywood. Each panel will be able to pivot to: (1) form a completely closed boundary (at night); (2) open passageways that allow people to use the new space as a shortcut from office buildings to the subway entrance; and (3) create a loggia-like situation that blurs the boundary between Lent Space and the sidewalk. Each panel incorporates a bench and openings at eye level to offer views in to or out of the new space. Depending upon how the panel is oriented these benches can face each other, face the same direction or face in opposite directions.

Interboro, Lent Space, New York, 2010. A temporary space for sculpture display in Tribeca is enclosed on one side by a 'fence' of movable panels, fitted with benches and windows. Panels can be placed in a great variety of positions creating different arrangements of the benches.

When differences are revealed, respected and explored, the new and unexpected can emerge. Instead of treating objections to a design as a threat and trying to close them down, they are treated as an opportunity to learn.[32] Holding opposites or apparent contradictions and the resulting tensions rather than compromising or choosing one over the other allows something new to emerge that otherwise may not have seen the light of day. The tension between different ideas generates what John Hunt describes as 'a kind of alchemy'.[33]

As the construction of Te Papa was nearing completion and the opening was looming, the museum board still needed to agree upon a logo. After the graphic designers had proposed many designs to the board, one design emerged as a strong contender: an x.[34] The designers explained that the proposed design was inspired by the handwritten mark Māori chiefs, unable to write their names, used to sign the Treaty of Waitangi. One Pākehā member commented appreciatively that it resembled 'x marks the spot' and many other Pākehā board members liked the design as well. Finally one of the Māori members of the board pointed out its negative connotations. Apirama Mahuika explained that he had received many 'crosses' at school signifying failure and felt insulted by the proposed logo. One of the designers, who was Pākehā, replied that Apirama was reading too much into the image.

The atmosphere in the meeting grew tense. Cheryl Sotheran was adamant that the museum could not adopt a symbol that was perceived to represent the oppression of Māori. As the entire purpose of the project

CHAPTER 6 TRANSFORMING • 193

was to create a bicultural museum that portrayed the stories, narratives and treasures of two cultures, the logo had to respond to the lives and perceptions of both peoples. She insisted that the design team develop an alternative. The graphic designers resisted Sotheran's insistence, muttering, 'We need something to be excited by. We shouldn't be designing the logo by committee'. As a result of Sotheran's respect for difference, her willingness to persevere despite opposition and her belief that something new would emerge, it did. The final logo resembles both a thumbprint, which is also a kind of signature, and a contour map of a mountain, perhaps Tongariro, one of New Zealand's many volcanoes.

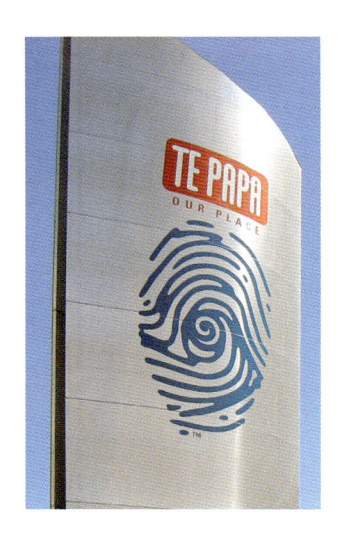

Jasmax, Te Papa Tongarewa Museum of New Zealand, Wellington 1993. The logo resembles a thumbprint and a contour map of a mountainous landform, perhaps the sacred mountain of Tongariro on New Zealand's north island.

NOTES

1. Ross W Ashby, *An Introduction to Cybernetics*, Chapman & Hall, (London), 1956, p 43.
2. Eva Hagberg, 'The long approach', *Metropolis*, July 2005, pp 130, 131, 156–7.
3. Roger S Ulrich, 'Health benefits of gardens in hospitals'. Paper presented at Plants for People conference, International Exhibition, Florida 2002; Roger S Ulrich, 'Visual landscapes and psychological well-being', *Landscape Research*, vol 4, 1979 pp 17–23.
4. Clare Cooper Marcus and Marni Barnes, *Healing Gardens: Therapeutic Benefits and Design Recommendations*, John Wiley & sons Inc (New York), 1999.
5. For initial reading on systems thinking, refer to Gregory Bateson, *Steps to an Ecology of Mind: Collected Essays in Anthropology, Psychiatry, Evolution, and Epistemology*, University of Chicago Press (Chicago), 1972.
6. Paul W Watzlawick, John Weakland and Richard Fisch, *Change: Principles of Problem Formation and Problem Resolution*, WW Norton (New York), 1974, p 12.
7. Karen A Franck, 'Types are us', in Karen A Franck and Lynda H Schneekloth, eds, *Ordering Space: Types in Architecture and Design*, Van Nostrand Reinhold (New York), 1994.
8. Ibid.
9. Tom Dixon, *The Museum of New Zealand Te Papa Tongarewa Building Design Brief*, Pepper Dixon Associates (Auckland), 1990, vol 1, p 1.
10. Ibid, vol 4, p 18.
11. Tom Dixon, *The Concept for the Museum of New Zealand Te Papa Tongarewa* (for the Architect Selection Competition), Pepper Dixon Associates (Auckland), 1989, p 1.
12. Thelma A Rogers, 'House of Biculturalism: A Study of the Cultural Constructs of Māori and Pākehā', A sub-thesis submitted in partial fulfilment of the B Arch University of Auckland, 1989, p 49.
13. The chair of the selection panel was California architect Joseph Esherick. The other members of the panel were: George MacDonald, a museum director from Ottawa; Richard Thorp, an Australian architect; John Hunt, lecturer in architecture at Auckland University; Ihakara Puketapu from the

Department of Internal Affairs and advocate for things Māori; Apirama Mahuiaka, a Māori sociologist from Gisborne and Chair of Ngati Porou; and Margaret Trotter, a company director and art curator from Wellington.

14 John Hunt, 'Process of selection', *Architecture New Zealand: Special Edition: The Designing of Te Papa*, February 1998, p 15.
15 Peter Bossley, 'Redirect, redevelop', *Architecture New Zealand: Special Edition*, p 23.
16 Cliff Whiting quoted in Anne French, 'Setting standards', ibid, p 72.
17 Cliff Whiting quoted, ibid, p 69.
18 Ibid, p 70.
19 Ibid, p 8.
20 Venturi, Scott Brown and Associates, *The Way of the People: National Museum of the American Indian (Master Facilities Programming, Phase I)*, Office of Design and Construction, Smithsonian Institution (Washington DC), 1991, p 2.
21 Ibid, p 3.
22 Ibid, p 103.
23 Richard W West, 'As long as we keep dancing', in Duane Blue Spruce, ed, *Spirit of a Native Place*, National Geographic (Washington DC), 2004, p 55.
24 George Horse Capture, 'The way of the people,' in Duane Blue Spruce, ed, *Spirit of a Native Place*.
25 Judith Ostrowitz, 'Concourse and periphery: Planning the National Museum of the American Indian', *American Indian Quarterly*, summer/fall 2005, pp 384–425.
26 OMA/LMN Concept Book, www.spl.org
27 Ibid.
28 Denise Chevin, 'Medical breakthrough, on site: Chelsea and Westminster Hospital', *Building*, 25 January 1991, pp 52–4
29 'The healthy hospital: We report, building analysis: Chelsea and Westminster Hospital', *Building Services*, July 1992, pp 19–22.
30 Patrick de Maré was one of Teresa's teachers in large-group analysis.
31 Edward Robbins, *Why Architects Draw*, MIT Press (Cambridge), 1994, p 61
32 Jeremy Till, 'The negotiation of hope,' in Peter Blundell Jones, Doina Petrescu and Jeremy Till, eds, *Architecture and Participation*, Spon Press (Oxford), 2005.
33 John Hunt, 'Process of selection', *Architecture New Zealand Special Edition*' p 16.
34 *Getting to Our Place*, Gaylene Preston Productions for New Zealand on Air (Wellington, New Zealand), 1999.

Architects and Clients

To gather information about the dialogue that shapes design, Teresa and Karen interviewed architects and clients in the UK, the US, Sweden, New Zealand, Israel and Hong Kong. Locations and dates listed below indicate the place and time of each interview.

Karen interviewed:

Brodie Bain and Bob Mohr, Mithun, Seattle, Washington, May 2005
Glynis Berry and Hideaki Ariizumi, studio a/b architects, Orient New York, June 2005 and November 2008
Louise Braverman, architect, New York, June 2006
Duane Blue Spruce, Facilities Planning Coordinator, George Gustav Heye Center, New York, March 2006
Christie Coffin, The Design Partnership, Berkeley, California, October 2005
Lauren Crahan, Freecell, Brooklyn, New York, July 2006
Justin Estoque, Director of Executive Planning Office, National Museum of the American Indian, Washington, DC, June 2006
Mark Gillem, architect, Oakland, California, October 2005
Diana Gordon, client of studio a/b architects, Greenport, New York, November 2008
Alex Harris, Director of Capital Fund, Seattle Central Library, Seattle, May 2005
John Hartmann, Freecell, Brooklyn, New York, July 2006
Denise Ho, architect, Hong Kong, March 2004 and Istanbul, June 2005
Johnpaul Jones, Jones and Jones Architecture and Landscape Architecture, Seattle, May 2005
Rosa Lane, architect, Berkeley, California, October 2005
Kava Massih, Kava Massih Architects, Berkeley, California, April 2006
Robert Miller, Bohlin Cywinski Jackson, Vera Cruz, Mexico, June 2008
Michael Mostoller, architect, Newark, New Jersey, November 2007
John Nesholm and Sam Miller, LMN Architects, Seattle, Washington, May 2006
Kristin Prentice, Chair of Site Committee for Rosa Parks Elementary School, Berkeley, California, April 2006
Michael Pyatok, Pyatok Architects, Oakland, California, October 2005
Joshua Ramus, REX, New York, November 2008
Denise Scott Brown, Venturi, Scott Brown Architects and Associates , Architects and Planners, Philadelphia, January 2008
Deborah Seidman and Lina Belle Seidman, clients of studio a/b architects, Orient, New York, June 2005
Joy Siegel, architect, Newark, New Jersey, November 2007
Georgeen Theodore, Interboro Partners, Brooklyn, New York, July 2008

Teresa interviewed:
Karl Alexanderson, White Arkitektur Stockholm, February 2008
Helen Bunder-Smith, Sheppard Robson, London, December 2008
Bob Allies, Allies and Morrison, London, September 2005
Trish Barry, psychologist, Winchester, UK, May 2007
Edward Cullinan, Edward Cullinan Associates, London, November 2005
Tom Dixon, Pepper Dixon Architects, Auckland, September 2005
Mats Fahlander, Mats Fahlander Arkitekt AB, Stockholm, May 2007
Anthony Furlong, Sheppard Robson Architects, London, December 2008
Ken Gorbey, exhibition designer for Te Papa Tongarewa, Wellington, New Zealand, April 2005
Judy Green and Carl Berg, clients of Jeremiah Eck, New Malden, Massachusetts, December 2007
Emma Gribble, architect and MA student at Bartlett School, London, July 2007
Guy Hermann, Director of Museum Planning, E Verner Johnson and Associates, Boston, November 2005
Helen Hitman, client of Nick Taylor, Francis Group Architects, Russell, Bay of Islands, New Zealand, October 2007, April and October 2008
Tim Hooson, Jasmax Architects, Auckland, April 2008
John Hunt, Professor of Architecture, Auckland University, Auckland, October 2007
Ada Karmi-Melamede, Ada Karmi-Melamede Architects, Tel Aviv, April 2006
Ram Karmi, Ram Karmi Architects, Tel Aviv, April 2006
Hans Landström, psychologist, Health Garden, Stockholm, October 2005
Ivan Mercep, Jasmax Architects, Auckland, October 2007
Maria Nordenberg, client of Mats Fahlander, Stockholm, September 2007
Bo Olofzon and Minako Nakatsuma, clients of Mats Fahlander, Stockholm, December 2007
Kara Puketapu, former Secretary of Māori Affairs, member of selection panel for Te Papa Tongarewa, Wellington, New Zealand, April 2005
Paul Robinson, Davis Langdon, Auckland, October 2007
Jenny Ryding, architect, Stockholm, March 2005
Cheryl Sotheran, Joint Chief Executive of Te Papa Tongarewa, Wellington, New Zealand, September 2005
Nick Taylor, Francis Group Architects, Auckland, New Zealand, October 2007
Margaret Trotter, member of the selection panel for Te Papa Tongarewa, Wellington, New Zealand, April 2005
Sarah and Bob Williamson, clients of Teresa, West Norwood, London, September 2008
Alison and Jim Wilson, clients of Teresa, Epsom, UK, June 2005
Yvonne Westerberg, project leader, Health Garden, Stockholm, November 2006
Cliff Whiting, joint Chief Executive of Te Papa Tongarewa, Russell, Bay of Islands, New Zealand, October 2004 and October 2008

Bibliography

Anderson, Harlene, 'Dialogue: people creating meaning with each other and finding ways to go on', in Harlene Anderson and Diane Gehart, eds, *Collaborative Therapy: Relationships and Conversations that Make a Difference*, Routledge (New York), 2007

Anderson, Harlene, 'The heart and spirit of collaborative therapy', in Harlene Anderson and Diane Gehart, eds, *Collaborative Therapy: Relationships and Conversations that Make a Difference*, Routledge (New York), 2007

Ashby, Ross W, *An Introduction to Cybernetics*, Chapman & Hall (London), 1956

Balint, Michael, Enid Balint, Robert Gosling and Peter Hildebrand, *A Study of Doctors: Mutual Selection and the Evaluation of Results in a Training Programme for Family Doctors*, Mind and Medicine Monographs, Tavistock Publications (London), 1966

Bateson, Gregory, *Steps to an Ecology of Mind: Collected Essays in Anthropology, Psychiatry, Evolution, and Epistemology*, University of Chicago Press (Chicago), 1972

Bion, Wilfred R, *Experiences in Groups and Other Papers*, Tavistock Publications (London), 1961

Blue Spruce, Duane, ed, *Spirit of a Native Place: Building the National Museum of the American Indian*, National Geographic (Washington, DC), 2004

Blythe, Alastair and John Worthington, *Managing the Brief for Better Design*, Spon Press (London), 2001

Bohm, David, *On Dialogue*, Routledge (London), 1996

Bohm, David, Donald Factor and Peter Garrett, 'Dialogue – a proposal 1991', http://www.infed.org/archives/e-texts/bohm_dialogue.htm.

Bollas, Christopher, 'Architecture and the unconscious', *International Forum of Psychoanalysis*, vol 9, 2000, pp 28–42

Bolton, Gillie, *Reflective Practice: Writing and Professional Development*, Sage (London), 2005

Bossley, Peter, 'Concepts in culture' *Architect New Zealand*, Special Edition on the Designing of Te Papa, February 1998, pp 18–19

Bossley, Peter, 'Redirect, redevelop', *Architecture New Zealand: Special Edition on the Designing of Te Papa*, February 1998, pp 22–3

Bronowski, Jacob, 'The logic of the mind', *American Scientist*, vol 54, 1966, pp 1–14

Brownlee, David B. and David G. De Long, *Louis I. Kahn: In the Realm of Architecture*, Universe (New York), 1997

Buber, Martin, *I and Thou*, Touchstone (New York), 1996

Burns, George W, *Nature-Guided Therapy: Brief Integrative Therapies for Health and Well-Being*, Psychology Press (London), 1998

CABE (Commission for Architecture and the Built Environment), *Creating Excellent Buildings: A Guide for Clients*, CABE (London), 2003

Calman, Ross and Margaret Sinclair, *The Reed Essential Maori Dictionary*, Reed (Auckland), 1999

Capra, Fritjof, *The Turning Point: Science, Society, and the Rising Culture*, Bantam Press (New York), 1983
Capra, Fritjof, *The Web of Life: A New Synthesis of Mind and Matter*, Flamingo (London), 1997
Cherry, Edith, *Programming for Design: From Theory to Practice*, John Wiley & Sons Inc (New York), 1999
Chevin, Denise, 'Medical breakthrough, on site: Chelsea and Westminster Hospital', *Building*, 25 January 1991.
Cramer, James, P and Scott Simpson, *The Next Architect: A New Twist on the Future of Design*, Greenway Communications (Norcross, GA), 2007
Cross, Nigel, *Designerly Ways of Knowing*, Birkhäuser (Basel), 2007
Cuff, Dana, 'The social production of built form', *Environment and Planning D: Society and Space*, vol 7, 1989, pp 433–447
Cuff, Dana, *Architecture: The Story of Practice*, MIT Press (Cambridge, MA), 1991
Dalal, Farhad, *Taking the Group Seriously*, Jessica Kingsley (London), 1998
Davis, Madeleine, and David Wallbridge, *Boundary and Space: An Introduction to the Work of D. W. Winnicott*, Karnac Books (London), 1981
Dixon, Tom, *The Concept for the Museum of New Zealand Te Papa Tongarewa* (for the Architect Selection Competition), Pepper Dixon Associates (Auckland) 1989
Dixon, Tom, *The Museum of New Zealand Te Papa Tongarewa Building Design Brief*, Pepper Dixon Associates (Auckland), 1990
Dong, Andy, 'The enactment of design through language', *Design Studies*, vol 28, January 2007, pp 5–21
Dorst, Kees and Nigel Cross, 'Creativity in the design process: co-evolution of problem-solution', *Design Studies*, vol 22, no 5, September 2001, pp 425–37
Douglas, Angela, 'Mapping the matrix: Healing vision and communication', *Group Analysis*, vol 35, 2002, pp 89–103
Downing, Frances, *Remembrance and the Making of Places*, Texas A & M University Press (College Station, TX), 2001
Duerk, Donna, *Architectural Programming: Creative Techniques for Design Professionals*, Van Nostrand Reinhold (New York), 1993
Eastman, Chuck, 'Automated assessment of early concept designs', in Richard Garber, ed, *Closing the Gap: Information Models in Contemporary Design Practice*, *Architectural Design*, vol 79, no 2, 2009, pp 52–7
Eck, Jeremiah, *The Distinctive Home: A Vision of Timeless Design*, Taunton (Newtown, CT), 2006
Ellis, Russell and Dana Cuff, eds, *Architects' People*, Oxford University Press (Oxford), 1989
Faga, Barbara, *Designing Public Consensus*, John Wiley & Sons Inc (Hoboken, NJ), 2006
Findley, Lisa, *Building Change: Architecture, Politics and Cultural Agency*, Routledge (London), 2005
Fisher, Thomas R, *In the Scheme of Things: Alternative Thinking on the Practice of Architecture*, University of Minnesota Press (Minneapolis), 2000
Forester, John, 'Designing: Making sense together in practical conversations', *Journal of Architectural Education*, vol 38, 1985, pp 14–20
Forty, Adrian, *Words and Buildings: A Vocabulary of Modern Architecture*, Thames & Hudson (London), 2000
Foulkes, SH, *Introduction to Group-Analytic Psychotherapy*, Heinemann (London), 1948; Reprinted Karnac Books (London), 1983
Foulkes, SH, *Therapeutic Group Analysis*, Allen & Unwin (London), 1964; reprinted Karnac Books (London), 1984
Foulkes, Elizabeth, ed, *Selected Papers of S. H. Foulkes: Psychoanalysis and Group Analysis*, Karnac Books (London), 1990
Franck, Karen A, 'Types are us', in Karen A Franck and Lynda H Schneekloth, eds, *Ordering Space: Types in Architecture and Design*, Van Nostrand Reinhold (New York), 1994
Franck, Karen A and R Bianca Lepori, *Architecture from the Inside Out: From the Body, the Senses, the Site, and the Community*, Wiley-Academy (London), 2007

French, Anne, 'Setting standards', *Architecture New Zealand: Special Edition on the Designing of Te Papa*, February 1998

Friedman, Alice, *Women and the Making of the Modern House: A Social and Architectural History*, Harry N Abrams (New York), 1998

Garber, Richard, ed, *Closing the Gap: Information Models in Contemporary Design Practice, Architectural Design*, vol 79, no 2, 2009

Glatzer, Nahum N and Paul Mendes Flohr, eds, *Martin Buber: A Life of Dialogue*, Schocken (New York), 1991

Hack, Gary and Mitsy Canto, 'Collaboration and context in urban design', *Design Studies*, vol 5, May 1984, pp 178–84

Hagberg, Eva, 'The long approach', *Metropolis*, July 2005, pp 156–7

Hale, Jonathan, *Ends, Middles, Beginnings: The Work of Edward Cullinan Architects*, Black Dog (London), 2005

Hershberger, Robert G, *Architectural Programming and Predesign Manager*, McGraw-Hill (New York), 1999

Hildebrand, Grant with Ann and Leonard K Eaton, *Frank Lloyd Wright's Palmer House*, University of Washington Press, (Seattle), 2007

Hinshelwood, Robert, *What Happens in Groups*, Free Association Books (London), 1987

Hobson, Peter, The *Cradle of Thought: Exploring the Origins of Thinking*, Macmillan (London), 2002

Howard, Pierce J, *The Owner's Manual: Everyday Applications from Mind-Brain Research* Bard Press (Austin, TX), 2000

Hunt, John, 'Process of selection', *Architecture New Zealand*: *Special Edition on the Designing of Te Papa*, February 1998, p 15

Isaacs, William, 'Dialogue', in Peter M Senge, Art Kleiner, Charlotte Roberts, Richard Ross and Bryan Smith, eds, *The Fifth Discipline Fieldbook: Strategies and Tools for Building a Learning Organization*, Doubleday (New York), 1994

Isaacs, William, *Dialogue and the Art of Thinking Together*, Currency (New York), 1999

Israel, Toby, *Some Place Like Home: Using Design Psychology to Create Ideal Places*, Wiley-Academy (London), 2003

Jones, Johnpaul, 'Carved by wind and water' in Duane Blue Spruce, ed, *Spirit of a Native Place: Building the National Museum of the American Indian*, Smithsonian Institution and National Geographic (Washington, DC), 2004

Jones, Peter Blundell, Doina Petrescu and Jeremy Till, eds, *Architecture and Participation*, Spon Press (Oxford), 2005

Karmi-Melamede, Ada and David S Robins, *Ada Karmi-Melamede Architect: Life Sciences Buildings, Ben Gurion University of the Negev*, Birkhäuser (Basel), 2003

Krens, Thomas, 'Developing the museum for the 21st century: A vision becomes reality', in Peter Noever, ed, *Visionary Clients for a New Architecture*, Prestel (London), 2000

Kumlin, Robert R, *Architectural Programming: Creative Techniques for Design Professionals*, McGraw-Hill (New York), 1995

Latham, Michael, *Constructing the Team: Final Report of the Government/Industry Review of Procurement and Contractual Arrangements in the UK Construction Industry*, HMSO (London), 1994

Lawson, Bryan, *Design in Mind*, Architectural Press (Oxford), 1994

Lawson, Bryan, *How Designers Think*, Architectural Press (Oxford), third edition, 1997

Lawson, Bryan, *What Designers Know*, Architectural Press (Oxford), 2004

Lawson, B, M Phiri Bassanino and J Worthington, 'Intentions, practices and aspirations: Understanding learning in design', *Design Studies*, vol 24, July 2003, pp 327–39

Leslie, Thomas, *Louis I. Kahn: Building Art, Building Science*, George Braziller (New York), 2005

Lewis, Paul, Marc Tsurumaki and David Lewis, *Opportunistic Architecture*, Princeton Architectural Press (New York), 2007

Ligtelijn, Vincent, ed, *Aldo van Eyck: Works*, Birkhäuser (Basel), 1999

Linzey, Michael, 'A fault-line at Te Papa: the use of a metaphor', *Fabrications*, BNET UK, June 2007, p 7

Maister, David H, Charles H Green and Robert M Galford, *The Trusted Advisor*, Touchstone (New York), 2000

Marcus Clare Cooper, *House as a Mirror of Self: Exploring the Deeper Meaning of Home* Conari Books (Berkeley, CA), 1995

Marcus, Clare Cooper and Marni Barnes, *Healing Gardens: Therapeutic Benefits and Design Recommendations*, John Wiley & Sons Inc (New York), 1999

de Maré, Patrick, Robin Piper and Sheila Thompson, *Koinonia: From Hate through Dialogue to Culture in the Large Group*, Karnac Books (London), 1991

Mattern, Shannon, *The New Downtown Library: Designing with Communities*, University of Minnesota Press (Minneapolis), 2007

Maturana, Humberto R and Francisco J Varela, *The Tree of Knowledge: The Biological Roots of Human Understanding*, New Science Library, Shambala (Boston, MA), 1987

Medway, P and B Clark, 'Imaging the building: Architectural design as semiotic construction', *Design Studies*, vol 24, May 2003, pp 255–73

Miller, Jeffery C, *The Transcendent Function*, State University of New York (Albany), 2004

Milner, Marion, *On Not Being Able to Paint*, Heinemann (London), 1957

Mitchell, C Thomas, *User-Responsive Design: Reducing the Risk of Failure*, WW Norton (London), 2002

Molnos, Angela, 'A Psychotherapist's Harvest', 1998, http://www.net.klte.hu/~keresofi/psyth/psyhthr.html

Moody, Fred, 'The spiral', *Metropolis*, October 2004, pp 108–11

Moore, Charles, 'Working together to make something', *Architectural Record*, vol 172, no 2, 1984, pp 102–3

Murray, Peter, *The Saga of the Sydney Opera House*, Spon Press (London), 2004

Nasar, Jack L, Wolfgang FE Preiser and Thomas Fisher, *Designing for Designers: Lessons Learned from Schools of Architecture*, Fairchild Publications (New York), 2007

Neasbey, Mark, Roy Barton and John Knott, 'Value management' in Rick Best and Gerard de Valance, eds, *Building in Value*, Elsevier (Oxford), 1999

Nitsun, Morris, *The Anti-Group: Destructive Forces in the Group and their Creative Potential*, Routledge (London), 1996

Ogden, Thomas, 'On potential space', in Dodi Goldman, ed, *In One's Bones: The Clinical Genius of Winnicott*, Jason Aaronson (Northvale, NJ), 1993

OMA/LMN Concept Book, www.spl.org

Ostrowitz, Judith, 'Concourse and periphery: Planning the National Museum of the American Indian', *American Indian Quarterly*, summer/fall 2005, pp 384–425

Pallasmaa, Juhani, *Eyes of the Skin: Architecture and the Senses*, Academy Editions (London), 1996

Pallasmaa, Juhani 'From an archipelago of authenticity: The task of architecture in consumer culture', in Gregory Caicco, ed, *Architecture, Ethics, the Personhood of Place*, University Press of New England (Lebanon, NH), 2007

Palmer, Mickey, ed, *The Architects' Guide to Facility Programming*, Architectural Record Books (New York), 1981

Pena, William, William Caudill and John Focke, *Problem Seeking: An Architectural Programming Primer*, Cahners Books International (Boston, MA), 1977

Potteiger, Matthew and Jamie Purinton, *Landscape Narratives: Design Practices for Telling Stories*, John Wiley & Sons Inc (New York), 1998

Prasad, Sunand, *Transformations: The Architecture of Penoyre & Prasad*, Black Dog (London), 2007

Preiser, Wolfgang FE, *Programming the Built Environment*, Van Nostrand Reinhold (New York), 1985

Pressman, Andrew, *Curing the Fountainheadache: How Architects and their Clients Communicate*, Sterling (New York), 2006

Pruitt, Bettye and Philip Thomas, *Democratic Dialogue – A Handbook for Practitioners*, GS/DAS (Washington, DC), 2007

Reid, Giles, 'Museo-logic' *Architecture New Zealand: Special Edition on the Design of Te Papa*, February 1998, pp 32–8

Robbins, Edward, *Why Architects Draw*, MIT Press (Cambridge, MA), 1994

Roberts, Jeff P, 'Foulkes' concept of the matrix', *Group Analysis*, vol 2, no 15, 1982, pp 111–26

Robinson, Julia Williams and J Stephen Weeks, 'Programming as design', *Journal of Architectural Education*, vol 37, 1983, pp 5–11

Robinson, Julia Williams, 'The question of type', in Karen A Franck and Lynda H Schneekloth, eds, *Ordering Space: Types in Architecture and Design*, Van Nostrand Reinhold (New York), 1994

Rogers, Thelma A, 'House of Biculturalism: A Study of the Cultural Constructs of Māori and Pākehā', sub-thesis submitted in partial fulfilment of the BArch, University of Auckland, 1989

Ruesh, Jurgen and Gregory Bateson, *Communication: The Social Matrix of Psychiatry*, Norton (New York), 1951

Salisbury, Frank, *Briefing Your Architect*, Architectural Press (Oxford), 1990

Schneekloth, Lynda H and Karen A Franck 'Type: prison or promise?' in Karen A Franck and Lynda H Schneekloth, eds, *Ordering Space: Types in Architecture and Design*, Van Nostrand Reinhold (New York), 1994

Schneekloth, Lynda H and Robert G Shibley, *Placemaking: The Art and Practice of Building Communities*, John Wiley & Sons Inc (New York), 1995

Schön, Donald A, *The Reflective Practitioner: How Professionals Think in Action*, Basic Books (New York, 1983

Schön, Donald A, 'Problems, frames and perspectives on designing', *Design Studies*, vol 5, July 1984, pp 132–6

Schön, Donald A, *Educating the Reflective Practitioner: Toward a New Design for Teaching and Learning in the Professions*, Jossey-Bass (San Francisco), 1987

Schön, Donald A, 'Designing Rules, types and worlds', *Design Studies*, vol 9, July 1988, pp 181–90

Schön, Donald A and Glenn Wiggins, 'Kinds of seeing and their functions in designing', *Design Studies*, vol 13, April 1992, pp 135–56

Seymour, Jane, Hillary Cotton, Grace Comely, Barbara Annesley and Sanjiv Lingayak, *School Works Tool Kit*, School Works Kit (London), 2001

Sharon, Yosef, *The Supreme Court Building, Jerusalem*, trans Alexandra Mahler, Yad Hanadiv (Israel), 1993

Silber, John, *Architecture of the Absurd: How 'Genius' Disfigured a Practical Art*, Norton (New York), 2007

Sluzki, Carlos E, 'A reflective consultation and some changes that resulted from it', *Human Systems*, vol 7, 1996, pp 103–16

Smith, Kendra Schrank, *Architects' Sketches: Dialogue and Design*, Elsevier (London), 2008

Song, Richard, 'Charles Moore and his clients: Designing St. Matthew's in Eugene J Johnson, ed, *Charles Moore: Buildings and Projects 1949–1986*, Rizzoli (New York), 1986

Steele, James, *Architecture in Detail: Salk Institute*, Phaidon (London), 1993

Stern, Daniel N, *The Interpersonal World of the Infant: A View from Psychoanalysis and Developmental Psychology*, Basic Books (New York), 1985

Stern, Daniel N, *The Present Moment in Psychotherapy and Everyday Life*, Norton (New York), 2004

Storr, Anthony, *The Dynamics of Creation*, Penguin (London), 1972

Stratford, Stephen, *Jasmax*, New Zealand Architectural Publications Trust (Auckland), 2007

Strauven, Francis, *Aldo Van Eyck: The Shape of Relativity*, Architecture & Natura Press (Amsterdam), 1998

Stumpf, SC and JT McDonnell, 'Talking about team framing', *Design Studies*, vol 23, 2001, pp 5–23

Sudjic, Deyan, *The Edifice Complex: How the Rich and Powerful Shape the World*, Penguin Press (New York), 2005

Tagore, Rabindranath, *Gitanjali: Song Offerings*, Full Circle (New Dehli), 2002,

Taleb, Nassim Nicholas, *The Black Swan: The Impact of the Highly Improbable*, Allen Lane (Camberwell, Australia), 2007

Tauroa, Hiwi and Pat Tauroa, *Te Marae: A Guide to Customs and Protocol*, Reed (Auckland), 1986

'The healthy hospital: We report, building analysis: Chelsea and Westminster Hospital', *Building Services*, July 1992, pp 19–22

The Architectural League of New York, 'Interboro' in *Young Architects 7: Situating*, Princeton Architectural Press (New York), 2006

Thompson, Sheila, *The Group Context*, Jessica Kingsley (London), 1999

Tilly, Charles, *Why?* Princeton University Press (Princeton, NJ), 2006

Till, Jeremy, 'The negotiation of hope', in Peter Blundell Jones, Doina Petrescu and Jeremy Till, eds, *Architecture and Participation*, Spon Press (Oxford), 2005

Ulrich, Roger S, 'Visual landscapes and psychological well-being', *Landscape Research*, vol 4, 1979, pp 17–23

Van der Voordt, Theo JM, and Herman BR van Wegen, *Architecture in Use: An Introduction to the Programming, Design and Evaluation of Buildings*, Elsevier (Oxford), 2005

Venturi, Scott Brown and Associates, *The Way of the People: National Museum of the American Indian (Master Facilities Programming, Phase 1)* Office of Design and Construction, Smithsonian Institution (Washington DC), 1991

Venturi, Scott Brown and Associates, *The Way of the People: National Museum of the American Indian (Master Facilities Programming, Phase 2)* Office of Design and Construction, Smithsonian Institution, (Washington DC), 1993

Ward, Jacob, 'The making of a library: The research', *Metropolis*, October 2004, pp 98–101

Watzlawick, Paul, Janet Helmick Beavin and Don Jackson, *Pragmatics of Human Communication: A Study of Interactional Patterns, Pathologies and Paradoxes*, Norton (New York), 1967

Watzlawick, Paul W, John Weakland and Richard Fisch, *Change: Principles of Problem Formation and Problem Resolution*, WW Norton (New York), 1974

West, W Richard, 'As long as we keep dancing', in Duane Blue Spruce, ed, *Spirit of a Native Place: Building the National Museum of the American Indian*, National Geographic (Washington, DC), 2004

Wheelan, Susan A, *Facilitating Training Groups: A Guide to Leadership and Verbal Intervention Skills*, Praeger (New York), 1990

Wheelan, Susan A, *Group Processes: A Developmental Perspective*, Allyn & Bacon (Boston, MA), 2005

White, Edward T, *Design Briefing in England*, Architectural Media (Tucson, AZ), 1991

Winnicott, Donald W, 'Primary maternal preoccupation' in his *Through Paediatrics to Psychoanalysis: Collected Papers*, Hogarth Press (London), 1956

Winnicott, Donald W, 'Morals and education', in his *The Maturational Processes and the Facilitating Environment: Studies in the Theory of Emotional Development*, Hogarth Press (London), 1960

Winnicott, Donald W, 'The Theory of the Parent-infant Relationship', in his *The Maturational Processes and the Facilitating Environment: Studies in the Theory of Emotional Development*, Hogarth Press (London), 1960

Winnicott, Donald W, What about Father? In his *The Child, the Family and the Outside World*, Penguin (London), 1964

Winnicott, Donald W, 'The location of cultural experience', in his *Playing and Reality* (London), 1971

Winnicott, Donald W, 'Communicating and not communicating' in Dodi Goldman, ed, *In One's Bones: The Clinical Genius of Winnicott*, Jason Aaronson (Northvale, NJ), 1993

Zeisel, John, *Inquiry by Design: Environment/Behaviour/Neuroscience in Architecture, Interiors, Landscape, and Planning*, WW Norton, Revised edition (New York), 2006

Index

Note: Page references in **bold** refer to Illustrations

Aalto, Alvar 130
Ada Karmi-Melamede Architects 26
Afonso, Nadir 41
Allies, Bob 98, 147, 150, 169
Allies and Morrison Architects 97-8, 147, **150**, 169, **170**
American Institute of Architects (AIA) 15, 37, 38, 97
Anderson, Gil 80
Anderson, Harlene 95, 97
anxiety 82-6, 109-11
Apodaca, Raymond 178
Ariizumi, Hideaki 64, 67-8, 78, **78**, 99, 100, **100**, 133, 139, 145
Arison School of Management 155, **155**
Auckland University School of Architecture 104, **105**
Auckland War Memorial Museum 173

Bain, Brodie 53, 96, 100, 111, 140, 147, 160
Balint, Michael 88
Barragan, Luis 11
Bateson, Gregory 84, 94
Beavin, Janet Helmick 112
Berg, Carl 62-3
Berg Green House, Columbia County, New York **63**
Berry, Glynis 64, 67-8, **78**, 99, 100, 139, 145
Bion, Wilfred R. 109
Birkdale Primary School playground, Auckland **105**
Bishops Square, Spitalfields, London 32, 69, **69**, 100, 110, 140
B'nai Keshet Synagogue, Montclair, New Jersey 75, **75**
Bohlin Cywinski Jackson 190, **190**
Bohm, David 103, 107
Bollas, Christopher 54
Bossley, Pete 176
Braverman, Louise **33**, 34, 41, 76, 87, 95, **95**, 96, 129, 132, 133, **135**, 139, 142, 147, 151, **151**
briefing 26-8
  and designing 36-40
  and the design 41-5
Bronowski, Jacob 187
Buber, Martin 10
Building Design Partnership 185
building information modeling (BIM) 17

Burgess, Greg 139
Burton, Richard 36

Calatrava, Santiago 100
Cambridge University, Faculty of Mathematics 87, **87**, 102, **102**
Canon's Marsh, Bristol 39, 65-6, **66**
Capra, Fritjof 93, 188
Cardinal, Douglas 45, 47, 48, 140, **146**, **179**
Centro de Artes Nadir Afonso, Boticas, Portugal 41-2
Chartres Cathedral 47
Chelsea and Westminster Hospital, London 134, **134**, 182-5, **182**, **183**, **184**
Chelsea Court, New York **95**, 135
Chic's Chinese Clinic, Hong Kong 152-3, **152**
choice of architect 62-5
Coffin, Christie 28, 64, 101, 121, 137, 138, 139, 149
Commission for Architecture and the Built Environment (CABE) 15, 27, 31, 38, **38**
Construction Industry Board 17
Courtyard Blot, 'Improve Your Lot!', Detroit **141**
Crahan, Lauren 143, 156
Cramer, James 17
Cress Nicholson 39, 66
Cross, Nigel 32, 34, 122, 130
Cuff, Dana 16, 32, 33, 77, 78, 129
Cullinan, Edward 39-40, 66, 75, 85-6, 87, 99, 102, 145, 191
Cultural Resource Center, Suitland, Maryland 120, 121, **121**, 146, 153, 158, **158**, 180

Dallas Theater Center 182, 185
Davis Langdon 113
Dayal, Antar: Flat Earth **129**
de Rijke Marsh Morgan Architects **16**
De Young Museum, San Francisco 136
Dead Malls competition 159, **159**
Dee and Charles Wyly Theater, Dallas **186**
dependency 109, 110, **111**
Design Brief 38
design champion 31
Design Partnership, The 28, 137, **137**, 149

Dixon, Tom 158, 173, 174
Donald W. Reynolds Community Services Center, Pine Bluff, Arkansas 53-4
Dong, Andy 122
Dorst, Kees 34
Downing, Frances 54
Downland Gridshell **74**, 75
Dutchess Mall, Fishkill, New York 159, **159**
dynamic matrix 106-7, **107**

Eck, Jeremiah 63, **63**
Eck MacNeely Architects 63, **64**
EDAW **45**, **146**, **179**
Edward Cullinan Architects 39, **39**, **65**, 66, **74**, **85**, **87**, **153**, 191, **191**
Eisenman, Peter 46
ELS Architecture **131**
Estoque, Justin 104, 119
Ethelred Estate, Lambeth, London **99**, 112, 188
Evelina Children's Hospital, St Thomas's, London 185

facilitating environment 81-9
Facilities Standards for the Public Building Service 37
Factor, Donald 107
Faga, Barbara: *Designing Public Consensus* 16
Fahlander, Mats 64, 68, 71, **86**, **98**, 188-9
Farnsworth, Edith 46
fight/flight 109-10, **111**
First Presbyterian Church, Berkeley, California 131, **131**, 132, 135
Fisch, Richard 165
Fisher, Thomas R 17
Flack, Christine **99**
Forester, John 94
Foulkes, S.H. 66-7, 106
foundation matrix 106-8, **107**
framing 119-24
Francis Associates 72, **73**
Franck, Karen A. 18, 120, 173
Freecell 36, **36**, 76, **142**, 143, **143**, 156-7, **156**
Friary Estate Options Appraisal, London **26**
Furlong, Anthony 183

Galford, Robert 17
Gallery of Israeli Art, Rishon Le'Zion, Israel **145**
Garden of Senses, Sabbatsberg Hospital, Stockholm 52, **52**, 168, **168**
Garrett, Peter 107
Gateway Commons, San Francisco **27**
GBQC Architects **45**, **146**, **179**
Gehry, Frank 41, 47
Gillem, Mark 131-2, **131**, 135, 136, 139, 146, 190
Gorbey, Ken 85
Gordon, Diana 64, **64**, 67-8, **67**, 78, **78**, 99, 133, 139
Gordon Residence, Greenport, New York 64, **67**, **78**, **100**, 133, **133**, **144**, 145
Graves, Michael 54, **55**
Gray, Eileen 130
Green, Charles 17

Green, Judy 62-3
Grudzien, Julien 35, 137, 139, 152
Grudzien apartment, Hong Kong 35, **35**, **138**
Guggenheim Museum, Bilbao 41, 47

Hadid, Zara 46
Haga Park Stockholm, Health Garden, 154, **154**, 168, **169**
Happold, Buro 75
Harris, Alex 28, 31, 43, 76, 97, 136
Hartmann, John 76, 156, 157
Health Garden, Haga Park Stockholm 154, **154**, 168, **169**
Henry Urbach Gallery, Manhattan 157
Hershberger, Robert 37, 39
Hertzberger, Herman 46
Herzog & Meuron 136
Heye, George 180
Heye Center, New York 180
Highlawn Branch Library, Brooklyn, New York 132, 133, 134, **135**, 151
Hinshelwood, Robert D. 52
Hitman, Helen 72-3, **73**, 84, 159
Ho, Denise 35, **35**, 76, 81, 130, **130**, 131, 137, **138**, 139, 152-3, **152**, 161, 170
Ho brothers' houses, San Shui, China 130, **130**
Hobson, Peter 19
Hooson, Tim 148
Hopkins Architects 185
Horniman Museum, London 147, 148, 169, **170**
House, Donna **45**, 48, **146**, **179**
Howard, Teresa von Sommaruga 18-19, 54
Hunt, John 174, 193

immersion 139
inner world 51-2
    architect's 54-7
    client's 52-4
Interboro 133, 141, **141**, 159, **159**, 160, 192, **193**
Isaacs, William 19, 94, 103, 115
Israel, Toby 52, 54, 139
'I-thou' 10

Jackson, Don D. 112
Jacobs, Deborah 31, 78-9, 122
Jasmax Architects **82**, 148, **148**, 149, 158, 174, **175**, 176, **176**, **194**
Jean, Jill 31
Jiricana, Eva 26, 99
Johnson, Philip 96
Jones, Allen: *Acrobat, The* 183
Jones, Johnpaul 36, 40, 45, 48, 49, 118, 140, **146**, 151, 155, 161, **179**
Jones & Jones 36, **45**, **146**, **179**
Jung, Carl G. 25

Kahn, Louis 10-12, **11**, 46
Karmi, Ram 29, **30**, 40, **44**, 56, 61, **61**, **145**, 152
Karmi-Melamede, Ada 26, 29, **30**, 36, 40, 43, **44**, 61, **61**, **116**, 152, 155, **155**

Keating, Michael 64, **64**, 68
Keene, Dakota 160
Kingsdale School, Dulwich, London **16**
Klee, Paul: *Conjuring Trick* **9**, 43
Koolhaas, Rem 32, 35, 40, 42, 43, 76, 78, 83, 96, 157
Krens, Thomas 47

Lambeth Community Care Centre, London **39**, 40, **153**
Lane, Rosa 28, 53, 54, 56, **56**, 71, 96, 117, 141
Lange, David 174
Latham, Michael 17
Laude School of Government, Herzliya 155, **155**
Lawson, Bryan 26, 36, 38, 99, 122, 144
Le Corbusier 96, 157
Lee Angel jewellery showroom, Manhattan 166
Lent Space, New York 192, **193**
Lepori, Bianca 130, 153
Lewis Tsurumaki Lewis 36
Life Sciences Building, Ben Gurion University, Beersheva 116, 155
Linzey, Michael 176, 178
listening and hearing 97-8
Lloyds of London 136
LMN Architects 40, 42, **42**, **43**, **51**, 77, 78, **80**, 96, 119, 122, **123**, 143, 180, **180**
London School of Contemporary Dance 150, **150**
Long Beach, Auckland **73**
Loop House, Millburn, New Jersey **117**
Loppert, Susan 183
Los Angeles Forum for Architecture and Urban Design 159, **159**

MacCormac, Richard 36, 37, 48
Mahuika, Apirama 114, 115
Maister, David 17
Mannheim Gridshell 75
Maranacook Performing Arts Center, Readfield, Maine **29**
Marcus, Clare Cooper 52, 139
Maré, Patrick de 114, 187
Mary Graham Children's Shelter, San Joaquin County, California 121, 137, **137**, 139, 149
Massih, Kava 31, 64, 79, 79, 95, 101, 122, **124**, 150
Maturana, Humberto 17
Medicine Wheel 103, **104**
Medway and Clark 115
Miller, Robert 190
Miller, Sam 78, 96, 119, 122
mission 146-7
Mithun Architects, Seattle 53, 96, 111, 117, 147, 160, **160**
Mohr, Bob 53, 96, 111, 117, 160
Moore Ruble Yudell (MRY) 12
Moore, Charles 12-13, **12**, 14, **14**, 15
Mostoller, Michael 68, 72, 75, **75**
Muschamp, Herbert 43
Myatt's Fields North, London Borough of Lambeth 171, **171**

naming 119-24
National Museum of the American Indian 18, 36, 40, 45, **45**, 47, 48-50, **48**, **49**, **50**, 104, 118-21, **118**, 140, 144, 146, **146**, 151, 153, 155-8, 160-1, 172, 173, 178-80, **179**
Native American Design Collaborative **45**, **146**, **179**
Nordenberg, Maria 64, 98, **98**
Nordfjell, Ulf 52, **52**, 154, 168, **168**, **169**
North Fork, Orient, New York 64
Northwest Indian College, Lumni Reservation, Washington 53, 100, 111, 117, 140, 147, **160**
NYC Velo, New York 156, 157

Office of Metropolitan Architecture (OMA) 40, 42, **42**, **43**, **51**, 63, 64, 68, **77**, 78, **80**, 83, 96, 97, **123**, 136, 143, 157, 180-1, **180**
Old Loughborough Estate, Lambeth, London 88-9, 108, 108
Outdoor Living Room, Venice, CA **167**
Outram, John 37

pairing 109, 110, **111**
Pallasmaa, Juhani 153
Palmer, Mary 77
Paradise Creek Community, National City, California **105**
Pemaquid Beach, Maine 56, **56**
Penoyre & Prasad 152, 154
Piano, Renzo 99, 144
Pine Bluff, Arkansas 141
Polshek Partnership Architects 45, **121**, **146**, **158**, **179**
Porter, William 122
Prasad, Sunand 41, 48, 117, 138, 139
Prentice, Kristin 31, 64, 66, 106, 120, 122
Pressman, Andrew 16
programming 26
Project Brief 38
psychotherapy 17-18
Puketapu, Kara 114, 115
Pyatok, Michael 55-6, 105, 106, 111
Pyatok Architects **27**, **55**, **105**

Ramus, Joshua 40, 42, 47, 63-4, 68, 76, 80, 83, 117, 132, 150, 166, 181, 182, 185-7
Rasmussen-Cancian, Steve 167, **167**
Ratcliff Architects 32, 64, **79**, **101**, **124**, **149**
'reflection-in-action' 18
Reid, Giles 158
relational approach 15-18
REX architects 83, 182, 185, **186**
Richard Rogers Partnership 136
Roberts, Jeff P. 106
Robins, David S. **116**
Robinson, Julia Williams 38, 144, 173
Robinson, Paul 113
Rosa Parks Elementary School, Berkeley 28, 31, 32, 51, 64, 66, 79, 79, 95, 100, 101, 106, 120, 122, 124, 149, 149
Ross, Charles **118**

Royal Alexandra Children's Hospital in Brighton 185
Royal Institute of British Architects (RIBA) 15, 38, 39, 62, 97
Ryding, Jenny 118

Sabbatsberg Hospital, Garden of Senses, Stockholm 52, 52, 168, 168
Sakiestewa, Ramona 45, 48, **146**, **179**
Salcedo, Doris: *Shibboleth* 165, **165**
Salisbury, Frank 38
Salk, Dr Jonas 10-12, **11**
Salk Institute for Biological Studies, La Jolla, California 11, **11**, 15
San Capistrano Library, California 55, **55**
Sarum Hall School, London 147
Scharoun, Hans 130
Schneekloth, Lynda H. 16, 103, 120, 173
Schön, Donald 18, 100, 121, 122, 144
Scott, Caudill Rowlett 37
Scott Brown, Denise 69, 118, 129
Seattle Central Library 18, 28, 31, 35, 40, 42-3, **42**, **43**, 48, 50, **51**, 63, 68, 76, 77-8, **77**, 80, **80**, 83, 96, 119, 122, **123**, 132, 136, 143, 150, 151, 153, 156, 157, 172, 173, 180-2, **180**
Seneca Group 31
Seymour, Jane 15-16, **16**
Shamgar, Meir 29
Sheppard Robson Architects 134, **134**, 183, 184
Shibley, Robert G. 16, 103
Shortwave Bookstore, Brooklyn, New York 36
Siegel, Joy 116, **117**
Silber, John 47
silence 111-15
Simpson, Scott 17
SIP, Brooklyn 143, **143**
Sluzki, Carlos E. 85
Smith Group 45, **146**, **179**
Smithsonian Institution 40, 118
Sotheran, Cheryl 83, 85, 88, 110, 174, 178, 193, 194
Southwark Building Design Service **26**
Spruce, Duane Blue 47, 49, 50, 178
St Mary's Church, Barnes, London 85-6, **85**, **191**
St Matthew's Parish Church, Palisades, California 12-14, **12**, **13**, 15, 27, 31
Steamboat Springs, Colorado 190, **190**
Stern, Daniel N. 18, 70, 72
Stockyards Exchange Building 54
studio a/b architects 64, **64**, **67**, **78**, 99, **100**, 133, **133**, 139, **144**
Supreme Court, Jerusalem 18, 28, 29-31, **30**, 40, 43-4, **44**, 47, **61**, 153
Swentzell, Rina 45
Sydney Opera House 41, 46, 52

Täby, Stockholm **86**
Tagore, Rabindranath 82
talking and showing 99-102
Tate Modern, London 165, **165**
Taylor, Nick 72, **73**
Te Papa Tongarewa Museum, New Zealand 18, **82**, 83-5, 88, 104, 110, 114, **114**, 158, 172-8, **175**, **176**, **177**, 180, 193, **194**
'technical rationality' 18
Thorp, Richard 174
Till, Jeremy 93
Tilly, Charles 140
Tower Apartments, Rohnert Park, California **55**
Townshend Landscape Architects **69**
Trotter, Sir Ron 115
Tucker, Sian **182**
Turoa, Hiwi 104, 115
Turoa, Par 104, 115

Ulrich, Roger 168
Uluru-Kata Tjuta Cultural Centre 139
University of Pennsylvania, Richards Buildings 11, 46
US Courts Design Guide 37
use and form 46-51
Utzon, Jørn 41, 46, 53

van der Rohe, Mies 46
Van der Veen, Ron 160
van Eyck, Aldo 130
Vemdalen, Sweden 188, **189**
Venice Community Housing Corporation **167**
Ventro de Artes Nadir Afonso, Boticas, Portugal **33**
Venturi, Scott Brown and Associates 40, 45, 69, 146
Verb Media **142**, 143, 156
Villa Monte Rosa 170
Vitra, Fire Station, Switzerland 46
Vodafone, Auckland 148, **148**, **149**

Walworth Surgery, London 152
Ward, Jacob 143
Ward, Tony 104
Watzlawick, Paul W. 112, 165, 172
Weakland, John 165
Weald and Downland Museum, West Sussex **74**, 75
Weeks, J. Stephen 38, 144
Weese, Cynthia 25
Weller, Lou 45, **146**, **179**
West, Richard 179
Westerberg, Yvonne 52, 154, 167
Wexner Art Center, Columbus, Ohio 46
Wheelan, Susan A. 110
Whiting, Cliff 83, 85, **114**, 115, 176, 177, **177**
Wiggins, Glenn 144
Wilford, Michael 43
Winnicott, Donald W. 70, 71, 81, 82-3, 88
Wood, Dan 166
Woodlands Nursing Home, New Cross, London 138, 154
Work Architecture Company 166, **166**
work group **111**
Wright, Frank Lloyd 62, 77

Young, John 136

Zeisel, John 139

Image credits

The authors and the publisher gratefully acknowledge the people who gave their permission to reproduce material in this book. While every effort has been made to contact copyright holders for their permission to reprint material, the publishers would be grateful to hear from any copyright holder who is not acknowledged here and will undertake to rectify any errors or omissions in future editions.

p 1(l) © Teresa von Sommaruga Howard; p 1(m) © Jasmax; p 1(r) © Denise Ho Architects; p 2(t,l) view/Peter Cook; p 2(t,r) © 2005 Elizabeth Felicella Photography; p2 (b,l) © Denise Ho Architects; p 2(b,r) © Freecell; p5(t,l) © Teresa von Sommaruga Howard; p5(t,c) Karen A. Franck; p5(t,r) Karen A. Franck; p 5(b) Interboro Partners; p 6 Hideaki Ariizumi; p 7(l) Karen A. Frank; p 7(m) Sheppard Robson; p 7(r) Karen A. Frank; p 9 ©2008 Artists Rights Society (ARS), New York/VG Bild-Kunst, Bonn; p11 © Karen A. Franck; p 12 ©Moore Ruble Yudell; p 13 © Moore Ruble Yudell; p 14 © Karen A. Franck; p 16 © Alex de Rijke; p 26 © Public Consultation Design Day by Chris Picton; p 27 © Mark Gillem; p 29 © Carol Fl Gillis, Design Group Collaborative; p 30(t) Ada Karmi-Melamede; p 30(b) © Teresa von Sommaruga Howard; p 32 © Dan Wetherwell/The Ratcliff Architects; p 33 © Louise Braverman, Architect; p 35 Denise Ho Architects; p 36 © Freecell; p 39(t) © Edward Cullinan Architects; p 39(b) © Teresa von Sommaruga Howard; p 42 © Metropolis Magazine; p 43 © Office for Metropolitan Architecture; p 44 © Teresa von Sommaruga Howard; p 45 © Tony Holmes; p 48 © Johnpaul Jones, Jones & Jones; p 49 © Johnpaul Jones, Jones & Jones; p 50 Courtesy of the Smithsonian Institution, National Museum of the American Indian; p 51 © Karen A. Franck; p 52 Yvonne Westerberg; p 54 © Teresa von Sommaruga Howard; p 55(t) © Karen A. Franck; p 55(b) © Michael Pyatok; p 56 © Janice Goldfrank; p 61 © Teresa von Sommaruga Howard; p 63 © Eck Macneely Architects, Boston USA; p 64 © Studio a/b Architects /Hideaki Ariizumi; p 65 © Edward Cullinan Architects; p 67 © Tony Holmes; p 69 © Teresa von Sommaruga Howard; p 70 © A. Inden/Corbis; p 71 © Goodshoot/Corbis; p 73 © Teresa von Sommaruga Howard; p 74(t) © A. Inden/Corbis; p 74(b) © Edward Cullinan Architects; p 75 © Michael Mostoller, Architect; p 77 © Karen A. Franck; p 78 © Tony Holmes; p 79 ©Radcliff Architects, drawing Kava Massih; p 80 © OMA/LMN; p 81 © Teresa von Sommaruga Howard; p 82 © Marilyn Higgins; p 85(l) ©Karen A. Franck; p 85(r) © Teresa von Sommaruga Howard; p 86 © Tove Falk-Olsson; p 87 © Edward Cullinan Architects; p 88 © Jose Luis Pelaez, Inc./CORBIS; p 94 © STScI/NASA/Corbis; p 95 © Kristine Foley; p 98 © Tove Falk-Olsson; p 99 © Teresa von Sommaruga Howard; p 100 © Studio a/b Architects /Hideaki Ariizumi; p 101 © Kristine Foley; p 102 ©Edward Cullinan Architects; p 103 © Teresa von Sommaruga Howard; p 104 © Teresa von Sommaruga Howard; p 105(t) © Teresa von Sommaruga Howard; p 105(b) © Michael Pyatok; p 107 © Teresa von Sommaruga Howard; p 111 © Teresa von Sommaruga Howard; p 114 © Museum of New Zealand Te Papa Tongawera; p 116 Ada Karmi Melamede; p 117 Joy Siegel Architect; p 118 ©Karen A. Franck; p 121 ©Karen A. Franck; p 123 © Office for Metropolitian Architecture; p 124 ©Karen A. Franck; p 129 © Antar Dayal/Illustration Works/Corbis; p 130 ©Denise Ho Architects; p 131 © Mark Gillem; p 133 © Studio a/b Architects /Hideaki Ariizumi; p 134 © Sheppard Robson; p 135 ©Michael Moran; p 137 © Denise Ho Architects; p 138 © The Design Partnership, photographer: Frank Domin; p 141 © Interboro; p 142 © Freecell; p 1431 © Freecell; p 144 © Studio a/b Architects /Hideaki Ariizumi; p 145 © Ram Karmi; p 146 © Karen A. Franck; p 148(t) © Jasmax Architects; p 148(b) © Simon Devitt photographer; p 149 © Karen A. Franck; p 150 © view/Dennis Gilbert; p 151 Louise Braverman; p 152 © Denise Ho Architects; p 153 © Karen A. Franck; p 154 © Teresa von Sommaruga Howard; p 155 © Teresa von Sommaruga Howard; p 156 © Freecell; p 158 © Karen A. Franck; p 159 © Interboro; p 160 © Mithun Inc; p 165 © Quentin Stevens; p 166 © 2005 Elizabeth Felicella Photography; p 167 Steve Rasmussen Cancian, Shared Spaces; p 168 Yvonne Westerberg; p 169 © Teresa von Sommaruga Howard; p 170(t) © Teresa von Sommaruga Howard; p 169(b) view/Peter Cook; p 171 © Teresa von Sommaruga Howard; p 175 © Jasmax Architects; p 175(b) Brian J McMorrow; p 176 © Jared Lee, lee.jared@gmail.com; p 177(r) Brian McMorrow and Cliff Whiting; p 177(l) Richard Nunns 'and the Melbourne Trust; p 179(l) © Tony Holmes; p 179(r) © Karen A. Franck; p 180 © Karen A. Franck; p 182 © Hospital Arts Chelsea & Westminster Health Charity: photo Lea Guzzo; p 183 © Hospital Arts Chelsea & Westminster Health Charity; p 184 © Sheppard Robson; p 186 © Josuha Prince-Ramus/REX; p 189 © Tove Falk-Olsson; p 190 © Bohlin Cywinski Jackson; p 191 © Edward Cullinan Architects; p 193 © Interboro; p 194 © Jared Lee, lee.jared@gmail.com